An Airman's Odyssey

An Airman's Odyssey

Walt Braznell and the Pilots
He Led into the Jet Age

William Braznell

Illustrations by C. Richard Clark and Tron Bykle

University of Missouri Press   Columbia and London

University of Missouri Press

Columbia and London

Copyright © 2001 by

William Braznell

University of Missouri Press, Columbia, Missouri 65201

Printed and bound in Hong Kong

5 4 3 2 1   05 04 03 02 01

Library of Congress Cataloging-in-Publications Data

Braznell, William

   An airman's odyssey : Walt Braznell and the pilots he
led into the Jet age / William Braznell ; illustrations by
C. Richard Clark and Tron Bykle.

     p. cm.

Includes bibliographical references and index.

ISBN 0–8262–1306–5 (alk. paper)

1. Braznell, Walt, 1907–1994. 2. Air pilots—United States—
Biography. I. Title.

TL540.B726 B73 2000

629.13'092—dc21

[B]

                    00-064774

⊚™ This paper meets the requirements of the
American National Standard for Permanence of Paper
for Printed Library Materials, Z39.48, 1984.

Design and composition: Kristie Lee
Printer and binder: Dai Nippon Printing Co.
Typefaces: Garamond Light and Caslon 224

Souls that have toiled, and wrought,
and thought with me—
That ever with a frolic welcome took
The thunder and the sunshine, and opposed
Free hearts, free foreheads—you and I are old;
Old age hath yet his honor and his toil;
Death closes all: but something ere the end,
Some work of noble note may yet be done,
Not unbecoming men that strove with Gods.

—Alfred Tennyson, *Ulysses*

Contents

Flight Plan

I don't know exactly how to describe this book. It is neither memoir, biography, nor history; it is, you might say, all of the above, with a random mix of tall tales, legends, flight-line humor, and operating instructions thrown in for good measure. It is a story about the early years of commercial aviation, going back to a time when air travel was still an exciting and dangerous novelty, and no one, least of all the pilots themselves, thought of flying for the airlines as just another occupation.

It is a story about a pilot named Walt Braznell and the airmen he flew with. In a way, it's about everyone who has ever flown for a living—or for the sheer love of flying.

The protagonist and occasional narrator of this story, my father, was born in 1907, four years, almost to the day, after the Wright Brothers launched their first airship at Kitty Hawk. He made his first solo flight in a Curtiss JN-4 "Jenny" at the age of eighteen. Two years later he took over Charles Lindbergh's former job flying the mail between St. Louis and Chicago for one of American Airlines' predecessor com-

panies, Robertson Aircraft Corporation. In 1937 he was named chief pilot of American's Chicago-based Midwestern Division and given the unenviable task of introducing the industry's first standardized flight procedures and instrument training techniques to a peer group of proudly independent, self-taught line pilots. This chief pilot role continued to evolve through successive title changes and increasing responsibilities until his retirement in 1968 as American's vice president–Flight.

A founding member of the airline industry's first pilot's union, the Air Line Pilots Association (ALPA), Walt Braznell remained preeminently a pilot's pilot throughout his forty-year career with American. Among his many firsts were two flights that could be considered the bookends bracketing the formative middle years—the Bronze Age—of air travel: the first commercial flight of the Douglas DC-3, on June 26, 1936, and the inaugural transcontinental flight of the last piston-engine airliner, the DC-7, on November 20, 1953. Five years later he played a leading role in ushering American Airlines and the American public into the Jet Age when he headed the team responsible for testing, proving, and certifying the nation's first domestic jetliner, the Boeing 707.

In addition to Walt's notes, flight logs, and tapes, George W. Cearley, Jr.'s *American Airlines, An Illustrated History,* Robert Serling's *Eagle: The Story of American Airlines,* Charles A. Lindbergh's *We* and *The Spirit of St. Louis,* James J. Horgan's *St. Louis: City of Flight,* R. E. G. Davies's *Airlines of the United States Since 1914,* T. A. Heppenheimer's *Turbulent Skies, The History of Commercial Aviation,* Dean Smith's classic *By the Seat of My Pants,* Jack Jaynes's memoirs, *Eagles Must Fly,* and Jim Mangan's *To the Four Winds* were important secondary sources of historical and technical information.

The beautiful pen-and-ink sketches were drawn by Dick Clark, a lifelong friend and the son of one of Walt's closest associates, American Airlines' legendary chief pilot, Harry "Red" Clark. Thank you, Richard. And thanks to artist/illustrator Tron Bykle for the handsome cover illustration.

I owe a considerable debt of gratitude to Beverly Jarrett, executive editor of the University of Missouri Press, for her guidance and encouragement during the many, many months it has taken to research and write this book. Aviation historian and Smithsonian Air and Space Museum curator R. E. G. Davies was also a source of inspiration and encouragement, particularly in the early going.

My guides, mentors, friends-in-need, and constant morale-boosters throughout the research phase of this project have been Captain Frank Nehlig, retired chief pilot of American Airlines and scribe of American's Grey Eagles, and

Captain William (Kelly) Owen, a retired AA line pilot, test pilot, and one of Walt's longtime friends and associates. I'm deeply grateful to them and to other retired AA veterans and FOWs (Friends of Walt), notably Jack Gibson, Glenn Brink, Charles Young, and Frank Atzert, for their notes and comments on this manuscript. I also want to thank my sister, Carole Carlin, for her voluminous tape transcriptions and interview notes and for contributing the bulk of the family photographs reprinted in this book. Finally, I'm indebted to my son, Bill, for getting this family project on track, to my wife, Judy, for her steadfast support and loving encouragement, and to my daughters, Leslie and Kate, for their invaluable artistic talents, assistance, and advice. *An Airman's Odyssey* has indeed been a family project from start to finish.

Many people and institutions contributed to the extensive collection of historical photographs contained in this book: Director Jay Miller and Curator Ben Kristy of American Airlines' C. R. Smith Museum; Tim Doke and Chet Snedden of AMR Corporation's corporate communications group; Missouri Historical Society Assistant Curator Kirsten Hammerstrom and rest of the MHS staff; Jean Robertson Pritchard and Frank Robertson, Jr., custodians of the Frank Robertson collection; Bette Davidson Kalash, curator of the Jesse Davidson Aviation Archives; and Lisa Constance of TWA.

This book is dedicated to Walt Braznell, who didn't live to see its long-awaited publication, and to a generation of airmen, eagles all, who set the standards of professionalism, resourcefulness, and valor by which airline pilots will forevermore be measured.

—William Braznell

Walt Braznell as he looked when he began flying the mail for Robertson Aircraft Corporation on CAM (Contract Air Mail) Route 2 between St. Louis and Chicago in September 1928. The plane appears to be a de Havilland DH-4. Walt was twenty years old.

Captain Braznell, roughly 15,000 flying hours later, as he approached the end of his forty-year career with American Airlines.

An Airman's Odyssey

Above the haze layer, with the sun behind you or sinking ahead, alone in an open cockpit, there is nothing and everything to see. The upper surface of the haze stretches on like a vast and endless desert, featureless and flat, and empty to the horizon. It seems your world alone. Threading one's way through the great piles of summer cumulus that hang over the plains, the patches of ground that show far below through the white are for earthbound folk, and the cloud shapes are sculptured just for you. The flash of rain, the shining rainbow riding completely around the plane, the lift over mountain ridges and crawling trains, the steady, pure air at dawn take-offs, and the smoke from the newly lit fires in houses just coming to life below—these were some of the many bits that helped pay for the tense moments of plunging through fog, or the somber thoughts when flying cortege for a pilot's funeral. It was so alive and rich a life that any other conceivable choice seemed dull, prosaic, and humdrum.

—Dean Smith, *By the Seat of My Pants*

Book One

The Education of
an Air Mail Pilot

Beginnings

The year is 1924: The Great War in Europe has been over for six years; twenty-one years have passed since Orville and Wilbur Wright launched the age of powered, heavier-than-air flight from a sand dune near Kitty Hawk, North Carolina.

Aviation has advanced prodigiously in a single generation. During the war "aeroplanes" rapidly evolved from motorized box kites fit only for aerial observation into deadly fighting machines such as France's SPAD, Britain's Sopwith Camel, and Germany's Fokker D.VII. Sturdy World War I–era biplanes like the Curtiss JN-4 "Jenny," the de Havilland DH-4, and the Lincoln Standard still abound, but their days are numbered. Within a few years they will be replaced by a new generation of sleek, stressed-aluminum monoplanes powered by lightweight, fuel-efficient radial engines such as Charles Lawrance's revolutionary Wright Whirlwind.

Flying is no longer merely a pastime for adventurers and playboys. Thousands of airmen, most of them trained at government expense during World War I, are now putting their flying skills to use barnstorming at air shows and county fairs, operating flying schools and regional air services, or running bootleg booze out of Canada or Cuba. War-surplus aircraft are cheap and plentiful. Five hundred dollars buys a serviceable JN-4 equipped with a 90-horsepower Curtiss OX-5 motor. Sellers will often toss in five or six hours of free flying lessons, or as many circuits around the airfield as it takes for the buyer to complete one successful unassisted takeoff and landing.

Aside from the brisk Prohibition-era trade in rum-running, commercial air transport has made very little progress in the United States up to this point. But all that is about to change. In early 1925 Congressman Clyde Kelly of Pennsylvania will introduce legislation authorizing the Department of Commerce to transfer air mail service from federal control to private contractors such as Boeing Air Transport, Western Air Express, and Robertson Aircraft Corporation—distant fore-runners of United, TWA, and American Airlines, respectively.

Meanwhile, the U.S. Post Office's six-year-old Air Mail Service is advertising three-day delivery from New York to San Francisco, weather permitting. Equipped with only the crudest flight instruments and lacking any communications or navigational aids, the service's lumbering DH-4 mail planes are incapable of operating in clouds or fog for more than a few minutes at a time. Furthermore, operations on many air mail routes are restricted to daylight hours pending completion of the Army Signal Corps' transcontinental network of high-powered navigational beacons.

In San Antonio, Texas, Army Air Service Cadet Charles Lindbergh is midway through the Army's twelve-month flight training program at Kelly Field and already laying plans for resuming his civil aviation career in St. Louis after he is released from active duty. And in St. Louis a young ROTC cadet named Walt Braznell is about to begin an apprenticeship in aviation that will eventually lead to the command of one of the world's largest fleets of commercial jet transports.

First Waltz

Walt Braznell's love affair with aviation began when he was sixteen. His first flame, a Curtiss "Jenny," was a few years younger, but vastly more experienced. They met at a Missouri National Guard encampment in southwest Missouri on a hot, dusty August afternoon in 1924. One aerial waltz around the camp grounds with an older cousin, Captain Ray Wassall, as chaperone, and Braznell was hooked for life.

Ray Wassall was one of a group of aviation-minded St. Louisans, most of them World War I

pilots, who banded together in 1923 to form the first air arm of the Missouri National Guard, the 110th Observation Squadron. After setting up shop in the back of a gas station belonging to one of the squadron members, they pitched in five hundred dollars of their own money and bought a war-surplus Jenny from another member—a used aircraft dealer named William Robertson. To cement the deal, they elected Robertson squadron commander. Wassall was named operations officer.

Originally the Guard squadron and its one and only aircraft operated out of a small grass field in Forest Park, not far from the St. Louis Zoo. But by the following summer, when Braznell enlisted, it boasted 124 members, a fleet of seven JN-4s, and a spacious new hangar at Lambert Field, about midway between St. Louis and St. Charles, in Anglum, Missouri.

The 110th was to be officially commissioned at the National Guard's summer encampment in Camp Clark, near the town of Nevada, Missouri, during the first two weeks of August. As operations officer, Ray Wassall had the job of preparing this bunch of World War I retreads and raw enlisted men for the federal inspection. He freely admitted he needed all the help he could get.

Wassall's uncle, George Braznell, suggested that his oldest son, Walt, a cadet officer on his high school's crack ROTC drill team, was just the fellow Ray needed to whip his National Guardsmen into shape. At the time, Braznell was preparing to move his family back to St. Louis from Dallas after an absence of four years. Walt was still in Texas, attending ROTC summer camp. Ray immediately wrote to his cousin and made him an offer no red-blooded ROTC cadet could resist—two weeks' wages (sixty-seven dollars), a sergeant's stripes, and the aforementioned introduction to Jenny.

Lambert Field

St. Louis's first municipal airport was established in Forest Park in 1918. The hundred-acre field was formally dedicated on August 16, 1920, with the inauguration of the Post Office's air mail service between St. Louis and Chicago. Almost immediately thereafter, Major Albert Bond Lambert, Major William Robertson, and other members of the Missouri Aeronautical Society began looking for a more suitable location for an airport. They settled on a 546-acre site in Anglum, Missouri, which was subsequently purchased by the city for $485,000. For several years thereafter Major Lambert continued to bankroll improvements and operating expenses while city bureaucrats dithered over the airport's development. By the time the "Lambert–St. Louis Municipal Airport" was officially dedicated and turned over to the city in 1930 it was already one of the Midwest's leading airports, served by three major airlines (American/Universal, Chicago & Southern, and TWA), and handling more than 170,000 airline, air mail, general aviation, and military arrivals and departures per year. This photo was taken during a Missouri National Guard summer encampment in 1928.

Airfields and Airports

The first airfields were simply pastures or public park land around which a few strands of barbed wire had been strung to keep sheep and cattle from getting in the way of traffic. There were no mown airstrips or surfaced runways, nor was there lighting of any sort. Aircraft were free to take off and land anywhere and in any direction the pilot chose. In the late 1920s and early 1930s progressive cities such as St. Louis began converting their local airfields into "airports" with control towers, beacon lights, paved or partially paved landing strips—even passenger terminals. Although the Air Corps continued to call its upgraded airdromes "fields" (Brooks Field, Kelly Field, Chanute Field, etc.), in commercial aviation usage was mixed: Lambert Field (St. Louis), Love Field (Dallas), Chrissy Field (San Francisco)—but Chicago Midway Airport, Newark Airport, etc. Purists in the Department of Commerce, which regulated civil aviation at the time, insisted that an "airport" had to be enclosed by a chain-link fence, or some similarly sturdy and secure structure— otherwise, it was a "field."

Bud

Walt Braznell was born December 16, 1907, four years, less one day, after the Wright brothers' first flight. Bud, as the family called him, was the second of four children born to George and Clarabel Cornick Braznell of St. Louis. From his father, a dapper traveling man for a large midwestern printing ink company, he acquired a love of the outdoors, of easy, relaxed male company, of automobiles and all things mechanical. Physically, young Bud favored his mother's side of the family—the dark-haired, fair-skinned, fine-featured Cornicks—and there was something of his mother's soft-spoken reserve as well as his father's bonhomie in the boy's complex nature.

His earliest memories were of growing up in the Braznell family compound on Lloyd Avenue, surrounded by grandparents, aunts, uncles, and cousins. There were fifteen children, all living on the same block, including Bud, his older sister, Alice, and younger brothers Babe (Stuart) and John. The Braznell patriarch and matriarch, William Henry and Amanda Green Braznell, had

moved to St. Louis in the 1880s after an unsuccessful attempt at homesteading government-owned land in Kansas. For as long as Bud could remember his grandparents had lived on Lloyd Avenue with their oldest son, John, and his wife, Emma. Their daughter, Kate Braznell Wassall, her husband, Charlie, and the Wassall's four boys, Ray, Cliff, Warren, and Jack, lived next door, in the biggest house on the block. On Sundays the entire clan gathered at the Wassall's for a command-performance family concert led by Aunt Kate on the piano. All the young people were taught to play a musical instrument (Bud was a violinist of sorts) and some, like Ray Wassall's younger brother Cliff and Walt's sister, Alice, eventually became accomplished musicians. Accomplished or not, everyone was expected to put in his or her licks at Aunt Kate's musicales.

Walt's musical education was cut short in 1920 when his father was assigned a new sales territory and the family had to leave Lloyd Avenue. For the next four years they were continually on the move—first to Indianapolis, then to Dallas, and finally back to St. Louis, where George, with

The Braznells of Lloyd Avenue

Young Walter, front row left, in Buster Brown collar, surrounded by his siblings and cousins—the Lloyd Avenue Dirties. His mother, Clarabel, is in the third row, far left; his father, George, is the tallest man in the back row. Grandpa William occupies the upper left corner, and white-haired Grandma Amanda sits with the ladies, a stair-step or two below him. The Braznell clan occupied nearly a full block of Lloyd Avenue for the better part of three decades. This picture dates from around 1914.

Walt, at sixteen, proudly poses in his high school ROTC uniform. He was captain of the rifle team.

a little help from his brothers and in-laws, started his own business, manufacturing and marketing printing inks under the Braznell label.

During his two years at Oak Cliff High School in Dallas, Walt fell under the spell of the charismatic commandant of the school's Reserve Officer's Training Corps program, a former Marine Corps captain named Day who considered the conduct of war to be man's noblest calling. By the end of his sophomore year, when Ray Wassall's letter summoned him back to St. Louis, the boy had risen through the cadet ranks to executive officer of Oak Cliff's crack close-order drill team and captain of its ROTC rifle team.

Walt earned his keep during that first National Guard summer encampment. Besides drilling the enlisted men for several hours a day, he taught them all the customs and courtesies of the service he had learned in ROTC—how to lay out company streets, prepare tents for inspection, conduct formal guard mount, and more. Any free time was spent on the flight line, helping the ground crews and mooching rides. Ray and the other pilots were too busy preparing for the federal inspection to spare time for joy rides or instruction, but enlisted men were permitted to tag along on squadron training flights if there was an empty rear cockpit.

A Feel for Flying

The boy became a proficient backseat driver. He learned by watching and pantomiming the pilots' control movements and trained himself to sense his aircraft's position and motion from seat-of-the-pants pressure, the hum of the guywires, the blast of the slipstream against his cheeks. Like all fledgling airmen, before and since, he was admonished to keep his head out of the cockpit. Pilots of that era flew almost

entirely by feel and by visual reference to the ground. Actually, they had little choice. Their only flight instruments consisted of a couple of crude pressure gauges (an altimeter and air speed indicator); a set of bubble gauges, which operated on roughly the same principle as a carpenters' level—or would, if the aircraft held still long enough for the bubbles to stabilize; and an undampened magnetic compass that spun like a top whenever the aircraft banked its wings.

In the flat midwestern farm country where Walt learned to fly, magnetic compasses were superfluous as long as a pilot maintained visual contact with the ground. The earth below was one enormous compass rose, with section lines, fields, and roads running due north and south, east and west as far as the eye could see.

An airman's primary visual reference was, of course, the horizon. The main idea was to "keep the blue side up." Coordinated turns were executed by rolling the airplane's wings until the leading edge intersected the horizon at a specific angle—say 30 degrees—while simultaneously applying just enough control pressure on the elevator and inside rudder to keep the weight on the cheeks of the butt in balance. A weight shift to the inside of the turn meant the plane was "slipping"—that is, sliding downward along the angle of the bank. Solution: Apply more rudder and a bit more back pressure on the elevator. A weight shift to the outside of the turn indicated an uncoordinated yaw, "fishtail," or skid. Solution: Ease off on the rudder or roll in more bank. Relying strictly on external references and physical sensations like these, an experienced pilot could make coordinated turns to precise headings without gaining or losing more than a few feet of altitude—and without a single glance at his flight instruments.

Climbs and descents were made by pointing the nose of the aircraft at the desired angle rela-

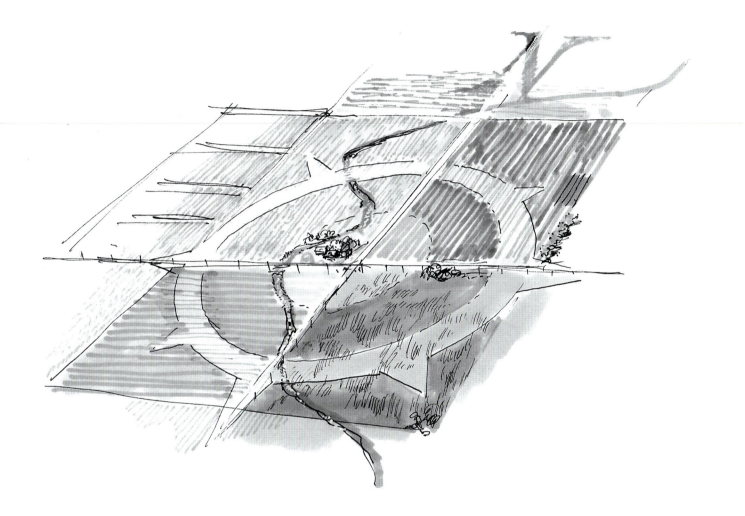

tive to the horizon and setting the throttle to maintain a constant air speed. A pilot could gauge his speed within a few miles per hour by such indicators as the wind pressure on his aileron and elevator controls and the pitch at which the wing wires vibrated. A lightness in the stomach, a slackening of pressure on the seat of the pants once the angle of climb or descent was established indicated the ship was mushing, or sinking below the intended vertical plane. Feeling that sudden sensation of emptiness, an alert pilot would add power and lower the aircraft's nose. If he ignored the warning or reacted too slowly, the wings would begin to buffet, indicating the approach of a stall; then the controls would go slack; finally, the plane would peel off into a spin—or simply drop from the sky as dead weight.

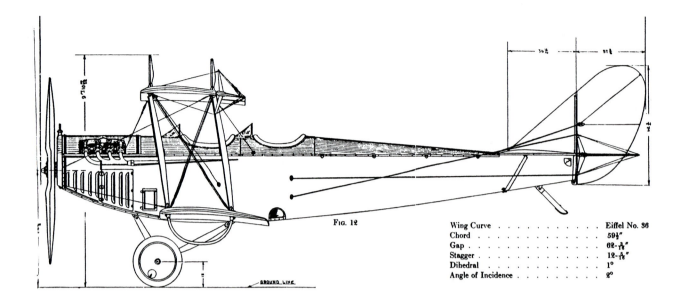

Fig. 12

Wing Curve	Eiffel No. 36
Chord	59½″
Gap	62-¹⁄₁₆″
Stagger	12-⁵⁄₁₆″
Dihedral	1°
Angle of Incidence	2°

The Jenny

Introduced in 1917, the Curtiss JN-4 "Jenny" trainer had the distinction of being the only American-designed aircraft mass-produced during World War I. Most of the more than ten thousand Jennies left over after the war were sold as surplus and snapped up by individual aviation enthusiasts, or by resellers such as Robertson Aircraft Corporation, for a few hundred dollars apiece—a fraction of their original cost. Most of these aircraft had never been removed from their original packing crates and had to be assembled at the buyer's expense. Each kit came with a handbook containing instructions for assembly and operation. It is said that an entire generation of American airmen learned to fly in Jennies. They were the Model Ts, the Tin Lizzies of aviation in the 1920s—awkward and underpowered, but stable, forgiving, and affordable. With the standard 90-horsepower Curtiss OX-5 engine, a JN-4D could do about 75 miles per hour straight and level and had a limited repertoire of aerobatic tricks, including a sissy version of the Immelman (a half loop with a roll out at the top) called the "Jenny Immelman." Later models were retrofitted with 150-horsepower Hispano-Suiza engines. The faster, more versatile JN-4Hs were used as primary trainers in the Air Corps until around 1926 and were still performing in civilian air shows and carnivals well into the 1930s.

"A Thrilling Aerial Rescue"

Toward the end of the 110th Observation Squadron's two-week encampment, an inspection team from the Air Service's 35th Division Headquarters arrived at Camp Clark to conduct its review. In honor of the occasion, Ray Wassall and the other squadron pilots staged an air show featuring a dazzling display of aerobatics, a squadron formation fly-by and, for the grand finale, a daring exhibition of wing-walking by a former barnstormer named Douglas. Sergeant Douglas was to conclude his act by diving off the wing in an apparent "leap of death" as the Jenny flew over the viewing stand. The leap—also known as a "breakaway" in standard barnstorming parlance—would be arrested by a stout, knotted rope cable, one end of which was attached to the plane's undercarriage, the other to the sky diver's leather body harness. After the breakaway, Douglas was supposed to pose for a moment, arms triumphantly outstretched as he dangled from the cord, and then hoist himself, hand over hand, back into the plane.

Walt remembers:

The actual performance came off beautifully, up to the point where Sergeant Douglas completed his jump. Maybe the knots in the cord were too far apart. Maybe he was simply out of shape and lacked the strength to overcome the combined effect of wind and gravity. Whatever the reason, he couldn't climb back into the aircraft, and the more he struggled, the more exhausted he became. So there he was, hanging helplessly from Ray's plane, in full sight of the Army brass and hundreds of visitors.

And there was Ray, circling around, trying to figure out what to do. Landing with Douglas trailing on a rope behind him was clearly out of the question. The only other possibility—and this was now becoming obvious not only to Ray, but to those of us on the ground—was to send another plane up to rescue Douglas. But how?

Ray's plan, which he explained in a note dropped from his Jenny, was to rendezvous over a nearby lake and have a crewman stationed on the rescue ship's wing cut Douglas loose, or pass him a knife so he could do it himself. A volunteer team was lined up in short order, and the wingman, Sgt. Jeddie Sharp, was armed with an assortment of knives and trussed to the wing of one of our squadron Jennies. That didn't work. The Jenny nearly tipped over trying to take off.

The only plane big and powerful enough to handle the off-center wing-load was a de Havilland DH-4 belonging to Lieutenant Fred Nelson, an Army Air Service officer on detached service with the squadron. As luck would have it, Nelson had taken the day off and was reported to be in town romancing one of the local belles. While Ray circled slowly, eking out his remaining fuel, a messenger was dispatched with a motorcycle and sidecar to find Nelson and bring him back. A quarter-hour later the three-wheeler roared up the road and skidded to a stop beside Nelson's plane. The de Havilland was already warmed up, with Sharp strapped securely to its wing. Nelson vaulted into the cockpit and off they went.

Meanwhile another rescue team had been sent to the lake to commandeer a boat. The first boat they borrowed filled with water and sank, but the rescuers managed to find another and row it to the designated splashdown area in the center of the lake.

Once aloft, the DH-4 made a beeline for Wassall's slowly circling Jenny, joined up, and snuggled in underneath, alongside the dangling aerialist. Sharp passed Douglas the knife and wished him luck. As soon as the DH-4 had veered off, Wassall dropped down over the lake and hovered there, slow-flying just above the surface, while Douglas cut himself free. Splashing down near the rescue boat, Douglas surfaced, sputtering and gasping for breath, but otherwise none the worse for his "leap of death."

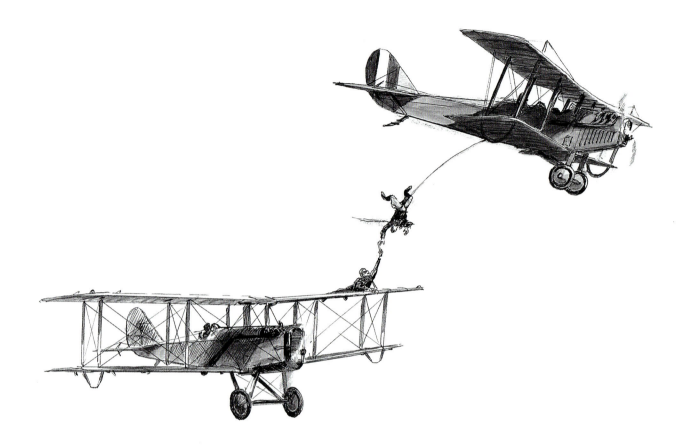

"Once aloft, the DH-4 made a beeline for Ray's slowly circling Jenny."

The incident made front-page headlines in newspapers throughout the state, and all those involved were proclaimed heroes. Being an eyewitness to this "thrilling aerial rescue" did nothing to dampen the enthusiasm of a sixteen-year-old already bitten by the flying bug.

Solo

The 110th passed its federal inspection, and Walt returned to Lloyd Avenue and his junior year at Grover Cleveland High School. In the months that followed, he and his brother Babe rode the trolley down to the St. Louis Armory every Monday night to drill with the Guardsmen. On Sundays, when the 110th's pilots gave the Jennies their weekly workout, the two boys were usually among the first to arrive at the flight line; first to help push the airplanes out of the hangar and get them ready to fly; and first to volunteer for duty as rear-cockpit "observers." Most of the squadron's senior pilots welcomed the young-sters' company and encouraged their interest in flying by occasionally giving them a turn at the controls. Gradually, Walt and Stu came to be rec-ognized for what they devoutly wished to be—apprentice airmen.

Walt:

I wonder if any pilot ever served a longer apprenticeship than we did. When I soloed at the age of eighteen, I had well over fifty hours of dual stick time and informal instruction. It seemed even longer, because those hours were stretched out over a two-year period—weekends and summer camps, scores of hours spent just milling around, boring holes in the sky, waiting for that glorious moment when the pilot would waggle the control stick back and forth—the signal that I had the controls.

On the other hand, I doubt that any pilot was ever more thoroughly prepared for his first solo flight. Typically, fledgling pilots are booted out of the nest after only ten or twelve hours of rudimentary instruction. At that point they are barely capable of taking off and landing a plane without hurting themselves. But, because I received most of my training on the job, flying actual missions, by the time they turned me loose I was already fairly proficient in more advanced aspects of flying such as aerobatics, combat maneuvers, formation flying, and simulated dead-stick landings.

Only Walt's age held him back from soloing. Even though the National Guard was somewhat loose on age requirements, Major Wassall felt that allowing a youth of sixteen or seventeen to go tooling around in the sky all by himself with an expensive piece of government property was stretching his authority—especially since the kid was his cousin.

Walt's big break came in the spring of 1926, when the Air Service—recently redesignated "Air Corps"—officially declared the Jennies obsolete. All Guard units were ordered to remove their engines and burn the airframes. On a Sunday afternoon, the last day before the order went into effect, Walt and his instructor, Captain Russell Young, had just finished a short training flight around Lambert Field and were taxiing back to

the National Guard hangar when Young motioned him to stop the plane, got out, tied a white handkerchief around the Jenny's tail skid (the customary warning to other pilots that a first solo was in progress), and jerked his thumb skyward. "I guess Russ figured the Guard had nothing to lose by allowing me to solo that old Jenny. If we crashed and burned, I'd just be sparing the squadron the trouble of scrapping it."

Slim and Phil

As a teenager, Braznell had no shortage of idols: Anyone with a pilot's rating and a few hundred hours of air time qualified. But about a year after he joined the Guard, two young airmen drifted into St. Louis who would, in time, exert an especially important influence on his career. One was Philip Love. The other was Charles Lindbergh.

Lindbergh and Love were no war-weary weekend warriors. They were young men like himself, barely out of flight school, but already seasoned professional airmen and superb pilots. And despite the gap in age, rank, and experience, they were not at all stuck up. "Slim" Lindbergh and Phil Love had been classmates at the Army Air Service's training school at Kelly Field in San Antonio. Lindbergh, the older of the two, had learned to fly—was, in fact, an accomplished barnstormer—before enlisting as an aviation cadet. Released from active duty in March 1925 after earning their Air Service wings and lieutenant's bars, the two headed north to St. Louis in hopes of landing jobs flying the mail for Robertson Aircraft Corporation when and if the company was successful in its bid for a commercial air mail route. When they reached St. Louis, they found they had plenty of time to kill: The Post Office was not expected to award the contract until fall, and the transfer of service from government to private carrier would not take place until the following spring. In the meantime, the company could offer them only part-time employment running test flights, giving flying lessons, hauling sightseers, and the like.

In August, at "Major Bill" Robertson's request, Lindbergh flew one of the company's new Curtiss Orioles down to Camp Clark to barnstorm the Guard's annual encampment and pick up a little cash selling plane rides to the local citizenry. Love went along to keep him company and help drum up business.

Walt remembers meeting Lindbergh and Love at the 1925 Guard encampment:

> Slim and Phil parked their Oriole on the squadron flight line, right next to our Jennies, and bunked in one of the Squadron's eight-man tents. When they weren't busy, which was most of the time, they burned off surplus energy organizing spot-landing contests, roughhousing, starting water fights, or playing practical jokes on one another. One morning, I recall, Slim was having trouble getting Phil out of bed. Finally, in exasperation, he picked up the huge center pole of the tent they shared and ran out into the street with it, burying Phil under a blanket of canvas that must have weighed a couple of hundred pounds. The next night, in retaliation, Phil and three tentmates waited until Slim corked off, then gently picked up his cot and carried it, tippy-toe, all the way out to the middle of the airfield, about a quarter of a mile from camp.
>
> At that point they gently lowered the cot to the ground, abandoned their sleeping bunkmate to the prairie dogs and jack rabbits, and returned to their tent to sleep the sleep of the just. I can imagine Slim waking in the pitch dark—and believe me, there is nothing darker than an unlit airfield on a moonless night—confused, disoriented, without a clue as to where he was, but knowing full well who put him there.

CAM 2

A few months after the 1925 encampment, the two roving barnstormers decided to tie down for the winter in St. Louis. Robertson Aircraft was officially awarded the Chicago–St. Louis air mail contract (Contract Air Mail Route 2, or CAM 2) in October, with service to begin the following spring. Lindbergh signed on as chief pilot, and Love was offered the number two slot. Both enlisted in the National Guard as well, so that when the Robertsons had nothing urgent for them to do, they could mosey over to the squadron hangar next door and roll out a ship for a spin, or lounge around the pot-bellied stove in the back of the officer's locker room, swapping stories with the other pilots. For added convenience Lindbergh boarded at a farmhouse on the edge of the field, a stone's throw from both Robertson's office and the Guard hangar, where he could walk to work in about as much time as it took to button his coveralls.

As spring approached, Lindbergh and Robertson's co-owner and director of flying operations, Frank Robertson, began surveying the air route from St. Louis to the Air Mail field at Maywood, Illinois (just outside Chicago) by way of Springfield and Peoria, Illinois. The airfields at Springfield and Peoria, as well as emergency landing strips en route, had to be checked out, properly fenced, and cleared of obstructions, including stray livestock. Facilities for taking on and discharging mail at Springfield and Peoria had to be set up and staffed. Work on the system of navigational beacons, which the Army Signal Corps had promised to complete by the time CAM 2 began operation, had to be pushed along: Rotating beacon lights were to be stationed every ten miles en route and 500,000 candlepower searchlights, visible for a hundred miles on a clear

Curtiss Oriole

Unlike the clunky Jennies and DH-4s of World War I vintage, the Curtiss Oriole sported a streamlined, bullet-nosed profile reminiscent of some of the great pursuit and fighter aircraft of World War II—the British Spitfire, German ME-109, and American P-36, P-39, P-40, and F-51 Mustang. The streamlining was accomplished by aligning the cylinders of its souped-up Curtiss K engine one behind the other, and encasing them in a circulating liquid coolant system. The pressurized liquid was supposed to maintain even temperatures on all cylinder heads, fore and aft. The main disadvantages of liquid-cooled engines like the Curtiss K and OX-5, the brutish Liberty engine, and the supercharged Rolls-Royce Merlin and General Motors Allison engines of World War II were the extra weight of the coolant jacket and—in battle—the vulnerability of the cooling system to enemy fire.

Air-cooled engines such as the Wright J5 Whirlwind and the Pratt & Whitney Wasp were lighter and more dependable than equivalent-horsepower liquid-cooled engines. But to keep them from overheating, their cylinders had to be mounted radially, around the crank shaft, rather than one behind the other. This frontal alignment created aerodynamic drag that tended to offset the air-cooled engines' 30 percent weight advantage. Later, designers partially solved the problem by enclosing radial engines in streamlined hoods or cowls, with trailing cowl flaps that could be cracked open to increase airflow over the cylinders, or closed to minimize drag. *Photo courtesy of National Archives*

night, installed at each major air field. For added assurance, Lindbergh, Love, and Robertson's third designated air mail pilot, Tom "Nelly" Nelson, flew the three-legged 279-mile route between St. Louis and Chicago again and again, charting prominent landmarks such as railroad crossings, bridges, steeples, and grain elevators, and logging times and headings from point to point.

Lastly, Robertson's fleet of tired old de Havilland DH-4s, along with their World War I Liberty engines, had to be modified, rebuilt, tested, and otherwise readied for the rigors of day-to-day, all-weather air mail service. Leaving as little to chance as the company could afford, Frank Robertson designated five DH's for air mail service—two to handle the regularly scheduled daily flights between Chicago and St. Louis, and three as backups. Since the Liberty engines were notoriously balky starters, Robertson decreed that at least two aircraft—one "goer" and one spare—should be fired up a half hour before each flight.

At 5:50 A.M. on April 15, 1926, Lindbergh took off from Chicago's Maywood Field, carrying Robertson's first load of mail to St. Louis. Later the same day, Love and Nelson flew north with two planeloads of inaugural mail from St. Louis, Springfield, and Peoria to Maywood, where CAM 2 connected with the Post Office's transcontinental eastbound and westbound air mail services.

Although Ford Motor Company's Aviation Division had the honor of flying the first contract air mail flight two months earlier (Detroit to Cleveland, February 16, 1926), Lindbergh's inaugural run made aviation history just the same: April 15, 1926, is still celebrated as the birthday of American Airlines, into which Robertson Aircraft's successor company, Universal Aviation Corporation, merged in 1929. Among his many other accomplishments and honors, Lindbergh

Beacon Signals

Mail route beacon lights served as milestones as well as directional beacons. Each transmitted its own unique series of long and short flashes (Morse Code) signaling its distance from the next major airfield. Here's how the system worked:

dot dash dash	(W)	10 miles
dot dot dash	(U)	20 miles
dot dot dot dash	(V)	30 miles
dot dot dot dot	(H)	40 miles
dot dash dot	(R)	50 miles
dash dot dash	(K)	60 miles
dash dot dot dot	(B)	70 miles
dash dash dot	(G)	80 miles
dash dash	(M)	90 miles

For distances of more than 90 miles, the sequence was repeated.

is recognized as American Airlines' first pilot. In this way American, no less than TWA and Pan American, to which he later lent his name, prestige, and considerable aeronautical expertise, can legitimately lay claim to a piece of the Lindbergh legend.

From Pin-Feathers to Wings

For Walt Braznell, the spring and summer of 1926, his eighteenth year, were also momentous times. High school was behind him. His father's new business was struggling, and he was needed in the ink plant. But long before Russell Young turned him loose in that doomed JN-4, Walt knew his future lay in the air. Now, following the lead of his two star role models, he decided to apply for admission into the Army Air Corps' flight school. In due course his application,

The de Havilland DH-4

Robertson Aircraft's original air mail fleet consisted of five de Havilland DH-4s equipped with 400-horsepower V-12 Liberty engines. Designed as a light bomber and observation craft, the DH-4 was first flown in 1918, but never saw combat in World War I. War surplus DHs became the workhorses of the Post Office's Postal Air Service, beginning around 1919, and were also used extensively by the contract airlines when they first began carrying mail. "They were called flaming coffins by pilots because their fuel tanks, set between engine and cockpit, were likely to explode in crash landings. Moreover, their landing speed was dangerously high; their landing gear was so weak it broke frequently on rough runways; visibility from their cockpits was poor; and they had, as pilots said, the gliding angle of a brick" (Kenneth S. Davis, *The Hero: Charles A. Lindbergh and the American Dream,* 139). In addition to their weak undercarriage and deplorable short-field landing and takeoff characteristics—qualities that made every forced landing a life-threatening gamble—DHs were heavy on the controls, a bit slow (95 miles per hour cruise speed, 118 miles per hour top speed), and outrageously awkward. Against these minor defects, one could count two overriding virtues: (1) They were cheap, and (2) They were plentiful. For Robertson and its pilots, they were an expedient—stop-gap equipment, long since obsolete, which would be replaced as soon as cash flow from mail service revenues permitted.

A Gathering of Eagles

A rare photograph of Charles Lindbergh (third from left) with his fellow CAM 2 pilots, Tom "Nelly" Nelson, Frank Robertson, Phil Love, Leslie Smith, Bud Gurney, E. L. Sloniger (mostly hidden), and Harry Perkins. Actually, when this photo was taken—on the occasion of a special air mail run in February 1928 commemorating the historic Lindbergh flight of the previous year—Lindbergh, Love, and Nelson, the original CAM 2 pilots, were no longer associated with Robertson. By the time Walt Braznell joined the group, in September 1928, Nelson and Smith had already died in air crashes.

An even rarer photo of CAM 2 Pilot Lindbergh before he became rich and famous. The shot must have been taken sometime between April 1926, when he started flying the mail, and early 1927, when he went on leave of absence from Robertson to prepare for his transatlantic flight. The pencil identification on the back of the photo reads simply, "LINDBERGH STL—CHI AM PILOT."

bearing the endorsement of 110th Observation Squadron Commander Ray Wassall, was accepted, and he was ordered to report to Brooks Field, Texas, for induction as a cadet.

At Brooks, the new cadet had barely un-packed his bag before he was on a train back to St. Louis. A half hour into his induction physical, the examining physician noted that one of his eardrums was slightly inflamed or glazed. Walt was summarily excused and told to get dressed. That was it: He was washed out. No hope of reprieve, no chance to show the Air Corps what he could do. Dazed and humiliated, the dream of an aviation career he had been nurturing for two years suddenly destroyed, he boarded the train for St. Louis like a condemned man facing life inprisonment.

By the time Walt returned home, Ray Wassall had heard the bad news from a friend—an offi-cer stationed at Brooks Field. According to this high-ranking officer, every one of the twenty-odd officer candidates inducted into Walt's class from various National Guard units throughout the country had been disqualified on physical or psychological grounds. Not one had seen the in-side of an Army cockpit before being dismissed. Puzzled, and more than a little bit suspicious, Ray arranged for Walt to get a second examina-tion from the squadron's flight surgeon, an emi-nent St. Louis physician. The flight surgeon, in turn, sent him to an eye, ear, nose, and throat specialist. Neither could find anything wrong with the young man's eardrum—or his hearing.

It was just one of those things, Wassall con-cluded. The peacetime services were constantly faced with budget squeezes and "reductions in force." If there had to be cutbacks in the Army's flight training program, the Air Corps was more likely to make them in its training commitments to the National Guard, rather than in its own ranks. Maybe someone at headquarters figured it

would be more expedient to wash out the Guard candidates en masse than to publicly admit the Air Corps was reneging on its obligations to the state air units. Expedient, perhaps—but rough on those young men.

This particular young man was in no mood for pity, however. Assured by the flight surgeon that he was not damaged goods, Walt quickly snapped out of the depression that had engulfed him on the long trip home. Wassall convinced him there were other ways, besides Cadet School, to earn his wings, if he was willing to work for them. *Damned right he was!*

Braznell became the 110th's special project. For the next six months the squadron's best pi-lots gave him a workout and a degree of per-sonal attention any Air Corps cadet would have felt privileged to receive. His trips to Lambert be-came an almost daily routine, his hours on the line devoted to study and practice. Each hour in the air was a continuous succession of loops, spins, barrel rolls, vertical reversals, chandelles, pylon eights, 180-degree and 360-degree "dead-stick" landings, short-field takeoffs and landings, and all the other precision maneuvers he would be expected to demonstrate to his examiners.

Braznell's description of this critical transition period in his young life is characteristically laconic:

> The summer and fall of 1926 were busy times for me. I studied hard and, early in 1927, I went to the Army's Chanute Field, in Rantoul, Illinois, to take the examinations for my Junior Air Pilot (JAP) rating. I toiled for thirteen hours over the written exam. My flight test the next day consisted of the usual precision maneuvers . . . It was a bitter cold morning, but I sweated for a solid hour as the Air Corps examiner put me through my paces. I never flew better in my life.
>
> A month later, a call came in to the family ink plant where I was working. It was the squadron

adjutant. My papers were in: *I passed!* I ordered a plane shoved out of the hangar, and my brother and I raced out to Lambert Field in the company truck. There I made my first flight as a certified pilot with Babe as my passenger. Up to that moment my total solo time was about thirty hours.

Jimmy Tate, one of our squadron mechanics, met the plane when Babe and I taxied in. After we shut down I asked Jimmy if he'd like to fly with me next weekend. Jimmy looked me up and down and said, "Ask me again when you have two thousand hours." Tate later became a regular passenger on my squadron missions.

Spirit of St. Louis

In February 1927 the 110th Observation Squadron's newest and youngest pilot was commissioned a second lieutenant. Among the privileges of his exalted rank was the right to hang out with the other officers around the pot-bellied stove in the pilot's locker room or at Louie De-Hatre's flightline hamburger stand. It was at Louie's one morning soon after his promotion that Braznell first heard Slim Lindbergh mention his intention to become the first airman to cross the Atlantic, New York to Paris nonstop:

Phil and one or two other close friends must have known what was going on for months, but to most us, this was incredible news. Not only was Slim talking about flying the Atlantic nonstop— something others had attempted and failed to do— but he was going to do it alone, in a single-engine plane—something no one had ever dreamed of doing. At first we wondered if this was just another of Slim's little practical jokes. But there was no faking the excitement in his voice as he told us his plan. We listened and we believed him. He really was going to do it.

By the time Braznell and most of the other squadron members heard the news, Lindbergh had already lined up his financial backers, drawn up a shopping list of aircraft, engines, and navigational equipment, and begun negotiating with Ryan Airlines of San Diego for the construction of a custom-built version of its popular single-engine monoplane, the M-2.

The unborn aircraft already had a name: *Spirit of St. Louis*. It would be powered by a 220-horsepower Wright J5 Whirlwind engine, carry 450 gallons of fuel, and have enough range— approximately 4,200 miles—to fly from New York to Moscow, if necessary. Aside from the fancy earth indicator compass he was thinking of ordering, Lindbergh would carry only the bare essentials for long-range navigation—altimeter and air speed indicator, tachometer, turn and bank indicator, eight-day clock, and both fore-and-aft and transverse levels or bubble gauges. Columbus had better navigation equipment: At least he had some means of estimating his latitude and ground speed.

By the end of February, Slim was off to the West Coast, where he would stay until the plane was built and ready to fly. The Robertsons, who were among the earliest backers of the venture, had given him an extended leave of absence from his duties as chief pilot. Phil, Nelly, and a new replacement pilot would fill in for him on the line. This was the official story. But I think we all knew that, one way or another, Slim was history as far as Robertson Aircraft and the 110th were concerned.

The thirty-three-hour solo flight of America's "Lone Eagle" from Roosevelt Field, Long Island, to Le Bourget Field, Paris, on May 20–21, 1927, stirred the imagination, admiration, and pride of

Aerial Maneuvers

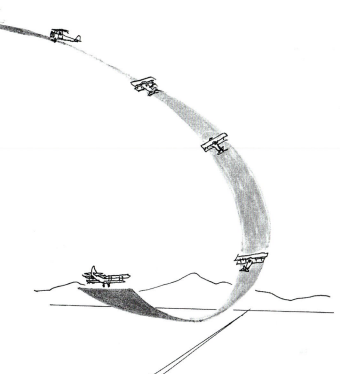

CHANDELLE: Loosely, any high-performance climbing 180-degree turn. In a classic chandelle, the aircraft's pitch and bank change constantly throughout the maneuver, until the plane rolls out in straight and level flight several hundred feet above its previous altitude, heading in the opposite direction from which it started.

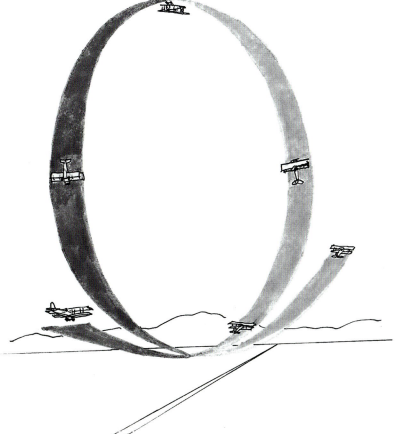

LOOP: Air speed control is crucial in the execution of a loop. The two extremes to be avoided are (1) running out of air speed (stalling) at the top—a very unpleasant sensation in inverted flight—or (2) overspeeding and pulling excessive "G" (gravitational) forces in the pull-out. The student pilot must also learn to keep the wings and nose of the aircraft square to the arc of the loop at all times, so that when he pulls out of the loop he is precisely lined up with his original heading.

VERTICAL REVERSAL (IMMELMAN): Literally a 180-degree turn performed on a vertical rather than a horizontal plane. The pilot pulls the nose of his plane straight up as if beginning a loop, but just as he reaches an inverted position at the top of the loop, he rolls into an upright position, facing in the opposite direction from which he started.

BARREL ROLL: Choosing an object on the horizon—the vanishing point of a road or section line, for example—the pilot attempts to describe a perfect arc around it with the nose of the aircraft, keeping his target in the exact center of the "barrel hoop" all the way through the roll. Unlike other rolling maneuvers, which generally involve snapping or rotating the aircraft on its longitudinal axis, this is a lazy maneuver requiring smooth coordination of bank, pitch, and rudder controls.

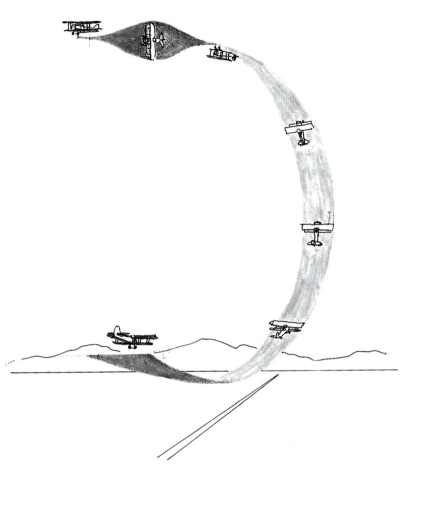

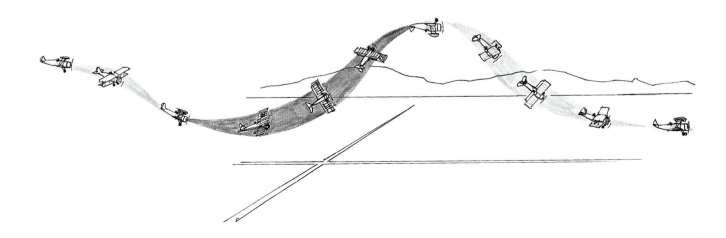

the American people in a way that bars comparison, even with the acclaim accorded the astronauts of the 1960s. The bashful young air mail pilot from St. Louis was suddenly transformed into the greatest popular hero of his era. The effect of his feat on public and governmental attitudes toward flight was so extraordinary, so intense and enduring, that aviation historians have given it a name—the Lindbergh Boom.

Walt:

The whole city turned out to cheer and wave when Slim and *Spirit of St. Louis* came home. After the official welcoming ceremonies, Colonel Lindbergh taxied into the Guard hangar, and the main

Homage to a Hero

St. Louisans hang from office and department store windows and line both sides of Olive Street twenty-deep to welcome home Charles Lindbergh and *Spirit of St. Louis* after their triumphal tour of Europe and the eastern United States. *Photo courtesy of Missouri Historical Society*

doors were closed to protect him and his plane from being ripped apart by the adoring throng. Inside the hangar, we squadron officers were lined up at attention, prepared to give the returning hero our own special welcome. As Slim crawled out of *Spirit's* cockpit and ducked under its wing, Phil Love let fly with a five-gallon bucket of water, drenching him from head to toe. Expressionless, and with all the dignity he could muster under the circumstances, Colonel Lindbergh removed his dripping tunic and draped it over *Spirit's* wing strut. Then he strode over to the nearest water barrel—there were a dozen of them, all marked "for emergency use only"—-scooped out a bucketful, and returned to where Phil stood, manfully holding his ground. Cracking the now famous Lindbergh grin, Slim unloaded the bucket squarely in Phil's face. That was the signal for the party to begin, and within seconds everyone in the hangar had grabbed a bucket and joined in. When we'd finished—that is, when the barrels were empty— we were a sad-looking bunch of officers, the hangar was ankle deep in mud, and Slim had been properly welcomed home.

Amusing or appalling, depending on your taste for practical jokes, there is an almost mythic quality to Braznell's story of the water fight: the newly anointed sun god bidding farewell to his mortal comrades, etc., etc. That he seems to have thoroughly enjoyed the dousing suggests that young Charles Lindbergh was not quite ready to be deified.

After a triumphal tour of the U.S., Slim returned to Lambert Field. On his last day with us, he joined Phil in a flying exhibition featuring a formation fly-over and a few stunts in the new Travel Air mail planes Robertson had just purchased. I watched them streak low across the field and burst upward in a graceful twin chandelle and thought I'd have given anything to be in Slim and Phil's place at that moment.

A year later, he would be.

The Education of an Air Mail Pilot

Two years after his historic transatlantic flight, the boom in aviation Lindbergh set in motion is still going strong. The North Atlantic has now been flown successfully several times, including the first nonstop flight by a woman, Amelia Earhart, on June 17, 1928. In 1929 Arctic explorer Richard Byrd adds another important chapter to aviation history with his aerial exploration of Antarctica in a Ford TriMotor; Major Carl Spaatz and Captain Ira Eaker of the Army Air Corps enter the history books for the first time by remaining aloft 150 hours, 40 minutes, and 15 seconds—an endurance record scores of aviators will surpass over the next two years; and in St. Louis, test pilot Dale Jackson scores the dizziest of records in this delightfully dizzy era by performing 417 consecutive barrel rolls in a Curtiss Robin monoplane.

Since the passage of the Air Commerce Act of 1926, the federal Department of Commerce, under Secretary of Commerce Herbert Hoover, has assumed responsibility for overseeing the development of the fledgling commercial aviation industry. The department's new duties include the licensing of commercial pilots and certifica-

tion of commercial aircraft, regulation and control of air traffic, production of aerial maps and navigation charts, preparation and dissemination of weather reports and forecasts, and the investigation of air crashes. With Hoover's victory in the 1928 presidential election and the appointment of his campaign manager, Walter Folger Brown, as postmaster general, commercial aviation now has two powerful allies in the administration.

Aircraft production has risen sixfold since 1926. Intercity airline passenger traffic, practically nonexistent three years ago, is expected to top 400,000 by the end of 1929. And enrollment in flying schools is soaring. Learning to fly has become a status symbol among the flaming youth of Scott Fitzgerald's and Cole Porter's generation—an experience Porter compares with "champagne, mere alcohol," and other popular "kicks" of the 1920s.[1] And where better to get one's kicks than at Lambert Field, St. Louis—"Where Lindbergh Learned to Fly"?

---

1. "I Get no kick from champagne . . . flying too high with some guy in the sky is my idea of nothing to do . . . but I get a kick out of you." Cole Porter, "I Get a Kick Out of You."

A Bad Day at the Office

In May 1928, at the age of twenty, Walt Braznell quit his job at the Braznell-Sylvester Ink Company and went to work at Lambert Field as an instructor pilot for Robertson Aircraft Corporation. With scarcely any guidance, supervision, or experience in the aircraft RAC used for instruction, he was immediately placed in charge of a motley group of farm boys and college students who had come to "Learn to Fly Where Lindbergh Learned to Fly." That was how RAC advertised its flying school. What the slogan lacked in precision it more than made up for in appeal to the hero-worshiping youth of that day.[2]

The flying school consisted of Walt and two other Robertson pilots, a dirt-floor classroom in the back of the company hangar, and a small fleet of Lincoln Standard biplanes equipped with Curtiss OX-5 engines. Ground school training aids consisted of a blackboard and a piece of chalk. For fees ranging from five hundred to a thousand dollars, depending upon what the traffic would bear, students were guaranteed a minimum of eight hours of dual flight time or sufficient instruction to "demonstrate proficiency"—that is, take off and land an airplane without hurting anyone. Unlike Robertson's air mail pilots, who earned a princely three hundred to four hundred dollars a month, instructors did not draw regular salaries. They were paid thirty-five dollars for every student they soloed, a small fee for taking students on cross-country flights, and a twenty-dollar bonus for every student who stayed on to com-

plete the full, deluxe course of twenty hours' dual instruction and solo time.

Braznell's first day at Robertson's flying school started out badly and got worse:

After the usual preliminaries, I selected a student—the son of a prominent St. Louis banker—and walked down to the line where a mechanic was adjusting the valve clearances on the Standard's engine. I asked the mechanic about the plane's condition. He said the engine would only turn 1100 rpm. Normal was 1300 rpm. He fiddled with the engine for a while without apparent success. Then he disappeared into the hangar and returned a minute or two later carrying something called a "toothpick" prop—a thin-bladed piece of lumber shaped like an oversized toothpick and, as I discovered, displaced about the same amount of air.

With this new prop, the engine turned over at a furious pace. The mechanic looked pleased with his work, and at this early stage in my career, I wasn't prepared to question his judgment. So I loaded the student in the rear seat and we taxied down to the far corner of the field. (I may have been naive and inexperienced, but I wasn't stupid, and I intended to give myself the widest possible margin of safety in case anything went wrong.) As it was, we used up the entire field on takeoff and barely managed to clear the telephone wires at the far end.

After nursing the plane up to 500 feet, I let the student take the controls and warm up with a few gentle climbing turns. By this time we were several miles from the field. I had just about decided we weren't going any further or higher that day, when—as if it had come to the same conclusion—the Standard's engine belched a huge sheet of flame and stopped cold. I immediately grabbed the controls and began looking for a place to set her down.

Compared to the aircraft I'd trained in with the National Guard, the Standard had the gliding range of a manhole cover. I had barely a minute to pick a landing spot and get the ship turned into the wind before we touched down. As we bumped across the clearing, a lone cow looked up and then

2. Actually, Lindbergh was largely self-taught. He took a few lessons from Standard Aviation in Lincoln, Nebraska, but never soloed. Later, he bought a Jenny, which he almost crashed on his first attempted solo flight. He stuck with it, however, and by the time he was admitted to the Army Air Service School at Brooks Field, Texas, was reputed to be a pretty fair country barnstormer.

resumed grazing. In the distance, a dog barked, a screen door screeched and banged, and in a moment I heard someone starting up a Model T—probably the owner of the spread, heading our way. I sat there in the cockpit, enjoying the stillness of the countryside and the firmness of the sod under our wheels, and let the adrenaline slowly drain from my veins.

"Well, pilot, what do we do now?" chirped the student, and I could tell from the breezy way he said it he was dying to get back to his fraternity house to tell the fellows about his first "deadstick" landing.

Company policy regarding forced landings was, "You put it there, you get it out." So, after bidding good-bye to my student, I arranged for a mechanic to drive out to the pasture, mend the broken gas line that had caused the engine failure, replace that ridiculous toothpick prop, and get the ship ready for an early morning return flight.

Shortly after dawn the next day the mechanic and I drove out to the farm. When we got there, two other cars were already parked alongside the road, and in the distance I could see my ship, its engine idling, my eager student at the controls. A half-dozen young men and women were clustered around the plane, shouting and waving. They appeared to be drunk as lords.

I started to run. But before I got halfway across the field, the OX-5 roared to life, the spectators gave a lusty cheer, and off went ship and student, bounding and zigzagging across the meadow like a scared deer. At first I was afraid they'd never make it. Then I began to worry that they might. To the best of my knowledge, this student had never landed an aircraft, drunk or sober.

The Standard, meanwhile, was heading straight for a small wash that cut diagonally across the pasture. Seeing he couldn't make it, the student veered sharply to the left. The plane, gathering speed and now totally out of control, hit the wash head-on, bounced hard, and flipped over on its back.

Fortunately, the student wasn't hurt. He was sent home, forfeiting the balance of his flying school tuition. Later we brought out a crew, righted the Standard, patched it up and I flew it back to Lambert Field.

Moment of Truth

"When I started flying," Walt wrote, many years later, "I wondered how I would react in a real emergency. That first deadstick was my moment of truth, and I handled it about as calmly and professionally as I had any right to expect. If I had behaved differently, I probably would have given up flying."

Like all good pilots, Walt had the knack of staying ahead of the aircraft—not just remaining alert to danger, but anticipating it, planning for it, and rehearsing his responses until they became second nature. "Stay ahead of your aircraft" was a mantra he often shared with me during my Air Force flying days—as I'm sure he did with generations of American Airlines pilots.

RAC: An Airline in Embryo

Robertson Aircraft Corporation, founded in 1919 and incorporated in 1921, got its start buying, reconditioning, and selling war surplus aircraft, engines, and parts. By 1925 the company boasted an armada of 333 ready-to-fly airplanes—Lincoln Standards, Curtiss Jennies, DH-4s, and the like—mostly purchased at public auctions in which the only bidders besides the Robertson brothers were scrap metal dealers. It is said that the brothers cornered the market for surplus Curtiss OX-5 engines, the standard power plant used in early model Jennies, Standards, Travel Airs, and other light planes of the postwar era. In 1927, when William Robertson formed an alliance with Curtiss to manufacture a new three-seater cabin plane called the Robin, part of the deal included selling RAC's inventory of nearly a thousand reconditioned OX-5 engines—the entire remaining stock—back to Curtiss for the sum of $400,000.

While Bill Robertson tended to the aircraft and parts business, Frank ran RAC's flight operations. These included regularly scheduled weekend sightseeing tours around St. Louis and environs, short-hop passenger taxi services, a bit of stunt flying at county fairs—and, of course, the now famous "Lindbergh" flying school.

In October 1925 Robertson was awarded the Contract Air Mail (CAM 2) route between St. Louis and Chicago, by way of Springfield and Peoria. Regular mail service over the 279-mile corridor began April 15, 1926, with Chief Pilot Charles Lindbergh making the inaugural morning southbound flight from Chicago and Lindbergh, Phil Love, and two reserve pilots, Dan Robertson and Ray Wassall, flying the first four planeloads of specially franked commemorative air mail out of St. Louis, Springfield, and Peoria later the same day. In its first full year of operation the fledgling airline flew 511 out of 513 scheduled flights and completed 490 of them, or nearly 97 percent of originations. In all, it carried 34,772 pounds of mail and ten paying passengers.

At the time Walt joined RAC, the company was going through the first of three rapid-fire reorganizations that would culminate in 1930 with the absorption of Robertson's flight operations into American Airways. Early in 1928 Bill Robertson resigned to become general manager of the new Curtiss Robertson Airplane Manufacturing Company. A group of investors headed by St. Louis investment banker Arthur Stifel purchased RAC's flying business, including its lucrative air mail contract, and immediately announced ambitious plans for expanding its scheduled airline operations. Frank Robertson remained manager of the reorganized operating company for a short time, then he too departed. In the months that followed, RAC extended its contract air mail service to Kansas City and Omaha; added several Ford TriMotor and Fokker F-10 trimotor passen-

ger planes to its fleet of single-engine DH-4s, Pitcairn Mailwings, Travel Airs, Ryan Broughams, and Stearmans; and commenced a $250,000 passenger terminal and hangar construction program at Lambert Field.

Then, in October 1928, the Stifel group sold out to a newly formed aviation holding company, Universal Aviation Corporation, and Robertson's operations were merged with Universal's five other operating companies to form the Universal Air Lines System, with headquarters in St. Louis and passenger and air mail contract services covering most of the Midwest and Great Plains, from Cleveland to Omaha and from Minneapolis to Tulsa. A year later Universal was, in turn, acquired by The Aviation Corporation (AVCO), a New York–based holding company, and merged into AVCO's American Airways System. We'll return to that story later.

The Phantom Air Mail Pilot

By the fall of 1928 the original three-man air mail team of Charles Lindbergh, Phil Love, and Tom Nelson had long since moved on. After his triumphal return to St. Louis in June 1927, Lindbergh invited Love to accompany him on a U.S. Department of Commerce–sponsored goodwill tour of the United States and Latin America. At about the same time, Nelson left Robertson to work for another mail carrier, National Air Transport. A few months later Nelson died in a plane crash in the notorious Hell Stretch of western Pennsylvania on a flight from Cleveland to Hadley Field, New Jersey.

Harlan "Bud" Gurney, another Lindbergh friend and sidekick from barnstorming days, was now chief pilot of RAC. In addition to Gurney, two veteran Air Mail Service pilots, E. L. Sloniger and Leslie L. Smith, filled in the three-pilot rota-

The Ryan Brougham: A Lindbergh Look-Alike

Frank Robertson, head of Robertson's Aviation Division, and Chief Pilot Bud Gurney proudly display their new Ryan Brougham. The year was probably 1928. The Brougham had a deservedly short career in air mail service, but a lingering impact on St. Louis's burgeoning aviation industry. Patterned after the famous Spirit of St. Louis, it enjoyed a great popularity among Lindbergh's many admirers in the area. Phil De Catesby Ball, a St. Louis industrialist and sportsman and one of Lindbergh's earliest backers, tried to order a Brougham soon after Slim's famous transatlantic flight and before the first commercial model had been built. But Ball was told that a rival St. Louis businessman, a Mr. Von Hoffman, had already purchased the Ryan distributorship for the area, and the order would have to be placed through Von Hoffman's office. This so incensed Ball that he bought the Ryan company lock, stock, and barrel and moved its factory from San Diego to St. Louis. *Photo courtesy of American Airlines C. R. Smith Museum*

tion on the St. Louis–Chicago mail run. Smith, an expert instrument pilot, didn't last long with RAC. On a courier flight for the *Chicago Tribune* between Chicago and the Democratic National Convention in Houston during the summer of 1928, he flew into a thunderstorm over the Ozark Mountains and never came out. A search party found his shattered DH-4 near the summit of a ridge, its throttle wide open.

Braznell:

Les Smith loved to fly in weather. For Smith, a day without rain, snow, or fog was like a day without sunshine for the rest of us. This was in the early days before we had anything as sophisticated as turn and bank indicators, gyro compasses, or artificial horizons. We had to improvise. One old-timer used a plumb bob consisting of a used spark plug and a piece of string tied to the instrument panel to tell up from down and whether his wings were level or banked. Another held a half-filled bottle of milk between his legs. There were no airborne radios or radio navigation aids at the time, so Smith had to navigate the short stretches between St. Louis, Springfield, Peoria, and Chicago by dead reckoning and by the glow of city lights through the overcast.

O. L. Spence, our station manager at Peoria, told me how, on nights when the field was socked in with "fog so thick you couldn't see from here to that barbed-wire fence," he would hear the familiar bat-bat-bat of a Liberty engine overhead—"and I'd know for sure it was Leslie Smith carrying the mail." If the field at Chicago was overcast, Les would head out over Lake Michigan, let down to a few hundred feet above the water, and try to sneak into Maywood Field under the cloud deck. If that didn't work, he would head for home, and on toward eight or nine o'clock anyone hanging around the airfields at Peoria or Springfield would hear that old DH-4 passing overhead again, heading south. To Smith there was nothing remarkable about flying all the way from St. Louis to Chicago and back on instruments. Yet, at the time, there

probably weren't a dozen pilots in the United States who could keep an aircraft upright without a visual horizon for twenty minutes, much less the four or five hours Smith's trip took.

A Spot Landing Contest

By late summer of 1928, Robertson Aircraft Corporation was facing an acute shortage of pilots. The company had recently bought four new Ford TriMotors and was planning to inaugurate daily passenger service between Chicago and St. Louis in addition to the usual early morning and evening mail runs. More pilots would also be needed to support the new air mail service (CAM 28) between St. Louis and Omaha, beginning in January 1929. Meanwhile, Gurney had hired Ray Fortner as Leslie Smith's replacement on the CAM 2 run and was looking for someone to take his own place in the three-day rotation. Having exhausted the available supply of veterans, Gurney now turned to Robertson's pool of young and relatively inexperienced instructor pilots.

Braznell continues:

One morning in early September I saw a notice on the bulletin board announcing that tryouts for

Dead Reckoning

Dead reckoning, a corruption of "deductive reckoning," is a method of navigation in which the pilot estimates or *deduces* his position based on the length of time flown on a given compass heading or sequence of headings at a given indicated air speed. In the following example, the pilot has vectored in the estimated wind speed and direction at his cruising altitude to arrive at an adjusted heading, ground speed, and estimated flight time.

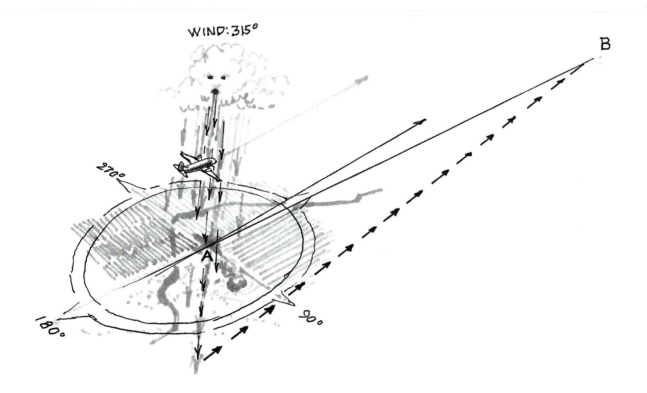

Destination (point B), 150 miles, true course 360 degrees.

Forecast winds en route, 315 degrees at 30 miles per hour.

Indicated air speed at 10,000 feet, 150 miles per hour.

True air speed (adjusted for temperature and barometric pressure at altitude), 171 miles per hour.

Ground speed (adjusted, per wind vector, for winds aloft), 149 miles per hour.

Estimated time en route: 150 miles at 149 miles per hour = one hour.

Magnetic heading: 360 degrees (TC), plus magnetic variation (+10 degrees), less wind vector (-8 degrees)

= 002 degrees.

the position of air mail pilot would be conducted the following Saturday. Anyone interested was invited to report to the flight line at 0800 Saturday.

Four candidates showed up Saturday morning—the two young pilots I shared instructing duties with, myself, and Dan Robertson, Frank and Bill's kid brother. Besides the contestants, a few spectators had gathered along the flight line to watch Bud Gurney put us through our paces. Promptly at 8 o'clock, he called us together and explained the rules of the competition. His next air mail pilot, he said, would have to demonstrate proficiency in landing a plane in a tight spot under emergency conditions—the sort of conditions we could expect to run into routinely once we went on the line. Accordingly, each of us would make three short-field or "spot" landings—two with power on, one "deadstick." On the deadstick approach we were supposed to simulate an engine failure by retarding the throttle to idle at a point 1,000 feet above and directly abeam of the landing area. Then we were to execute a 180-degree gliding turn to final approach and land without adding power. To make the test as realistic as possible, Bud had rigged up a "hedge" consisting of a tape stretched between two poles at a height of about ten feet. The object, he explained, was to land as close as possible to the hedge without breaking the tape. The pilot who set the DH down the shortest average distance from the obstacle would be declared the winner and new CAM 2 air mail pilot.

We drew numbers out of Bud's helmet to decide the order of competition. The first contestant made a couple of pretty fair power-on approaches and landings, but came up short on his deadstick approach and had to add throttle. He was automatically disqualified. The next pilot also did well on his two power-assisted landings, but overcompensated for the first pilot's mistake and missed the landing spot by a good hundred yards on his simulated engine-out approach.

With the contest now narrowed down to just the two of us, it was obvious that Dan had become the prohibitive favorite among the sideline gamblers and kibitzers. He clearly had the edge in experience. On the other hand, I figured if the boss's brother wanted the job as bad as I did, he would have had it by now. Desire had to count for something.

They tell me that I practically tore down Bud's makeshift goal posts on my first two approaches, grazing the tape with my tail skid and touching down within thirty yards of the barrier. But on the final deadstick approach, I played it a bit too safe, came in high and hot and drifted fifty yards down the field before sticking her down. Now there was nothing to do but stand on the sidelines and watch Dan take advantage of the easy set-up shot I'd left him.

Dan was a slick pilot—no question about it. He made the first two spot landings look insultingly easy, slipping that lumbering brick of a DH-4 over the hedge and setting her down as light as a feather, practically in the shadow of the goal posts.

On his third approach, he really rubbed it in. No *simulated* deadstick for Dan. At the point over the landing spot where he was supposed to idle back, he raised the de Havilland's nose to lose speed, cut his engine, and stopped the prop. Since the DH's Liberty engine could not be restarted in the air once the prop stopped, he was now committed to a real deadstick landing. (This was how it was done in the high-stakes spot-landing contests Dan was fond of organizing. I'd seen him do it many times.)

Somewhere between his base turn and getting set up on final approach it must have dawned on Dan that there were distinct differences in the sink rates of the DH-4 and the sleek little Curtiss Oriole he was used to flying. He was now making a beeline for the landing zone, with none of the flashy fishtailing and side-slipping an expert spot-lander used to kill excess altitude and air speed. You could see he had little of either to spare. Now, with a hundred yards to go and the DH sinking fast, Robertson was clearly in trouble. I'm thinking, *"Be smart, Dan— forget the dumb competition. Save your bacon."* But Dan's no quitter. One last stretch, a slight lift of the nose, and he's over the tape!

Well, almost.

For an instant the DH seemed to hang in the air above Bud's makeshift goal posts like a tethered balloon. Then it gave a little shudder and dropped straight down, hitting the ground so hard its undercarriage was rammed clear up through its lower wing panels. When the dust settled, there was Danny, grinning sheepishly up at us from the cockpit of the lowest-slung de Havilland I ever saw.

A few months after this episode Dan left RAC. When last heard from he was somewhere south of the border, flying for a wealthy Mexican landowner, cattleman, and aviation promoter.

True to his word, Bud Gurney named Braznell his replacement on CAM 2. There was, however, more than the usual amount of field gossip and second-guessing about the promotion. Word had it that Gurney didn't like Guard officers, that Braznell was too young and inexperienced for the job, that he would probably quit and run home to Mama when winter set in and the weather turned ugly. At least the gossips were right about Braznell's inexperience: On the eve of his first flight as an air mail pilot his logbook showed fewer than four hundred total hours of flying time and not a single night landing.

"Neither Snow, Nor Sleet . . . Nor Gloom of Night"

Under the original CAM 2 terms, the Post Office paid Robertson a flat 15.5 cents per ounce to transport mail from St. Louis to Chicago. To encourage public patronage, air mail postage was deliberately pegged below cost—ten cents per ounce. In 1928 the rate was further reduced to five cents per ounce.

On a good day—that is, when the weather cooperated and everything else went according to plan—mail received at the downtown St. Louis post office by 3 P.M. would depart Lambert Field at 4:15 and arrive in Chicago by way of Springfield and Peoria three hours later. At

Chicago, eastbound mail would be transferred to planes departing that evening for Cleveland and, ultimately, Hadley Field, New Jersey. Arriving at Hadley early the next morning, the mail would be delivered to its destination in Manhattan before noon, a full business day ahead of the regular St. Louis–New York mail service.

In really foul weather, the afternoon flight from St. Louis to Chicago might be delayed for hours or scrubbed outright. But since weather reports were notoriously unreliable, pilots typically took off whenever local conditions permitted and kept going until low visibility or icing forced them to turn back or land at emergency fields en route. If the weather got better, they would try again. If not, they would haul their mail pouches down to the nearest railroad station, entrain them, and head for home as soon as the clouds lifted.

Expensive, unreliable, and not much faster than regular mail even on good days, the early air mail service could never have justified its existence on the grounds of market demand or public necessity. The fees paid by the Post Office to its contract carriers were, in effect, federal subsidies established to promote the development of a strong, healthy, competitive commercial airline industry. That was how the White House, the Post Office, and the Commerce Department looked at it, anyway. On the other hand, many contract carriers, including RAC's Robertson brothers, felt the rates did not begin to compensate their stockholders for the risk of their capital—much less encourage them to spend huge sums of money equipping their pilots with modern aircraft and navigation aids or pampering their occasional passengers with such expensive luxuries as heated cabins, coffee, and box lunches.

To compensate for the stinginess of postal subsidies, the carriers took maximum advantage of the disparity between the 5-cents-per-ounce postal rate and the 15.5-cents-per-ounce contract carrier rate. Month in, month out, diligent Robertson staffers posted a phenomenal quantity of air mail: company sales brochures, greeting cards, telephone books, Sears Roebuck and Montgomery Ward catalogs, registered letters (which required a special leather pouch sealed with a heavy metal clasp and lock)—even the occasional packaged brick—all of which generated a handsome profit for their smiling employers.

Maiden Flight

The daily departure of the RAC mail plane from St. Louis to Chicago was a spectacle guaranteed to impress anyone who happened to witness it with the swiftness, precision, and machine-like efficiency of the contract air mail service. It seldom failed to attract an admiring crowd.

Braznell:

The mail plane would be parked on the ramp just outside Robertson Aircraft's office, all gassed and ready to go. Promptly at 4 P.M., RAC's chief mechanic would fire up the engine and start warming her up. This was the signal for all the loiterers in the area to gather around. A few minutes later the pilot would lumber out of the locker room dressed in heavy, fleece-lined leather flying suit, boots, and helmet; goggles up; service revolver in its shoulder holster; parachute slapping against his backside. While he climbed into the cockpit and exchanged a few words with the engineer, bystanders would crane their necks toward Natural Bridge Road, watching for the mail truck from downtown St. Louis. It always appeared in the nick of time, trailing a cloud of dust. Around the corner of the hangar it would fly, pulling up along side the mail plane with a screeching of brakes and a slamming of doors. Mail pouches and official papers changed hands at

a feverish pace; the leather straps that held down the cover of the mail bin were cinched and buckled; and the afternoon mail was on its way.

On this particular day, Sept. 28, 1928, I was at the controls of one of the company's new Wright J-5 Whirlwind-powered Travel Airs, and this was my first flight as an air mail pilot. In keeping with local custom, I blasted the plane's tail around, blowing dust and debris all over the onlookers, and immediately began my takeoff roll. Once airborne, I held the ship a few feet off the ground to gather speed, then, rotating her wings into a steep bank, I cut diagonally across the field and rolled out with the late afternoon sun over my left shoulder, on course to Springfield.

It was one of those golden fall afternoons, with just enough breeze to clear away the mid-day haze and make the lengthening shadows stand out black and crisp. I flew on the deck until the sod runway at Springfield was under my nose, crossed the fence at the beacon house wide out, and pulled up into a steep chandelle. Cutting the throttle at the top of my turn, I put the Travel Air into an exaggerated nose-high slip and followed that with a fish-tail or two to kill air speed and altitude. A moment later I was down and taxiing toward our Springfield mail truck driver. I had wasted this performance on an audience of one. It was a shameful bit of hot-dogging, but then, I was twenty years old and this was the greatest day in my young life, the realization of a dream.

As the driver handed up his mail pouch he smiled and said, "Thought you was Slim Lindbergh, comin' in like that. That's how he done it when the wind was from the South."

I reached Chicago well after dark. Approaching the airport's pitch black cinder runway I landed over the lights—which is to say I was still several feet from the ground and rapidly running out of air speed when my wheels should have been rolling. Fortunately, the Travel Air was a forgiving ship with excellent stall characteristics and a good strong undercarriage. My first flight as an air mail pilot—and my first night landing—ended without damage to anything but my pride.

The Travel Air

Built by the Travel Air Company of Wichita, Kansas, the Travel Air was one of several light, sturdy, open-cockpit biplanes developed in the mid-1920s as replacements for the converted World War I bombers and observation craft that had been used to fly the mail since 1918. Unlike the clunky trimotors and single-engine passenger planes of the postwar era, the Travel Air was designed specifically to carry mail, and nothing but mail, at the lowest possible cost per mile. The original 90-horsepower Curtiss OX-5 engine gave it a cruising speed of 85 miles per hour—almost as fast as the DH-4s, with their balky, gas-guzzling Liberty engines. The Travel Air was also one of the first commercial aircraft equipped with brakes, which made it much easier to maneuver in tight spots than the DH-4. About the time Braznell started flying the mail, Robertson's Travel Airs were refitted with 220-horsepower Wright J-5 Whirlwind air-cooled engines, which boosted cruising speed to around 100 miles per hour and greatly improved the aircraft's short-field takeoff performance. *Photo courtesy of Frank H. Robertson Collection*

Wake-up Call

After landing the mail in Chicago around 7 P.M., RAC pilots typically killed the evening at a steak house, speak-easy, movie theater, or bowling alley near the field, then hit the sack in anticipation of a dawn wake-up call and an early return flight to St. Louis. Sometimes they bunked at the field, in a small room in the loft or balcony of the company's Chicago hangar; sometimes in a two-bedroom apartment near the airport shared with pilots from Minneapolis-based Northwest Airlines.

Braznell:

The time of our departure for St. Louis the following morning depended on when the mail arrived from the West Coast. There was no need to consult a schedule or call operations for an ETA (estimated time of arrival). No one knew when the mail would arrive. But everyone within ten miles of the airport knew precisely when it *did* arrive. The inbound Boeing Air Transport pilots saw to that. Anywhere from 5 A.M. on, depending on the winds and weather, they would come barreling in, ripping across the field with the throttles of their Boeing 40Bs wide open and those tremendous Hornet engines making enough racket to give nosebleeds to half the population of Chicago. That was the wake-up call for the National Air Transport pilot waiting to complete the transcontinental mail run, and to airmen from all the regional feeder lines connecting with Chicago—Robertson, Embrey Riddle from Cincinnati, Thompson Aeronautical from Detroit, Northwest from Minneapolis, and N.E.T. from Kansas City and Dallas.

After breakfast, we would check in at our respective field offices, glance at the day-old Department of Agriculture weather maps, and then taxi our ships across to the northeast corner of the field and line up six or seven abreast, props ticking, looking for all the world like the LaFayette Escadrille preparing to launch a strike on the Jerries. Soon after we assembled, our mechanics would come trotting out of the post office with our mail bags, sling them aboard, and batten down the cargo hatches. From then on it was every man for himself—no one to read us climb-out instructions, no tower to signal us into position for takeoff, no radios, no green lights, *no tower*—just go!

Imagine a covey of bobwhite quail exploding out of a cornfield on a fine October morning. Multiply the mass by a factor of four or five thousand. Add sound effects—the combined acoustical wallop of six or seven high-performance internal combustion engines, more than 2,000 horses in total, each at full takeoff power. Boy, oh boy, that was something!

The Life of an Air Mail Pilot

Air mail pilots were still a rare and exotic breed in 1928, when Walt Braznell took his place on CAM 2's three-man roster. At the time, fewer than 120 pilots were employed in flying the nation's thirty-odd contract air mail routes. The rosters of the commercial air mail carriers included a richly assorted mixture of former barnstormers, carney operators, crop dusters, rum runners, farm boys, college dropouts, aeronautical engineers, writers, dreamers, adventurers, free spirits, mavericks, and eccentrics.

Braznell:

They came from all sorts of backgrounds. Some were college educated; some could barely write their names. One of the great ones used to perform in circuses, riding a motorcycle around the near-vertical walls of a bowl-shaped track. Another was a carnival magician.

One of my best friends, Joe Hammer, grew up on a farm in Marshall, Missouri. When Joe was about sixteen, a Curtiss Pusher made a forced landing and cracked up in a field near his home. The plane's owner said he'd had enough of flying and offered to sell it to Joe "as is" for eight hundred bucks. Joe borrowed the money from his widowed mother and rebuilt the Pusher with parts salvaged from an old Buick. Then he taught himself to fly it. That's how Joe became a pilot.

Most of the older, senior air mail pilots had learned to fly in the military service. Some had seen combat in World War I. Many were veterans of the Post Office's Air Mail Service. In fact, when Boeing Air Transport and National Air Transport (the combined forerunners of United Airlines) took over the "Main Line" transcontinental air mail route in 1927, the forty-three remaining Air Mail Service pilots transferred en masse from government to BAT or NAT payrolls without changing jobs.

The Air Mail Service veteran, with his studied coolness in the face of danger, his disdain for bragging and bravado, his independence and distrust of authority, set the style for the first generation of airline pilots and for generations to come. In his classic memoirs, *By the Seat of My Pants,* Dean Smith eloquently described that model pilot and what made him tick:

The air mail pilot's life was anything but routine. His trips were an uninterrupted series of extraordinary events. He learned to live with the chill of high danger; he met a constant challenge to his personal skill, was paid a lot of money, and had a whale of a lot of fun. . . . [The combination of high pay and plenty of leisure time] made for a merry life, even if indications were that it would be a short one. As a normal thing we worked two or three days a week, five or six hours a day, plus standing reserve perhaps one day a week, which only meant keeping the field advised how they could reach us. I spent my time as unproductively as possible: learning to play golf, chasing girls, reading omnivorously and indiscriminately; investigating dives and joints in the area; and—an interest that has remained with me ever since—trout fishing.

FUI (Flying under the Influence)

Drinking was also a part of the air mail pilot's "merry life," and not all of it was confined to leisure hours. Smith writes:

The flying heroes of the war had been hard-living and nonchalant in their recklessness, and perhaps their behavior gave us [Air Mail Service pilots] our standards. Then too, the end of the war and the onset of prohibition brought on a general increase in consumption of liquor during the 1920s. In any case, I can remember few pilots who did not drink, and many who really put it away.

Smith tells the story of Air Mail Service pilot Slim Lewis, who had a bit too much to drink on the night before a scheduled morning flight from New York to Cleveland. Arriving at Hazelhurst Field at 5:30 A.M., Slim stumbled into his flying suit and weaved out into the fog, calling for the mechanics to come and start his plane. When they refused, he became violent and started wrecking the operations hut. "After he picked up and threw the pot-bellied stove out the window, they finally gave in," Smith recalls. With the fog barely improved and the ceiling on the deck, the mechanics cranked up the engine, lowered Slim into his cockpit, and fastened his seat belt. Immediately, Slim gave it the gun. As soon as his wheels lifted, he rolled into a near-vertical bank with one wing tip not a foot from the ground and, flying like an angel, held it there without faltering an inch as he did a full 180-degree turn, flattened out, and came roaring back up the field directly at us. Just as he reached us he pulled back on the controls and the plane shot up in a steep climb, disappearing instantly into the fog. Two hours later Bellefonte telephoned a report that Slim had come in over College Ridge flying upside down, had made a series of slow rolls during his approach, landed perfectly, and gone on to Cleveland.

Everything to See

Why did men choose the life of an air mail pilot? More compelling than the money and the high life, far more important than the excitement and the thrills, according to Smith, was "the beauty and exaltation of flying itself."

Above the haze layer, with the sun behind you or sinking ahead, alone in an open cockpit, there is nothing and everything to see. The upper surface of the haze stretches on like a vast and endless desert, featureless and flat, and empty to the horizon. It seems your world alone. Threading one's way through the great piles of summer cumulus that hang over the plains, the patches of ground that show far below through the white are for earthbound folk, and the cloud shapes are sculptured just for you. The flash of rain, the shining rainbow riding completely around the plane, the lift over mountain ridges and crawling trains, the steady, pure air at dawn takeoffs, and the smoke from the newly lit fires in houses just coming to life below—these were some of the many bits that helped pay for the tense moments of plunging through fog, or the somber thoughts when flying cortege for a pilot's funeral. It was so alive and rich a life that any other conceivable choice seemed dull, prosaic, and humdrum.

Death, the dark side of that flashing coin, was an ever-present specter. Smith writes:

The Service was in existence for less than a decade and was never in any sense large. When I joined the Air Mail Service in 1920 there were perhaps twenty pilots employed by the Post Office Department. There were forty-three when the service ended in 1927. Forty-three were killed and

twenty-three suffered serious injuries during its brief history.

In 1921, the first year of transcontinental operation, and the worst year in the service's history in terms of fatal accidents, mail pilots flew 1,770,658 miles and had 1,764 forced landings—810 mechanical, and 954 weather—or roughly one forced landing for every thousand miles flown. Fifty-six mail planes crashed, twelve pilots and four mechanics were killed, and thirty-six others were injured. "Statistically, every pilot flying the mail that year might expect to crash at least once. One out of four (would) be killed, and all the rest injured."

The life expectancy of air mail pilots depended to some extent on the routes they flew. The narrow, fog-shrouded valleys of western Pennsylvania's Allegheny Mountains and the jagged peaks of California's Sierra Nevadas took a heavy toll on the lives of airmen and passengers all through the 1920s and 1930s. But even the relatively safe route from St. Louis to Chicago across the flat farmlands of central Illinois was no milk run—as Braznell would soon discover.

The Post Office paid pilots on a sliding scale, based on years of service, or total miles flown, plus a per mile bonus that varied with the difficulty of terrain covered—seven cents per mile for the Sierras and Alleghenies, six for the Rockies, five for the Midwest. The Rockies were considered safer than the Alleghenies because their valleys tended to be U-shaped, with wide, flat floors that made forced landings comparatively easy, whereas the valleys and gorges of western Pennsylvania were narrow, V-shaped, and studded with trees and boulders. Besides, the weather over the Rockies was better, on average, and the passes were wide enough so that a pilot had room to circle or turn back if need be.

Duty and Authority

In the early days of the Air Mail Service, station managers—most of them non-pilots—were given the final say about whether a flight was flown or scrubbed. A pilot ordered to fly a mission did so, despite his own misgivings and objections, or faced instant dismissal. In 1919 a group of Air Mail Service pilots walked out in protest against this rule and threatened to continue their strike unless a pilot who had been discharged for refusing to fly a mission was reinstated. Under pressure, management agreed to rehire the pilot. As a face-saving measure, the rule giving station managers "authority" remained on the books as long as Post Office employees continued to fly the mail, but henceforth and forever afterward no air mail pilot was ever ordered to fly a mission he considered unsafe, or threatened with dismissal if he refused to do so.

Still, the pressure to perform—much of it self-imposed—was intense and unremitting. For many young and inexperienced pilots, just about the worst thing, the most embarrassing and demeaning thing, that could happen was to be overflown by another pilot—to be shown lacking in courage or ability when someone else accepted and completed a flight that he, possibly for the best of reasons, refused. This macho attitude probably contributed to more aviation fatalities during the 1920s and 1930s than engine failures, foul weather, bad luck, and all manner of "pilot error" combined.

At twenty, Walt was as indestructible, as full of testosterone, as any of his young comrades. He was, in short, an accident in waiting.

One night I battled snow storms until 3 A.M., making one emergency landing after another. I sat in one of the company's emergency airfields for hours, climbing the beacon tower every few min-

utes to check the ceiling and visibility. By the time I judged the ceiling to be high enough to let me clear the Illinois River bluffs and sneak into Chicago, I was dead tired and half frozen. Settling into bed at our Chicago apartment with a deep sigh of relief, I was just about to cork off when the phone rang and I heard Bud Gurney say "Congratulations, kid. You really stuck with it tonight."

A little praise went a long way. But the company had other ways of impressing on us that the mail must go through. For example, we had a calendar hanging in the mail office with the names of the three pilots written in on the days we were scheduled to fly. If the trip was not completed, that day of the month was blocked out in red, with the pilot's name PROMINENTLY DISPLAYED. We took our work seriously, and we had one of the finest records in the service. But, as I discovered one night, a sense of duty was no substitute for brains.

It was an evening in the late fall of 1928, soon after I started flying the mail. I left Springfield at dark for Peoria. The ceiling en route was low and forward visibility was obscured by rain. Later, the mail driver at Springfield told me he had waited for some time at the strip, certain that I would turn back. I kept peering over the side of the cockpit, looking for lights, ground objects, terrain features— anything that would help keep me oriented to the earth below. Somehow I hit my check points as I remembered them and landed in Peoria right side up. But then I foolishly decided to go on.

The field man at Peoria was shaking his head as I taxied out. Sure enough, I was in trouble within minutes after takeoff. Low clouds obscured the ground and I struggled unsuccessfully to "keep the blue side up." By sheer luck I broke out of the clouds directly over the field beacon, landed, and called it a night.

The next morning, weather still very bad, I repeated my mistake. In similar straits, I again lost my horizon—and my equilibrium—and literally fell out of the clouds. This time I popped out of the soup directly over the Illinois River. On the near bank of the river, I could see an old man staring

Vertigo

When sight is lost we must get our sense of balance and motion from the muscles and from the fluid movement sensors in the vestibular canals (of the ear). . . . (after spinning in a chair, or plane) it may take from 5 to 25 seconds for the fluid motions (in the canal) to stop. During this period an individual can experience the false sense of motion we call vertigo.

—General Jimmy Doolittle, quoted by Caroll V. Glines in
Jimmy Doolittle, Master of the Calculated Risk.

up at my plane. He was motioning to me, and I could almost read his lips. He seemed to be saying, "Get the hell down from there, you idiot!"

But once again, fortune smiled. I identified my position and, sneaking along under the cloud deck, crossed the river, cleared the bluffs, and pressed on into Chicago.

I had come close to spinning in, not once, but twice, on the short leg between Peoria and Chicago. That evening I got into a conversation with Fred Whitmore of Northwest Airlines at the crew quarters our two companies shared. Without going into the embarrassing details of my recent experience, I asked Fred whether veteran pilots like him ever experienced, um . . . *disorientation* . . . or maybe even *vertigo* . . . when they lost visual contact with the ground?

"Never," he said.

What's the secret? I asked.

"Simple," he said, "*I never lose contact with the ground.* Anytime I can't see the beacon light ahead of me before I lose sight of the one behind me, I do a snappy 180 and get the hell out of there."

But what about the mail? I asked. The mail must go through!

"Yep," Fred replied, "Weather permitting."

Flying in those days was not just man against the elements, but man against his own ignorance and inexperience. We learned from our mistakes—if we were lucky enough to walk away from them—and from other pilots who had been similarly fortunate. As a rookie air mail pilot, much of my education—my survival training—came from bull sessions like

this. Fred Whitmore is long gone, and he didn't die in bed. But he may have saved my life that night, and I'm forever indebted to him.

Weather Permitting

Next to his own ignorance and an occasionally balky engine or fuel system, nothing made a CAM 2 air mail pilot's occupation more interesting or perilous than that combination of fast-moving squall lines, blizzards, sleet, freezing rain, and pea-soup fog that characterized winter on the midwestern plains. With the limited range and ceiling of their open-cockpit biplanes, lacking instruments and radio navigation aids to penetrate storm fronts or rise above them, without even the means of sheltering themselves from winter's icy blast, the airmen of the 1920s and early 1930s were sitting ducks, their flimsy aircraft exposed to some of the worst punishment nature could inflict on a flying object. Like ducks, they had but two choices—fly low, or land and take cover.

In his entertaining memoirs, *Eagles Must Fly,* former CAA Administrator Jack Jaynes provides a vivid firsthand description of an air mail flight through a raging Great Plains blizzard during the winter of 1931–1932, in the waning months of the open-cockpit era. The pilot was one of the greats of that or any other period in aviation history, Hamilton Lee.

Jaynes, then working as a Department of Commerce airline inspector, was on a scheduled westbound inspection ride with Boeing Air Transport out of Chicago. On the first leg of the trip BAT pilot Cy Coppin had barely managed to drag his Boeing 80 trimotor and its eight passengers into Omaha under "deteriorating weather conditions" and a ceiling that was "truly below authorized minimums" (a breach of regulations for which Jaynes forgave him). With Omaha reporting a ceiling of less than 500 feet and heavy blowing snow, Jaynes "concluded the flight westward would be canceled or at least delayed." Not so. Entering the operations office, Jaynes found the famous Ham Lee dressed in helmet, goggles, and heavy flying suit, looking over the weather reports. The passenger flight had been scrubbed, of course, but Lee had decided to continue on to Laramie with the mail in an open-cockpit Boeing 40B-2. Jaynes asked if he could ride along in the Boeing's enclosed two-seater passenger compartment. Not wanting to cramp Lee's style so far as altitude and ceiling restrictions were concerned, Jaynes assured him he wished to be considered "just another bag of mail."

"Ham said 'Welcome Aboard,'" Jaynes writes— and we can just imagine the Cat That Is About to Swallow the Canary grin on Lee's face as he uttered those words.

"Our takeoff was a lulu," Jaynes continues. "Just as we gained flying speed, Ham rolled over on a wing and took off down the streets of Omaha, sliding in and out between buildings." It was snowing hard and, as Jaynes remembers, "I had a feeling we were already lost." After recovering from the shock of Lee's unorthodox and definitely nonregulation departure, Jaynes pulled out his notebook and began "jotting down to the best of my ability the description of

our maneuvers" in the hope that some record of the flight might be preserved after they crashed. "I hoped the aircraft wouldn't burn," he adds.

"I was thrown around quite a bit by his almost constant S turns, and only after gluing my face to the small window (in the aircraft's vestigial passenger compartment) did I realize what he was doing. He was banking around haystacks, barns, houses, trees, etc."

Lee was flying this obstacle course in heavy snow with practically zero forward visibility, maybe a hundred-foot ceiling, and an ambient air temperature of 27 degrees below zero. Forget the wind-chill factor—to a pilot flying at more than 100 miles per hour in an open-cockpit biplane, it must have been off the chart. But, fortunately, relief was just around the bend. About twenty-five miles out of Omaha, Lee intercepted the Platte River. For the next 250 miles, all the way to North Platte, he tracked the river's snaking course, taking full advantage of the twenty-foot increase in ceiling and slightly improved visibility the riverbed afforded. That's how Ham Lee got through with the mail on a nasty day in March 1932. Nothing special—just part of the routine of flying the mail for one of commercial aviation's true pioneers.

Weather Reports

Aeronautical meteorology was primitive and weather forecasting practically nonexistent until the mid-1930s. Weather maps issued by the Department of Agriculture, the principal source of meteorological information before the Department of Commerce got into the act, were of purely historical interest. They provided a reasonably accurate picture of what the weather was like *yesterday*. Compounding the problem, most of the aircraft flown by air mail carriers during the 1920s lacked radios, so there was no reliable way of warning pilots of changes in weather en route or at their destinations after they took off.

Braznell:

> We had an arrangement whereby a farmer about forty miles southwest of Chicago was supposed to light a red flare at his beacon site whenever our man in Chicago called to say the field was socked in. The system never worked for me. Somehow I always passed over the beacon before the phone message got through.

Efforts by airlines and individual mail pilots to enlist volunteer weather spotters along their routes proved equally fruitless. Dean Smith records this telephone conversation with a rural stringer:

> "Is it raining?"
>
> "Yup. Pouring."
>
> "How far can you see?"
>
> "I can see as far as the next man. I don't wear glasses or anything."
>
> "What I want to know is about the clouds. How far up can you see now?"
>
> "I don't know, it's pretty foggy; about a mile I guess."
>
> "Foggy, and you can see a mile straight up? Then the mountains should be all clear, are they?"
>
> "How can I tell? They're all covered with clouds."

Foul Weather Gear

The Midwest is a meteorological battleground on which dry, cold continental air masses whistling in off the Great Plains are constantly colliding with the cool, moist southward flow of air out of Canada and the Great Lakes and warm, moisture-laden air moving up from the Gulf of Mexico. When warm and cold air masses clash, the warm air tends to rise—to slide over the denser, colder air—causing an abnormal temperature inversion: Warmer air aloft, colder air below. Inversions are most common in spring and summer. When they occur in winter, rain falling out of warm, moist upper air often freezes and turns to sleet when it passes through the colder layer below. Or the precipitation may be transformed from super-chilled rain to clear ice when it hits a cold surface. In either form, icing could be deadly to the low-flying air mail ships of the 1920s and early 1930s.

Braznell:

> When I first began flying the mail, it was standard practice to carry a long stick in the cockpit during the winter months. No one bothered to tell me why. Flying into freezing rain late one winter afternoon, my Travel Air soon became encrusted in a sheath of ice that set its flying wires and struts to vibrating so hard I thought she was going to tear herself apart. At the same time I could see she was getting heavier and the ice forming on the leading edge of her wings was increasing her stall speed. Flying just fast enough to avoid stalling and slow enough to keep the wings from shaking off, I limped into the nearest emergency field. Landing with a thump, I taxied up to the beacon house, got out, and began beating the ice off the wings and struts with the stick my employer had so thoughtfully provided for that purpose. Then it was on to the next emergency field, and the next, and the next, repeating the de-icing operation at thirty- to fifty-mile intervals. This sort of thing went on all winter.

Ray Fortner, one of the other pilots on the St. Louis–Chicago run, took on a heavy load of ice one day. When he landed, the center section wing struts buckled under its weight. It would not have occurred to Ray to find a phone and call for help. After all, it was his problem. Borrowing some 2x4s and bailing wire from a farmer, he rigged the 2x4s outboard of the bent struts. Then he inserted a stout stick between the wires and started twisting. When the center-section was about in its original position, he jumped back in the plane and

Structural Icing

Structural icing does not develop at a steady rate. It builds up geometrically. In severe sleet storms, it can form so quickly that an airfoil without de-icing equipment may lose its aerodynamic shape and efficiency in minutes. As ice thickens and spreads around the leading edges of a ship's wings and propeller blades, the air flow over those surfaces is disturbed, causing a loss of lift and an increase in drag. Eventually the leading edge becomes a solid, blunt-nosed wall of ice, and no matter how much power is added, the plane can no longer sustain level flight.

Before propeller de-icing systems came along, ice on propeller blades tended to build up until thrown off by centrifugal force. This often happened asymmetrically—one blade at a time. The imbalance could shake an airframe so violently that aircraft sometimes shed a propeller, an engine, even a wing as a result.

flew on to St. Louis. I wish I had a picture of that jury-rigged ship, just to prove that old business about holding aircraft together with glue and bailing wire was not just a figure of speech.

Ground Sailing

Learning to fly the early open-cockpit air mail planes was only half the battle. Often, the real test was maneuvering them and keeping them under control once they landed.

Braznell:

Before the Travel Air came along, no one had seen any point in putting brakes on airplanes. Without brakes, taxiing one of those overgrown kites in a cross-wind or on the side of a hill was a testy maneuver. You progressed by a series of ground-loops. When the ship got away from you, you let it ground-loop and stop. Then you would gingerly try again, making sure you had plenty of sea-room so as not to run into fences, parked planes, and other stationary objects. It's no wonder the Army's flight school referred to taxiing as *sailing.*

One winter morning I flew a Ryan Brougham into Peoria. The Brougham was a cabin plane modeled after Lindbergh's *Spirit of St. Louis,* except that it had a conventional cockpit, with a windshield up front, and had been equipped with extra large wheels to keep it from digging into the mud on emergency landing fields. The over-sized wheels gave it an awkward nose-high angle at rest and made taxiing extremely difficult, even under ideal conditions. Naturally, it had no brakes.

On this particular morning, the field at Peoria was glazed with ice, having been pelted by snow, sleet, and freezing rain the night before. I made a low, slow approach, landing at the near edge of the field. Even so, by the time I was halfway to the opposite fence, I could see the Ryan was not going to stop. It had barely slowed down. I gave it hard left rudder and swung it into a high-speed ground-loop, praying I wouldn't catch a wing as its tail spun around. Our ever-alert field man, O. L. Spence, half-ran, half-skated onto the icy field and tried to grab hold of the horizontal stabilizer as I whipped past the second time. I looped it again, and again, blasting the tail around in ever tightening circles, while O. L. dodged, darted and stumbled after me like a maddened terrier. On about the fifth attempt, he threw his upper body over the stabilizer, dug in his heels, and brought the exhausted beast to ground. O. L. and I changed mail pouches on the spot. Then I headed the Ryan as close to the wind as possible and got the hell out of there.

"You Got Into It"

Air mail pilots had plenty of practice getting into tight spots. Sometimes the hardest part was getting out of them.

Braznell:

One bitter cold day in January 1929 my Travel Air's engine suddenly quit on me a few minutes after takeoff from Springfield. The only clearing within my glide range was a small pasture surrounded by trees. I dragged my tail skid through the snowy pine boughs at the approach end of the field and still barely managed to stop before running out of open space. Breathing a little prayer of thanks for all those hours my instructors had made me work on my short-field landings, I shut her down, unbuckled and, with my mailbags over my shoulder, trudged to a nearby farmhouse to call the office. Bud Gurney immediately came on the line. After I'd reported the ship's condition and location, he told me to hang on—he and a mechanic would hop into the company's new Cessna monoplane and be there within an hour. I offered the unsolicited opinion that he might find this field a bit tight for a ship as hot as the Cessna and suggested he pick another landing field.

"You got into it, didn't you?" he snorted.

I decided not to pursue the point.

An hour later, Bud and his Cessna arrived with a roar. After the customary low pass and chandelle, he squared away and started his approach. On the first attempt, he overshot and had to go around. His next approach was low, slow, and cautious, but again the Cessna overshot the field. After several more passes Bud and the mechanic landed in a bigger field and got someone to drive them over. I didn't dare crack a smile. Bud was a great pilot— one of the best. Nobody could have put a Cessna in that tiny field, and I wouldn't have wanted to try it in the Travel Air again, even with power. But I guess everyone enjoys seeing the boss make a mistake now and then—and treasures those sweet memories.

The repair work didn't take long. As soon as it was finished, Bud departed for home, leaving me, the guy who "got her in there," to get her out.

I figured I was going to need a fast start. So, with the help of the pasture's owner, I rigged a rope around the Travel Air's tail skid and tied the rope to a good stout tree. With the farmer standing by, ax in hand, I advanced the throttle to full take-off power. On my signal he cut her loose and off I sailed, high-tailing it over the icy sod. I'm not exaggerating when I say the Travel Air's prop wash bowed the tips of the pines as we brushed over them at the end of the clearing. That was about as close as I ever came to nicking an aircraft.

Thoughts While Idling in a Snowy Field

As we've already observed, an air mail pilot's education progressed more by trial and error than by training. Any mistake an airman was fortunate to walk away from was a learning experience that improved his chances of survival. Another case in point:

One of my earliest passengers was the great baseball player, Rogers Hornsby. It was a midwinter flight in a brand new Boeing 40B-4 from St. Louis to Chicago, and the weather between the two points was steadily deteriorating. I carried Mr. Hornsby as far as Springfield, where I was advised to put him on a train and scamper back to St. Louis before the airport socked in. Chicago was already closed. Soon after I took off, snow began to fall, thick, wet, and hard. I was flying by compass, looking straight down for visual reference to the ground, and not paying much attention to my engine gauges. But I could feel the ship growing sluggish, and a quick glance at the tachometer confirmed I was losing power. Within a few minutes, the prop was barely turning over, even with the throttle wide open, and I was starting to lose

Boeing 40B-4

The last of the great open-cockpit mail planes, the sturdy, long-nosed Boeing 40B-4 cruised at "a snappy 110 miles per hour" (124 miles per hour according to the manual) and carried as many as four passengers in a pinch. Note the cabin windows just forward of the open pilot cockpit.

Braznell, in summer flying gear, poses on the turtledeck of his beloved 40B-4. Robertson Aircraft was acquired by Universal in late 1928. The sign reads "Universal Air Lines System / Robertson Aircraft Division."

altitude. Having little altitude to lose—I had been flying at about three hundred feet—I turned north-east to avoid the heavily wooded area directly in my line of flight and began feeling for the ground.

The Boeing settled smoothly into a snowy field not far from a farmhouse. With the engine idling, I sat there for a minute or two, thinking about the experience. Eventually it dawned on me that the loss of power I'd just experienced must have been caused by carburetor icing, a condition I'd heard about but never experienced before. The 40B-4 was, in fact, the first ship I'd ever flown that was equipped with a carburetor heat control. During my descent I had tried everything I could think of to increase rpm, including yanking on that unfamiliar carburetor heat lever. Now, as I sat idling the engine, the ice blocking the carburetor intake began to thaw, and before long I could advance the throttle to full power. Without wasting any more time, I took off and completed my flight to St. Louis, having learned a lesson about foul-weather flying and the effects of visible moisture on internal combustion engines that would stick with me for the rest of my flying career.

Like Aiming Down the Muzzle of a Cannon

The Boeing 40B-4 was a rugged open-cockpit biplane designed and built to carry mail and passengers over the mountainous mail routes of the western United States. The "-4" designation stood for the number of passengers that could be squeezed into the coach compartment, which consisted of two enclosed cubicles over the wings, well forward of the open cockpit. Robertson Aircraft, by then a division of Universal Aviation, acquired a couple of 40B-4s in early 1929. Despite their ungainly appearance, they were great flying machines, much favored by Braznell and the other Robertson Division pilots. Walt explains why:

The Boeing had a fuselage that stretched about a mile and a half from the nose to the open cock-pit just forward of the vertical stabilizer. Flying it was comparable to aiming down the muzzle of a cannon. Like the Travel Air, it had primitive instruments and no radio, but it was still a great ship. With its brutish 525-horsepower Pratt & Whitney Hornet engine and light wing-loading you could practically hang it on its prop, riding it to the ground nose-high in a near stall. Even in a full stall, it showed no tendency to fall off on one wing or the other, as many planes do. And where the Travel Air cruised at 90 to 100 miles per hour, the 40B-4 ate up the miles at a snappy 110 per hour! It proved to be a very practical aircraft, and despite its size, we soon found we could put it into the same emergency fields we used for the Travel Air.

Pilots had a special reason for liking the 40B-4: That long nose served as a marvelously effective shock absorber. One of Braznell's pals, Axel Swanson, discovered this the hard way.

On a night flight from St. Louis to Omaha, Axel landed in Kansas City to refuel. It was raining and the field was muddy, so after topping off his tanks, he decided to take off directly from the concrete fueling ramp. In the darkness and rain, with the 40B-4's long nose further obstructing his forward visibility, he didn't see the fuel truck parked at the end of the ramp until he was practically on top of it. The force of the crash at near-takeoff speed compacted the Boeing like an accordion. From the engine to the cockpit there was nothing left of the fuselage but a mass of twisted and mangled steel tubing. It must have been an awesome collision, but Axel walked away from it.

A Dazzling White Light

Unscheduled landings at emergency airports, clearings, and pastures were regular occurrences for air mail pilots of the 1920s. When squall lines and low visibility blocked the way ahead, they generally preferred to land wherever they could find a level clearing, wait for the storm to pass or the ceiling to lift, and then press on. Genuine *forced* landings due to engine failure or a plugged fuel line were less common, but hardly rare. Walt logged a half dozen engine-out (deadstick) landings in his first two years on the line—a fairly typical record. The least common and most dreaded emergencies were nighttime forced landings. They were uncommon because, given a choice between making a deadstick night landing or bailing out, many air mail pilots elected to hit the silk. The one time an engine quit on Walt at night, he did not have that option.

One Friday evening in December 1928, about two months after I started flying the mail, I took on my first passenger. It was O. L. Spence, our Peoria station manager, who was on his way to Chicago to visit a lady friend. The Travel Air I was flying was strictly a one-seater, with an enclosed cargo compartment or mail bin forward of the pilot's cockpit. But O. L. assured me he had stowed away in mail bins many times before, and would be quite comfortable down there. So he stuffed himself in among the mail bags and, after assuring myself he had room to breathe, I snapped down the hatch. Since it was company policy not to wear a parachute when carrying passengers, I took mine off and stowed it in the operations shack before takeoff.

Everything went well until, approaching Chicago, I reached up and flipped the fuel switch from the main tank to the reserve. At that point the engine quit. I switched back to my main tanks and rocked the wings to get the last dregs of fuel. At the same time I changed direction, heading for a stretch of relatively open country along the Sag Canal. The engine surged back momentarily and then quit for good.

Another first: Ever since I began flying the mail, I'd wondered how it would feel to make a forced

landing at night. Now I knew. It felt terrible.

I gave a tug on the flare ring and, my, what a beautiful sight it was—a blaze of dazzling white light floating in the night air, clouds of smoke streaming off into the mist. Checking the wind direction, I picked out a snowy field within gliding range,[3] slipped the Travel Air in over a power line, and landed without any further problem.

During all this maneuvering I was uneasily aware of O. L. and his frantic efforts to pry the hatch off the mail bin in which he was trapped. Later he told me how, when he saw the light and the billowing smoke of the flare, he was certain the ship was on fire and wished he had brought his parachute. I admitted to similar feelings. If O. L. Spence is alive today, I'm sure he's still telling the story of how he and Walt Braznell lit up the skies over Chicago one winter night.

Parachute Flares

Parachute flares were standard equipment aboard single-engine open-cockpit mail planes of the 1920s. With the possible exception of human parachutes, they probably saved the lives of more airmen than any other safety or survival equipment of that era. Flares came in two sizes. The smaller 200,000-candle-power version burned for approximately one minute. The larger 600,000-candlepower flare was good for four minutes. At 1,000 feet, it brilliantly illuminated nearly a square mile of terrain.

3. "Field" is a slight exaggeration. It was a vacant lot near the intersection of 79th Street and Joliet Avenue, and Walt's forced landing was almost certainly the last successfully negotiated by an airline pilot within Chicago's city limits.

Low-Level Navigation

Pilots accustomed to flying the transcontinental routes over the Sierras, Rockies, or Appalachians considered midwestern runs like CAM 2 duck soup. But the very flatness, the sameness of the farmlands that stretched across the midsection of the country and made the 278-mile run between St. Louis and Chicago one of the most hospitable of air mail routes, also made it relatively difficult to navigate in marginal weather. At 150 to 500 feet above the terrain, typical cruising altitude for airmail pilots, all cornfields look pretty much alike.

By night CAM 2 was lit by navigation beacons spaced ten miles apart. But beacons were useless on gray winter days or on nights when clouds nestled in the treetops and forward vision was obscured by fog, rain, or snow. At such times, getting the mail to its destination or finding a safe haven in a storm often depended on the pilot's knowledge of the terrain—his ability literally to *feel* his way from one dimly perceived landmark to another, like someone walking in darkness through a familiar room.

Before he was checked out on the mail run, Braznell had been required to memorize the major topographical and political features of his route to and from Chicago as well as the location and configuration of every airfield and emergency landing strip along the way. By the onset of winter he was also familiar with all the roads, farmhouses, barns, windmills, and silos in his path—knew them so well he could pilot his way from point to point in practically zero visibility without straying from his course by more than a few dozen yards. At least once in his career as an air mail pilot, this local knowledge saved Robertson an aircraft:

On a night flight from St. Louis to Chicago the weather outlook for Chicago was so questionable I put my lone passenger on a train at Peoria and buckled into my parachute. Near Chicago a low stratus moved in. I stayed on top, navigating by compass and checking my position by the glow of the towns through the wispy undercast. Over Chicago the broken cloud layer turned solid, so I turned around and headed back to Peoria, hoping I had enough fuel to make it. The terrain I had flown over less than a half hour earlier was obscured in low clouds and fog, and I could no longer pick up the route beacon lights. I recalled how, twice during his service with Robertson, Slim Lindbergh had been trapped on top like this and forced to bail out, and I confess the thought of doing the same thing crossed my mind.

Flying southwest, I spotted a glow of lights that looked to be the town of Wenona. If I was right, another five miles on this heading would bring me to a beacon and, just beyond, a large, open pasture surrounded by cornfields. I was lucky: The undercast turned from solid to ragged as I began my timed descent, and at about 300 feet I spotted the wink of the beacon straight ahead. At 150 feet I turned on my wing lights. All I could see below was cornstalks. Figuring I was close to the open field, I popped a flare. The effect was dazzling. With the low clouds acting as a reflector, I could clearly see where the corn stopped and the open field began. The flare's backlighting was so intense that, for a few seconds, every cornstalk in the swath of my landing lights stood out in vivid detail.

By the time I had landed and secured my ship, a dense ground fog was settling in, and even though I knew a farmhouse was nearby, I doubted I could find it in the murk. So I sat there on the ship's turtleneck, firing my government-issue .38 automatic into the air in bursts of three, hoping to rouse the farmer. By and by he came chugging along in his Model T, and I spent the night as his drop-in guest.

Fifty years later Braznell could still visualize the prominent features of the route from St. Louis to Chicago the way a movie fan recalls highlights from *Casablanca* or *The Wizard of Oz*.

From Lambert Field the course runs northeast, past the Jesuit monastery on the outskirts of Florissant, Missouri. Halfway between Florissant and the Missouri River you hit the Number One beacon, then a house with a water tower perched on the bluffs of the Mississippi. From there, you pass the Monticello Seminary campus near Godfrey. Wave to the girls lining the dormitory windows, then head straight up the C&A railroad tracks from Godfrey to Brighton, Illinois. Pass over Shipman and Carlinville, and proceed north to the forty-acre sod field at Springfield, about eight miles west of the state capitol. Continuing north from Springfield, you pass just to the left of the railroad bridge over the Sangamon River, alongside a switchman's tower. At Mason City, you'll want to stay to the left of the 150 foot hillock or mound northeast of town. Next you hit Pekin. There's an emergency field a mile east of town, the last before you cross the bluffs of the Illinois River at Peoria. Peoria airfield lies to the northwest, beyond the downtown area.

A cup of coffee and a bit of gab with the Peoria station manager, and you're on your way, again, heading northeast, about 60 degrees magnetic, over the bluffs, across the broad Illinois River valley, past the bluffs once again, and down the main streets of Wenona and Grand Ridge. Before heading into Chicago for landing, you'll want to buzz Grand Ridge at treetop level so you can check and reset your altimeter against the town's known elevation. Past Marseilles and the emergency field at Stavenger, the grain elevator and quarry at Plainfield are usually visible from several miles. Northeast of the elevator you intercept the Des Plaines River where it bends to the northeast, near Lockport. Once over the river you continue to the Argo Starch Plant on the outskirts of Chicago.

Don't worry about missing this landmark—if you can't see it, you'll smell it. Turn right at 63rd Street, and you're all lined up for your approach to Chicago Airport, about a quarter mile dead ahead.

A Sure Cure for the High Lonesomes

Why did they fly so low, those brash young air mail pilots? Why, when weather conditions permitted them to cruise at a safe, comfortable 3,000 or 4,000 feet, did they still insist on putting their planes and their backsides in jeopardy by flying so close to the ground that there was no margin for error, and little room to maneuver, if they suddenly lost an engine?

Had I asked Walt that question, I'm sure he would have given me a perfectly logical explanation: "Headwinds are lighter at low altitude"; "Early air mail planes were slow climbers; it took too long to reach altitude," etc., etc. Of course, he would have said it with a wink and a grin. Anyone who has ever buzzed a sorority house, or kicked up dust chasing jackrabbits across a western prairie, knows why airmen like to fly low: because it's fun! Nowhere else, except perhaps skimming through canyons of billowing cumulus, does one experience the sensation of speed, the wonder and joy of flight, quite like this.

But, having given the matter further thought, permit me to offer an additional explanation: I think they flew low partly to keep in touch.

The higher an airman flies, the more he distances and isolates himself from his fellow beings. As we climb, living creatures are the first to disappear, then cars and tractors and all other man-made machinery. Gradually, houses and barns, office buildings and factories, schools and churches shrink into mere grains of sand. Above 10,000 feet, the last traces of civilization recede. With the approach of night, they dissolve into faint webs and pin-pricks of light, remote as stars.

Try cruising alone on a clear, moonlit night high over a sleeping city. It's an unforgettable experience—beautiful, serene, and unspeakably lonely. You wonder if maybe God felt like this before he created man and woman.

The airmen of the 1920s had no one and nothing to keep them company on their nightly vigils. No wonder they hugged the earth. What better cure for the High Lonesomes than dragging down the main street of Grand Ridge at dusk, or swooping low over the Illinois River bluffs on a fine spring morning to wave to a pretty girl?

People who lived along the air mail run from St. Louis to Chicago grew accustomed to being buzzed twice a day, three hundred days a year. Even the barnyard animals were used to the airmen's presence—so much so that if a cow or chicken spooked under a low-flying plane, the pilot knew he had strayed off course. Farmers told time by the morning and afternoon mail flights. When a plane was forced down, they were always the first to the rescue—always on hand to help the pilot pull his ship out of the muck and patch it up with glue and bailing wire; to help him deliver his mail bags to the post office in their pickup trucks or Model Ts; to feed him and give him shelter until he was ready to move on.

Walt and his fellow air mail pilots knew all the best farm pastures and frequently used them as emergency or "unscheduled" landing fields. In those days, airmen thought nothing of making short stops en route to relieve themselves, or have a cup of coffee with a neighborly farmer or, time permitting, sample the ribs at an outdoor barbecue.

The old tales of winsome milk maids and dashing aviators are not pure fiction. Farm girls did develop crushes on pilots. Some lit bonfires or set out lanterns to guide them on their way at night. Some sent demurely romantic notes and home-baked cakes and cookies, care of the Peoria airport. Pilots would show their appreciation by performing roof-raising buzz jobs or by dropping gifts tied in long red streamers onto their ladies' doorsteps.

Braznell remembers:

> One fall afternoon, years after the beacon lines had been torn down and the last of the ground-hugging open-cockpit mail planes had gone to pasture, I found myself at the controls of a small,

twin-engined Cessna on a cross-country flight from Chicago to Dallas. With the afternoon to myself, I had the happy thought of flying the first leg of my flight down the old air mail run from Chicago to Peoria, Springfield, and St. Louis, to see how much of it I could remember—how much it had changed over the years.

Off I went, flying as low to the ground as modern civil aviation rules permitted, and maybe a little lower. It was an experience I'll never forget—men jumping off their tractors, running across pastures waving their hats; women standing on their back porches fluttering their aprons, gesturing "Come on down, stay for dinner!" They remembered. At each greeting I circled low and waved back. It was long after dark when I landed in Dallas.

Growth and Obsolescence

With the introduction of reliable airborne communications equipment in the early 1930s, something of the air mail pilots' proud independence and self-reliance was lost forever. In a few years, crusty old-timers such as E. L. Sloniger would listen in to the chatter on the company radio channel and shake their heads, flabbergasted, as younger pilots pleaded, *"My oil pressure is dropping and the oil temperature is going up. What should I do?"*

Gone, too, was the star status that news media and the public had bestowed on the dashing young airmen of Slim Lindbergh's and Ham Lee's generation. How quickly yesterday's aviation he-

roes became—in the immortal words of airline owner E. L. Cord—mere "overpaid chauffeurs."

Two-way radios; increasing passenger travel, with all the attendant constraints and responsibilities; enclosed cockpits and passenger cabins; the first serious efforts by federal authorities to regulate or standardize flight procedures; fancy uniforms—*even gold-braided yachting caps, for crissake!* What were the grimy, rough-and-ready, seat-of-the-pants air mail veterans of the postwar decade to make of all this folderol?

Some adapted. Some quit. And some simply couldn't cut it. By 1932, pilots who had once considered flight instruments all but useless adjuncts to contact flying would be expected to demonstrate a level of proficiency in "blind" flying and radio navigation that had been considered physically impossible just a few years earlier. Many fine contact pilots never got the knack of flying on instruments. In a year or two they would be as obsolete as the breezy biplanes they loved to fly.

Aviation was changing, becoming big business, and just about everyone in the industry recognized it would have to be run like a business henceforth. For a young airman who idolized the old-timers and copied their free and easy ways, the transition would be a wrenching experience. But he, too, was changing and growing. No longer a rookie, not yet a leader; no longer a boy, nor yet a man of responsibility, Walt Braznell still had a lot of growing to do.

Flightline Snap Shots, Lambert Field, 1928–1932

UNIVERSAL AIR LINES AIR MAIL PLIOTS, C. 1930: From top left to bottom right: Wayne Williams, Axel Swenson, unidentified, Bob Rentz, Bobby Jewell, Leslie Smith, George Wade, Walt Hunter, unidentified, Walt Braznell, unidentified, Joe Westover, rest unidentified. *Photo courtesy of Frank H. Robertson Collection*

THREE OF A KIND: All they had in common was superb airmanship, a love of flying, and distinctly offbeat personalities—but
that was all the bond they needed. Left to right: Bobby Jewell
had a profitable sideline as a circus magician. One of his acts
involved sawing Mrs. Jewell in half. "Smokey Joe" Westover
wouldn't have been Smokey Joe without a cigarette dangling
from his lip and an inch-long ash poised to drop into his coffee
mug. Joe never removed a butt with his fingers. He just popped
it out of the corner of his mouth with a flick of his tongue. Anywhere—living room, cocktail lounge, ramp, cockpit. George
McCabe, commonly called "The Walrus" (but never within his
hearing) later served as American's Chief Pilot–New York
(Newark). Pilot-novelist Ernie Gann trained under him during
the late 1930s and undoubtedly used McCabe as the model, or
one of the models, for the gruff, gravelly-voiced, heart-of-butter
chief pilots who populated many of his early aviation novels.
Photo courtesy of Missouri Historical Society

Dashing Wayne Williams attracted momentary fame in the late
1920s by being photographed in a slow-flying RAC mail plane
hovering motionless in a stiff breeze over the dome of the Illinois
state capitol. A news photo of the stunt, appearing in newspapers all over the country, nearly cost Wayne his job. Williams
was the pilot in the 1942 TWA plane crash in which film star
Carole Lombard was killed.

LOUIE'S SHACK: Louis DeHatre's hamburger shack, famed in song and legend, was for many years the favorite hangout for pilots and idlers around Lambert Field. An avid amateur photographer, Louie plastered the walls of his shack with photos of all the resident aviators and any transient pilot of note who happened to wander within the scope of his camera lens.

Photos courtesy of Missouri Historical Society, Louis De Hatre and George J. Herzig Collections

Phil Love

Walt Braznell retained close ties with his old Missouri National Guard unit, the
110th Observation Squadron, and its commanding officer, Major Philip Love,
until 1934, when American transferred him to Chicago. Walt writes:

About the time I began flying the mail for Robertson, Phil Love was
elected commanding officer of the squadron. I was putting in one hundred
hours a month on the mail line and had looked forward to doping off and
getting a little rest on my weekends with the Guard. I should have known
better. Under Phil's leadership the squadron was constantly on the go. We
went places and did things that no Air Guard and few regular Air Corps
units had ever attempted. We flew seven-ship night formation takeoffs and
landings, often on unprepared strips where the dust was so thick you could
barely see your leader's wing lights. At a time when few commercial or military pilots felt comfortable flying blind, Phil would routinely pull up into an
overcast on cross-country flights to give us practice flying instruments in
formation. During summer maneuvers we flew night reconnaissance missions for two solid weeks, spotting and pinpointing the positions of enemy
convoys and artillery units hidden on side roads and cul de sacs deep in the
Ozark hills. We were invited to all sorts of state ceremonies, celebrations,
dedications, and balls—always arriving in show formation, wearing our
dress blouses, cavalry boots, breeches, and Sam Brown belts under our flying overalls. Bridge dedications were a specialty. We would fly in on a Saturday, make a formation pass at the bridge—over or under it, depending on
Phil's mood—then land in a nearby pasture or hayfield and spend the rest
of the day giving stunting exhibitions and free rides to the local citizenry.
Individual cross-country training flights were not only tolerated, but encouraged. And for a year or so I logged more than a few landings and one-
man aerial exhibitions at Columbia, Missouri, where my future bride, Miss
Celeste (Diddy) Fleming, was attending college.

Phil shaped the 110th into a crack unit—one that aroused a great deal of
public interest in aviation throughout the state during the 1930s and distinguished itself in World War II.
Phil himself was in line for a senior command, had he lived. Diddy and I lost a dear friend, and the nation
a natural leader, when he died in a plane crash just before the United States entered the war.

Photo courtesy of Frank H. Robertson Collection

Walt and Diddy

Walt Braznell met Celeste M. (Diddy) Fleming at a party at her parents' home in Ferguson, Missouri, not far from Lambert Field, in the summer of 1929. Walt was introduced to the Fleming family through a cousin, Belva Braznell, who was a close friend and Washington University classmate of Diddy's older sister, Helene. Diddy was eighteen, semi-engaged to a high school sweetheart named Harold Tuthill, and about to depart for her freshman year at the University of Missouri when the handsome young aviator showed up at her doorstep. Walt's favorite song, a snappy Jazz Age number titled "Somebody Stole My Gal," was playing on the Victrola when he danced with Diddy for the first time. That was it. From then on, Harold was history. Walt and Diddy were married on Valentine's Day the following year.

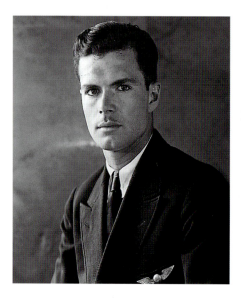

Airline Pilot

Walt in dress uniform, circa 1931, sporting a brand-new mustache—standard equipment for airmen of that era—and the wings of a Universal Air Lines pilot. Universal later became a division of "the American Airways System"—a name gradually phased out as American Airway's operations were consolidated.

The press notice on the back of this photo is dated November 24, 1931: "St. Louis to Chicago in 92 minutes! Pilot Walter Braznell of American Airways System on November 23 clipped 8 minutes from the flight record of the Chicago–St. Louis run established in March 30 by Robert (Bobby) Jewell. Braznell was flying a new Pilgrim 9-passenger plane manufactured and used exclusively by the American Airways System." Notice the absence of the now-standard honorific, "Captain." American didn't begin calling its pilots "captains" until 1938.

SUNDAY, APRIL 13, 1930

FLIES AIR MAIL

WALTER W. BRAZNELL.

RISE OF ST. LOUIS AIR MAIL PILOT RAPID

W. W. Braznell, 22, Has Been Instructor in Flying School —One of His Thrills.

Walter W. Braznell, 22 years old, who has been flying mail planes between Chicago and St. Louis for nearly two years, is one of the youngest mail pilots in the service.

Long before he attained voting age, Braznell determined that his future would be in aviation. He enlisted in the Thirty-fifth Division Air Service, Missouri National Guard, and subsequently was designated to take the Army flying course. After receiving military rating at Chanute Field, Braznell was elected an officer of the National Guard Air unit, and obtained a job as an instructor in the flying school conducted by the Robertson Aircraft Corporation—now part of the Universal Airlines System—which operates the Chicago-St. Louis air mail service under contract.

Braznell increased his flying time as an instructor, and, because of his skill, was selected to fill a vacancy in the mail pilots' group, of which he is now senior pilot.

Like others who fly regularly, Braznell has had a number of experiences calling for the utmost display of nerve and resourcefulness. One forced landing he has not forgotten was made in the residential district of Chicago.

Steamer Pilot in Mail Cockpit.

On the night of Dec. 8, 1928, Braznell, en route to Chicago, landed at Peoria to pick up mail. An aircraft exposition was in progress at Chicago and O. L. Spence, field manager at Peoria, expressed a desire to go along and attend the show that night. Spence, a master mariner and pilot of ocean steamers, who is seeking new thrills in aviation, proposed riding in the mail cockpit of the plane, a single-seater.

"I'll get in with the sacks," Spence announced. "I've ridden in the crow's nest of a ship in heavy seas, and this should be a lot easier."

Spence climbed in, and Braznell took off for Chicago. It was a cold, dark night, and the passenger, who wore a felt hat and an overcoat instead of regulation flying togs, made himself as comfortable as possible.

The engine of the plane had shown a tendency to "miss" on the way from Springfield to Peoria, but "revved up" to perfection while the ship was on the ground. After taking off Braznell climbed to several thousand feet above the airport to test the engine further, and, as it continued to run smoothly, headed for Chicago. All went well until the ship was over the city, when the engine began to sputter. Braznell nosed earthward and the engine picked up, only to cut out again.

Rocked Craft to Drain Fuel.

"Presuming that the trouble was caused by water in the reserve gasoline tank, Braznell began rocking the ship to drain fuel from the wing tanks, which previously had been practically emptied. Spence, in the mail cockpit, was unaware of the true state of affairs and later said he thought the pilot was endeavoring to give him a thrill. As a result of the various maneuvers employed by Braznell the plane lost altitude, and Braznell decided it was time to seek open country. Neither pilot nor passenger wore a parachute, and a landing at that particular spot would have ended in disaster.

The motor continued to act badly and finally, despite all the rocking and diving resorted to, "quit cold." Braznell knew he was over the outskirts of the city, but could see lights twinkling on all sides below, with no sign of open country. Spence, now sensing that something was wrong, thrust his head out of the mail compartment, and lost his hat. He immediately began piling mail sacks in front of him in anticipation of the expected crash.

Mail planes are equipped with flares for emergency landings. As the plane neared the ground Braznell released a flare and was relieved beyond expression to see a narrow strip of vacant ground in the thickly populated area below. That strip of open country was a much needed port and the mail pilot and his passenger made a safe landing at Sixty-ninth street and Joliet avenue, Chicago.

Spence never found his hat, but had an experience that he can tell his fellow mariners when he returns to sea.

STORM DOESN'T HALT CHICAGO AIR MAIL

Service To and From Here Continues Despite Bad Weather.

Despite the reports of storms and snow over the Midwest, which prevented all other mail planes from leaving Chicago yesterday and caused the mail to be forwarded instead by train, the air mail between St. Louis and Chicago was carried by plane as usual. Walter Braznel, mail pilot for the Robertson Aircraft Corporation, was the only pilot to undertake the flight out of Chicago, arriving here at 3:30 o'clock yesterday afternoon.

The outbound plane, carrying mail for Chicago, also left on schedule time, despite the bad weather, with R. R. Newton as pilot. Newton took off in the teeth of a heavy wind, and encountered considerable resistance, but made good time, despite the handicap.

The big Robertson Ford trimotored passenger plane also made the trip to Chicago successfully, with one passenger and an extra pilot aboard. Ben Howard was at the controls when the big plane took off at 10:30 o'clock yesterday morning, with W. L. Jammeson of Chicago, also a mail pilot, accompanying him. D. L. La Chance of Chicago was the passenger.

Braznel left Chicago yesterday afternoon, instead of in the morning, as he had to wait for the air mail, which was sent to that city by train. He was delayed a total of six hours in all, of which only one and one-half hours was due to bad weather. Between Peoria and Chicago he ran into snow and a high gale.

News Clippings

Air mail pilots were always good newspaper copy. Walt probably got more than his share.

Passages

In late 1928, less than ten years after they started Robertson Aircraft Corporation with a couple of war surplus Jennies and a garage full of spare parts, the Robertson brothers sold out to a group of midwestern bankers and businessmen for the then-princely sum of $300,000. In the event, RAC became one of fourteen operating units of a new multimillion-dollar combine called Universal Aviation Corporation. Six months later, Universal was snapped up by another new holding company, The Aviation Corporation (AVCO), in a one-year sweep that netted AVCO not only Universal and its subsidiaries but also Colonial Airways, Southern Air Transport, Interstate Airlines, Embry-Riddle Company, Bendix Aviation, Alaska Airways, and a minority interest in Western Air Express.

AVCO's acquisition binge was financed with the $37.5 million proceeds from an initial public offering of two million shares of common stock. The timing of the offering, May 1929, was fortuitous. In the giddy days preceding the great stock market crash of October 1929, there was no shortage of investors willing to pony up twenty dollars per share for a company with no operations and no operating history—with only the promise of future rewards implicit in that outrageously presumptuous name: *The* Aviation Corporation.

Early in 1930 the directors of AVCO decided to consolidate their newly acquired airline subsidiaries and sub-subsidiaries into a single organization. American Airways, incorporated in January 1930, was the chosen vehicle. Despite the new name and corporate structure, American Airways remained an agglomeration of small, independently operated units and mail routes, none of which connected. It was a system without system, "an airline to nowhere" as the savvy young vice president of American's Southern Air Transport Division, C. R. Smith, would later observe.

To insiders such as Smith it was painfully evident that AVCO's directors had no idea what to do with the sprawling aviation empire they had cobbled together. Ironically, the vision and drive needed to mold American Airways into the prototype of a great transcontinental airline

Vision in Brown

Almost all of (the air mail contractors) were refusing to carry passengers. They were using little open-cockpit ships to move the mail with great dependability, but no real progress was being made. I believed it was my duty to force them to get revenues from nonpostal sources. The purpose was to develop an industry that could live without subsidies. At any rate, I decided to take the responsibility, and I used the power of the Watres Act to compel the carrying of passengers.

—Former Postmaster General Walter F. Brown, testifying before Congress in 1934

would come, not from the company's senior management or board of directors, but from the postmaster general of the United States, the Right Honorable Walter Folger Brown.

Upon his appointment in April 1929, Walter Brown began a year-long review of the commercial aviation industry President Hoover had placed under his administration and patronage. The main conclusion Brown drew from the study was that the nation's airlines needed to be weaned from their near-total dependence on air mail subsidies and "compelled" to develop the long-neglected passenger and freight-hauling aspects of their business.

The postmaster general set out to achieve this worthy goal by rigging air mail rates and contract awards in favor of the largest and strongest carriers. Henceforth, rates would be based on the contractors' load-carrying *capacity* rather than the actual poundage of air mail they transported. Under the new formula, the base rate rose from fifty-five cents per mile for the smallest mail planes to a maximum of ninety-five cents per mile for aircraft capable of carrying up to two thousand pounds of air mail. As an added incen-

tive to upgrade their fleets, carriers were offered bonuses of ten cents per mile for mail trips flown by ships with two-way radios and seating capacity for ten passengers or more.

Among other things, the new rate structure put an end to the ancient and dishonorable practice of stuffing mail sacks with Sears Roebuck catalogs and waffle irons. By basing fees on capacity and mileage rather than poundage, it also doomed the "little open-cockpit ships" and shoestring carriers of the 1920s. Indeed, the revised rates virtually guaranteed that no airline, regardless of size, would ever again make a profit strictly from carrying mail. For larger airlines, the keys to survival would be to extend their routes, modernize and expand their fleets, and get busy filling their new ships with paying passengers.

Using the expanded powers vested in him by the McNary Watres Act of 1930, the postmaster general convened a conference of industry leaders to reveal his plans for their future. What Brown had in mind was to consolidate the nation's forty-odd regional carriers into a system of four or five major trunk lines, supported, where necessary, by regional feeder lines. United Airlines, created just a few weeks earlier through the unfriendly takeover of Clement Key's National Air Transport by Seattle-based Boeing Air Transport, provided the role model for his grand scheme: a few strong, well-managed enterprises with linked air mail route franchises stretching from coast to coast.

Brown next arranged a shotgun wedding between Transcontinental Air Transport and Western Air Express, with WAE's fiery Pop Hanshue playing the reluctant bridegroom. The combined lines, relabeled Transcontinental and Western Air, or TWA, formed the central tier of what the postmaster general visualized as a three-tier transcontinental route structure anchored by United to the north.

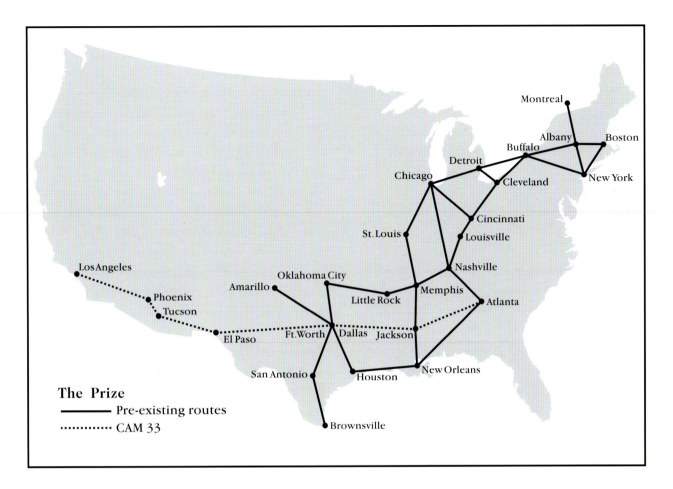

The Prize
Pre-existing routes
CAM 33

The Prize

On September 16, 1930, to absolutely no one's surprise, the Post Office Department awarded American Airways Contract Air Mail Route 33, the prized southern transcontinental route from Atlanta to Los Angeles by way of Birmingham, Jackson, Shreveport, Dallas, El Paso, Tucson, and Phoenix. Subsequently, American's CAM 16 (Cleveland-Louisville) and CAM 20 (Cleveland-Albany) were spliced and extended at both ends to create a New York–Dallas connection of sorts. Thus a traveler from New York to Los Angeles who didn't mind going a bit out of his way might board an American Airways plane in Newark, zip up the Hudson to Albany, cross Lake Erie on a line from Buffalo to Cleveland, cut diagonally through the nation's heartland to Dallas, with intermediate stops at Louisville, Nashville, Memphis, Little Rock, and Oklahoma City, and after four or five more westbound stops, stagger into Los Angeles late the second day. Most travelers preferred to take the train.

AVCO's five-month-old American Airways won the nod for the southern tier, even though it lacked anything approaching a transcontinental route structure, and despite stiff resistance from Oklahoma-based Southwest Air Fast Express (SAFE). For more than a year SAFE's owner, wealthy oilman Erle P. Halliburton, had been bankrolling a money-losing passenger airline serving Tulsa, Oklahoma City, Kansas City, St. Louis, and Dallas. Now Halliburton threatened to disrupt the conference and blow Brown's grandiose plans out of the air if SAFE was not permitted to bid on at least a portion of the southern route. To resolve the conflict, Brown arranged for American to buy out Halliburton for $1.4 million, or roughly twice SAFE's net worth. By an odd coincidence, this was precisely the sum TWA had agreed to pay American for its minority interest in Western Air Express—another transaction masterminded and brokered by the postmaster general. With a little more high-handed finagling—a strategic acquisition here, a route restructuring there—American Airways ended up with a system that "went somewhere," and Walter Folger Brown achieved his grand design for the airline industry.

Flying Indoors

Despite Postmaster General Brown's statements to the contrary, many progressive air mail contractors had recognized the importance of promoting air travel long before he forced the issue. Universal's Robertson Aircraft Division, for example, began passenger service between St. Louis and Chicago in August 1928, when it took delivery of the first of four new twelve-passenger Ford TriMotors. By mid-1929 it had assembled a sizable fleet of trimotors and six-seater single-engine transport planes and was operating combined passenger and mail flights twice daily to

and from the seven cities on its route system.

Universal's twelve-passenger Fords and six-passenger Fokker Super Universal monoplanes were used on the deluxe "Skyline Express" and "Skyline Limited" flights, which departed from St. Louis, Chicago, and Omaha around midday, Monday through Saturday. The six-days-per-week evening and predawn mail runs were flown in old warhorse Boeing 40B-4s. Though technically classed as four-passenger cabin planes, the Boeings seldom carried a fare. Walt Braznell was one of the Universal pilots regularly assigned to the Chicago–St. Louis mail flights during the winter and spring of 1930. He recalls that, on the rare occasions when the evening Air Mail Limited booked a paying customer, "we would stuff our parachutes in the mail bin and sulk all the way to Chicago."

During this transition period, pilots might be assigned to fly the evening and dawn mail runs one month and the deluxe midday passenger flights the next. Some air mail veterans objected to this arrangement and made their disdain for flying "indoors"—that is, flying in closed-cockpit cabin planes—abundantly clear. CAM 2 pilot Joe Hammer reported for his first TriMotor passenger flight wearing an elegant velvet-collared Chesterfield coat, white silk scarf, black derby, navy-blue suit, and gray spats. His sartorial statement was an immediate hit, and for several months the de facto uniform for Skyline Limited pilots remained Chesterfield, derby, and spats.

A few pilots actually enjoyed, or professed to enjoy, the heightened status associated with flying the bigger, costlier passenger ships. Braznell's friend Benny Howard spoke for this upwardly mobile element one rainy afternoon over cups of coffee in Louie's flightline canteen:

> "Look at the two of us. I fly a real ship—a Tri-Motor. I wear a white cap and trousers and a blue flannel coat with shiny brass buttons. Like any civi-

Benny and Mike

During the 1930s Benny Howard gained fame as a successful designer, builder, and pilot of racing planes. Here he is, with "Mike," one of the four pint-sized racers he designed with Gordon Israel and flew to victory again and again in the National Air Races of the 1930s. Not even the loss of a leg in a near-fatal crash while competing in the 1936 Bendix Cup race could ground the irrepressible Howard. As a test pilot for United Airlines and Douglas Aircraft he continued to make important contributions to the advancement of aviation all through the 1940s and 1950s, particularly in the development and refinement of automated instrument approach and landing systems. Braznell remembers him as "a virtuoso—the most talented aircraft handler I have ever known."

lized man, I quit work when the sun goes down, and when I walk off my ship people address me as Mister Howard. There is stature and dignity in what I do, Walt—whereas you mail pilots . . ."

He didn't have to finish. There I sat in my dirty coveralls, soaked and bleary-eyed from a long, wet flight from Chicago. The comparison was ridiculous. But I wouldn't have changed places with Benny for a minute, and he knew it.

The next time I ran into Benny, the passenger airline he worked for had folded and he had landed a job with Universal, flying the mail on the St. Louis–Omaha run. Meanwhile, I'd been temporarily reassigned one of the new Fokker F-10 trimotors, flying passengers over the same route. Naturally, I couldn't wait to commiserate with my old friend over the turn in our respective fortunes. "Gosh, Benny," I said, "I really worry about you, flying at night and in all kinds of weather in that little mail plane. No fancy uniform, no dignity— what a comedown!"

"Ah, Walt," he said, "how quickly you've forgotten the romance, the freedom, the thrill of the open cockpit—not to mention the extra bucks *we mail pilots* get for flying at night."

A few months later Howard was reassigned to the F-10 passenger run. Benny flatly refused the assignment ("Sorry, Boss, I'm an *air mail* pilot") and was promptly fired for insubordination. It was not the first time this free-spirited and immensely gifted airman ran afoul of authority. Nor would it be the last.

Idle Hands

In an open-cockpit mail plane, an airman always had the wind for company, and if he grew tired of drilling holes in the sky, he could always divert himself by playing tag with the clouds or buzzing a barnyard and frightening the chickens.

Flying one of those pokey cabin cruisers was a different matter. Alone in a big empty plane, lacking even radio communications with the outside world, pilots found the daily transit from St. Louis to Chicago a dull and lonesome routine. Low-level flying and horseplay were out, of course. Whether or not he carried passengers, an airline pilot of the 1930s was expected to maintain a degree of dignity and decorum befitting the captain of a modern airship. Or so said the company handbook. Braznell remembers somewhat differently:

The Fokker Super Universal, like its big brother, the trimotored Fokker F-10, was a remarkably stable aircraft. Sometimes, just to break the monotony, I would trim one up to fly straight and level, then go sit in the small, empty passenger compartment and see how close I could come to my destination without touching the controls. On one flight from Chicago to St. Louis, I was hunched down in the cockpit, practicing flying on instruments, when out of the corner of my eye, I saw a Stinson Trimotor cruising up alongside me, just off my right wing. Having gained my attention, the pilot of the other plane smiled and waved—with both hands. It was Eddie Schmidt, a friend who flew for Century Airlines. Smitty obviously wanted me to see what a fine, stable aircraft he was flying: "Look, ma, no hands!"

I maneuvered my Fokker over the Stinson so I could look down into his cockpit and, as I suspected, Eddie had his knees clamped around the control column. I pulled back into formation and sat there for a minute, exchanging mildly obscene gestures with my traveling companion. Then, trimming the stabilizer one notch down to compensate for my weight, I climbed out of the pilot's seat, yawned, stretched, and ambled back to the passenger section. When Eddie saw me waving from the cabin window, he immediately lost interest in formation flying and we went our separate ways.

The Trimotors

The Ford TriMotors were hot in the summer, cold in the winter, and noisy all the time. The stick force needed to maneuver their control surfaces was awesome. But they were sturdy and dependable. Passengers felt safer flying in one of Henry Ford's airplanes. Most pilots, however, preferred the Fokker F-10 Trimotor. It had a plywood wing and a noise-dampening linen-covered fuselage, and though its Wasp engines were the same as the Ford's, the Fokker's three-bladed propellers ran quieter and smoother. With its lighter weight, the F-10 was also a good 10 miles per hour faster than the Ford—an edge that Braznell and his fellow Universal pilots used to advantage.

On the Tulsa–St. Louis run, our F-10s would take off from Tulsa a few minutes after the Ford TriMotors flown by our rival, Safeway Airways. Our standard procedure was to climb a thousand feet or so above the Safeway ships as soon as we had them in sight, then swoop down like hawks, streaking past them and, we hoped, dazzling the Safeway passengers with Universal's superior performance. It was a silly, childish trick—and great fun.

The fun lasted until one of our pilots, not content with a thousand-foot advantage in altitude, dove upon a Safeway flight minutes out of St. Louis from about 12,000 feet. He was going so fast when he passed the Safeway ship that both the F-10's ailerons ripped clear off their wings. Fortunately, the pilot was able to land the crippled Fokker safely, but that episode marked the end of the Tulsa–St. Louis air races. We got the ailerons back by advertising in the local newspaper.

It was in a Fokker F-10 that Braznell first experienced the phenomenon known as wind shear.

Diddy and I had just returned home after a big evening in St. Louis, shortly after we were married, when I got a call from the field. Our hangar at Chicago had burned down earlier that evening and, with it, all of our Chicago-based F-10s. I was ordered to report to Lambert at once and ferry a replacement aircraft to Chicago. When I got to the field I learned there hadn't been time to round up a copilot, so I would have to fly the ferry mission alone. No problem, I thought.

With a strong tailwind out of the southwest, I was making good time. Nearing Chicago, just before dawn, I could see a thick pall of smoke drifting toward me out of the northeast quadrant. There I was, riding a tail wind with smoke blowing more or less straight at me. Had I been wide-awake, alarm bells would have been ringing. At least I might have had the sense to tighten my safety belt.

I was descending through 500 feet when I hit the edge of the smoke. It was like driving a car into a brick wall. One moment the plane and I were flying along together, the next I was flying all by myself. My head hit the cockpit overhead hard enough to drive my metal cap ornament into my scalp. The concussion must have knocked me out for a second or two, because the next thing I knew, I was lying in the baggage bin beneath the cockpit, blood dripping down my brow, with the broken remains of my pilot seat lying on top of me. The violence of the down-draft had been strong enough to separate the seat from its deck mounting. Lurching back into the cockpit, I climbed into the copilot's seat and leveled out with a few hundred feet to spare. The brief remainder of the flight was uneventful: The plane was delivered safely to Chicago, and the pilot gained a new and profound respect for the power of clear-air turbulence.

Braznell liked to finish this story by mentioning that the only plane not trapped in the company's Chicago hangar when the fire broke out was an early model Dutchwing Fokker, which

A Gallery of Early Cabin Planes

The Ford TriMotor, affectionately known as the "Tin Goose," featured a radically new cantilevered wing and a corrugated aluminum body that made it look like a flying toolshed. The original 4A-T models, built in 1927, were powered by three 220-horsepower Wright J5 Whirlwinds—the same engine that powered Lindbergh's *Spirit of St. Louis*. Conversion to 400-horsepower Pratt & Whitney Wasp engines boosted the Goose's cruising speed about 10 knots, to an honest 110 miles per hour. A remarkably stable aircraft, the Ford responded only to he-man stick forces.

Pilots who flew both aircraft preferred the Fokker F-10 trimotor. With its plywood wings and fabric-covered fuselage the Fokker was lighter, faster, quieter, and more maneuverable.

Introduced in 1929, the six-passenger Fokker Super-Universal was retired from service with American just three years later, a victim of the rapid engineering advancements typical of the period. With its single Pratt & Whitney Wasp engine and a full passenger load (rare), the Super-Universal cruised at 105 miles per hour. It was so stable in calm air, pilots could trim it up and literally fly "hands off" for an hour or so at a time.

Built to American Airway's specifications in early 1931, the Fairchild Pilgrim 100 carried nine passengers in comparative comfort, offered excellent pilot visibility, and was among the first airliners equipped with wing flaps and operable two-way radios. These advantages were offset by its slow cruising speed (110 miles per hour) and its dangerously short three-hour cruising range.

Braznell writes,

The Pilgrim was so short-winded it could barely make it from Chicago to Springfield in a stiff south-westerly breeze without adding fuel at Peoria. The route between Springfield and St. Louis paralleled a major highway and there were occasions when I suffered the indignity of watching cars below pass me as I staggered along in 40- to 50-miles-per-hour headwinds. Lacking sufficient fuel reserves to hold over a destination until the field cleared—or proceed to an alternate, if it didn't—made every flight in marginal weather a calculated risk. A bad guess could cost you your job or your neck.

The Pilgrim was built expressly for American Airways by another AVCO subsidiary, Fairchild Aviation Corporation. Sherman Fairchild, its president and founder, was also a founder, director, and officer of AVCO. Similarly, the Fokker F-10 and Fokker Super-Universal were built by Fokker Aircraft Corporation of America, a company in which an AVCO subsidiary, Universal Air Lines, owned a considerable stake. Tony Fokker, the famous Dutch designer and president of Fokker Aircraft, sat on Universal's board of directors. Later, after industrialist E. L. Cord gained control of American Airways, American acquired millions of dollars worth of aircraft, propellers, and engines from companies Mr. Cord owned or controlled. Directori conflicts of interest and intracorporate hand-washings of this nature were common in the aviation industry before the Roosevelt administration forced the breakup of holding companies such as North American, AVCO, and Boeing. After passage of the Air Mail Act of 1934, airlines could no longer be affiliated with aircraft or engine manufacturing companies. *Photos courtesy of American Airlines*

"flew like a crate full of loose parts." "The Dutch-wing was parked on a ramp when the fire started, but all the boys on the flight line got together and pushed it into the blaze."

Growing Pains

In retrospect, the Post Office's decision to launch its air mail carriers into the travel business seems to have been remarkably ill-timed. The nation's financial markets were still in chaos following the crash of October 1929. All over the country companies were firing workers, reducing inventories, cutting expenses to the bone. The world's economy was slipping into the abyss called the Great Depression. These conditions alone would surely have given pause to anyone less single-minded than Walter Folger Brown. But there are more and better reasons to conclude that the postmaster general acted prematurely.

Saddled with an immense burden of debt for the purchase of passenger ships that flew empty as often as not, the airlines gushed red ink all through the early 1930s. To make matters worse, the ships they impoverished themselves to buy were dogs: awkward, sluggish, expensive to operate, and damnably uncomfortable. Practically every passenger aircraft put into service between 1930 and 1933 would be retired by 1936, rendered prematurely obsolete by rapid advances in aircraft design and engineering.

Municipalities also felt the pinch of unpreparedness. Even progressive, aviation-minded cities such as St. Louis lacked suitable airport facilities to serve the hordes of passengers whose air fares were expected to replace the loss of mail subsidies. At Lambert Field, ticket-holders for the noon Skyline Express flight to Chicago were directed by a small sign to Universal Air

Lines' operations office, a one-story brick building sandwiched between the old National Guard and Robertson Aircraft hangars. There they were shunted into a drafty vestibule furnished with wooden benches, a potbellied stove, an overhead fan, and a single overhead light, and left to await word of when—or whether—their flight would depart.

The go–no-go decision might hinge on the condition and temperament of the ship scheduled for that day's flight, or that of the pilot, or, more likely, on the latest weather reports from Chicago. In marginal weather, the St. Louis station manager might decide to cancel the flight entirely or send the mail on alone rather than expose passengers to unnecessary risk.

For passengers and pilot alike, the risks of flying in bad weather far outweighed the inconvenience of having a flight canceled. At the time the new air mail rate structure went into effect, not one airline pilot was qualified to fly passengers under instrument conditions—officially described as visibility of less than three miles and ceiling of less than a thousand feet. The Commerce Department bureau responsible for certifying pilots and establishing and enforcing air safety regulations was still getting its act together. None of its examiners were themselves qualified for instrument flight. Airline standards for training and supervising flight crews ranged from nominal to nonexistent. Weather reports provided by the Department of Agriculture were unreliable, and the manner of collecting, analyzing, and broadcasting meteorological data remained better adapted to the pace of farming than of flying. To top it all off, few of the passenger aircraft of that day were equipped with functional two-way radios or radio navigation equipment. Without these aids, descending through an overcast was, at best, a crap shoot and, at worst, suicidal. Unfortunately, the alter-

Universal Air Lines Passenger Depot and Hangar, Lambert Field, St. Louis, 1929.
Photo courtesy of Frank H. Robertson Collection

natives—getting trapped on top of a solid stratus layer or becoming trapped beneath a lowering cloud deck and having to weave across country at tree-top level—were equally unappealing.

In short, the airlines were entirely unprepared to provide the safe, reliable, all-weather operations that the traveling public had every right to expect. Accidents, often fatal, always costly, occurred with alarming regularity. In 1930 and 1931 the airlines experienced by far the highest annual fatality rates in commercial aviation history—28.6 and 23.5 per 100 million passenger miles, respectively.[1] Adverse weather conditions—thunderstorms, clear air turbulence, icing, fog, or low ceilings—were factors in the vast majority of these crashes.

As for the life expectancy of air crews, Braznell recalls:

The good news was, we were never pestered by insurance salesmen. On the contrary, until the mid-1930s airline pilots couldn't buy life insurance at any price. So we organized our own pilots' benevolent association. Whenever one member of the association was killed, the others were assessed a few dollars for the pilot's family. There were about seventy of us. On Christmas Eve 1930 we lost two pilots—three percent of the Association membership—in two separate crashes over the Allegheny Mountains. The plan fell apart soon after that. Too many claims, too few policy holders.

All-Weather Operations

Up to 1931, what few passengers the airlines carried were flown exclusively during daylight hours and according to visual flight rules. The mail traveled any way the pilot chose to fly it, with no questions asked as long as it got to its destination on time. Now the rules were suddenly changed, and for the first time the technical and managerial aspects of operating a safe, round-the-clock, all-weather commercial transport service began to receive the attention they deserved.

Braznell:

Shortly after I began my flying career, I read an article by a famous Air Corps pilot and aviation writer of that era, Ira Eaker. Eaker claimed there were not a dozen pilots who could fly twenty-five miles in solid fog and come out alive. I doubt that many airmen would have disputed his statement at the time.

The introduction of the gyro-operated turn and bank indicator in the late 1920s considerably improved the air mail pilot's odds of survival. This lifesaver was followed around 1931 by the gyro compass and gyro-operated artificial horizon, an improved altimeter, and a device called a vertical speed or rate of climb indicator. With this array of instruments, a reasonably proficient airman could climb into a solid overcast and perform precision turns, climbs, and descents to his heart's content.

Learning how to use these new gauges was the individual pilot's responsibility. We had no training program as such, no check pilots, no instructors—just one instrument trainer, an obsolete Fairchild Razorback cabin plane that had been outfitted with an extra set of controls, instruments, and radio navigation equipment in the aft compartment. We signed up for the trainer on our days off and arranged for another pilot to come along as observer. Except on takeoffs and landings, the trainee flew in back with the window shades drawn, while an observer rode up front in the cockpit, ready to take the controls if he screwed up.

I practiced whenever and wherever I could—in the trainer or on the job. Flying the mail on overcast days, I'd nose up into the clouds like a trout rising to a mayfly hatch and stay there as long as I dared. In fair weather, I'd take off my parachute and hunch down in my seat with my eyes well below the cockpit rim and fly that way from one

1. By the end of the decade, the ratio had declined to 1.2 per 100 million passenger miles.

stop to another. (No need to worry about watching out for air traffic in those days—aside from migratory birds, there was no traffic.)

All this was great training. But, like most other line pilots, I decided to wait until our ships were outfitted with reliable air-ground voice communications and radio navigation equipment before making the big plunge.

Riding the Range

Braznell continues:

By 1930 the Department of Commerce had erected a network of low-frequency radio airways linking major U.S. cities throughout the country. There were about three hundred radio range stations in all. On the ground, with the engine off, our radio receivers could pick up the Chicago range station nearly a hundred miles away. But as soon as we fired up, all we could hear was static— the staccato pop-pop-pop of electrical discharges from the engine's ignition system. Those early radios were marvelous ignition analyzers.

Our radio headsets hung on their hooks until 1931, when the company began installing ignition shielding. That solved the static problem. Unfortunately, whenever the new ignition harnesses got wet, our engines quit. For months we flew across country dodging raindrops.

In the summer of 1932 the Department of Commerce came out with its first instrument rating for airline pilots—the Scheduled Air Transport Rating (SATR). I flew into St. Louis with the Chicago mail one morning in mid-October and was told that a Department of Commerce inspector was on the field. I ran the inspector down, took the test, and passed. Mine was the second instrument rating awarded in St. Louis. I was lucky to make it on the first try. Many of my friends didn't. Some never made it.

It was as if someone flicked a switch and a whole generation of seat-of-the-pants World War I and Air Mail Service veterans suddenly vanished.

By 1934 any pilot who couldn't fly by the gauges was unemployable in the air transport business. Simply to keep his job an airline pilot had to demonstrate levels of instrument flying proficiency aviation experts had considered impossible only a few years earlier.

Benny's Unorthodox Approach

Navigating by low-frequency radio range signals could be a tricky and dangerous business. Radio beams had an annoying tendency to bend around mountains or shorelines, leading the unwary astray. Occasionally, for no good reason, a loop might reverse itself, broadcasting an A instead of an N signal, or an N instead of an A. Static caused by thunderstorms or falling snow might temporarily drown out a range signal. And, invariably, just when it was needed most, the signal would disappear entirely. Braznell tells a story of how this happened to Benny Howard soon after Howard left American to fly for United Airlines.

One miserable, rainy night, Benny was inbound to Chicago in a Ford TriMotor with United's president, Pat Patterson, as a passenger. He was within a mile or two of the Chicago range station when the signal went dead and a CAA operator began broadcasting weather reports for the Chicago-Cleveland region.

In those days, it was common practice to interrupt range signals with intermittent voice broadcasts. Without an aural signal or direction finding antenna, a pilot unlucky enough to be at a critical point in his range approach, as Benny was, had no choice but to break off, "take it around," and home in to the range station once again.

Benny executed a gentle banking turn, reversed course, and then, after proceeding outbound for the prescribed two minutes, did another gentle

Flight Instruments of the 1920s and Early 1930s

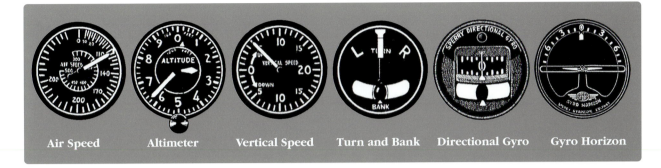

| Air Speed | Altimeter | Vertical Speed | Turn and Bank | Directional Gyro | Gyro Horizon |

AIR SPEED INDICATOR: The air speed indicator measures ram air pressure created by the motion of an aircraft through its surrounding atmosphere. Altitude and air temperature affect ram air pressure as well as barometric pressure and must be taken into account in calculating an aircraft's true air speed. In the relatively thin atmosphere above 10,000 feet, for example, an indicated air speed of 150 miles per hour may translate to true air speed of more than 170.

ALTIMETER: Altimeters are basically barometers that have been preset and calibrated to measure atmospheric pressure in feet above sea level rather than inches of mercury. The Kollsman Sensitive Altimeter, introduced around 1929, was the first equipped with two-handed dials that simultaneously measured altitude in hundreds as well as thousands of feet. The sensitive altimeter's improved design eliminated the indicator lag that made earlier altimeters dangerously unreliable during low-altitude instrument approaches.

VERTICAL SPEED INDICATOR: Similar to the altimeter, this ultra-sensitive pressure instrument registers a ship's vertical movement through a column of air by measuring the rate of change in the weight of the air column as the plane climbs or dives.

TURN AND BANK INDICATOR: Turn and bank indicators combine two elements—a gyro-operated turn needle and a bank indicator consisting of a weighted ball floating in an arched fluid race. In straight and level flight, both needle and ball are centered. In a coordinated turn, the ball remains centered while the needle swings to the left or right to indicate the direction and rate of turn. Displacement of the ball to either side of the race indicates the aircraft is in an uncoordinated slip, skid, or spin. In all three instances, the proper correction is to center the ball with rudder pressure ("step on the ball"), then use aileron and elevator controls to center the needle.

DIRECTIONAL GYRO: Directional gyros developed and manufactured by Sperry Gyroscope Company made their first appearances on airliner instrument panels around 1931. Although similar in appearance to the airborne magnetic compasses of that period, DGs had no built-in direction-finding ability. They had to be manually preset to the correct compass heading before each flight and required frequent resetting during flight. Once up and running, however, the DG served as an invaluable directional instrument, permitting the pilot to hold a steady course in turbulent air and make precise turns without the oscillation, dip, and swing error typical of magnetic compasses.

ARTIFICIAL (GYRO) HORIZON: With the introduction of the Sperry Artificial Horizon in 1931 the average pilot's proficiency and confidence in flying on instruments improved dramatically. Here, for the first time, was a means of visualizing an aircraft's position or attitude relative to an invisible earthly horizon, and of making small, precise adjustments in pitch and bank, air speed, and rate of climb. The instrument featured a fixed image of an aircraft (rear-view perspective) against a gyro-stabilized, semi-spherical horizon.

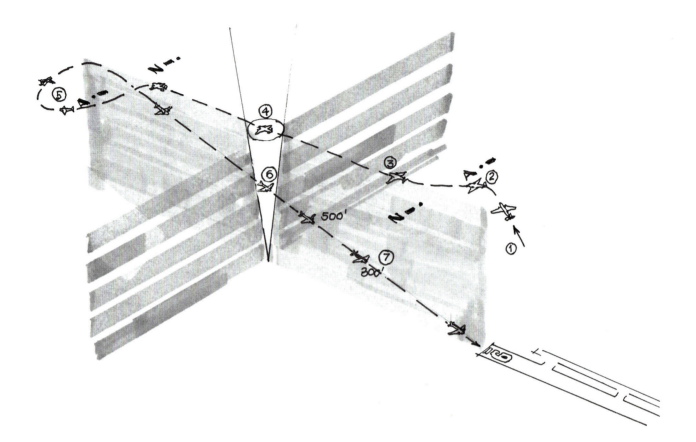

Riding the Range

A low-frequency radio range consisted of four transmitters broadcasting an overlapping clover-leaf pattern of aural signals—"N" (dah dit) in the north and south quadrants and "A" (dit dah) in the east and west quadrants. Thus, a pilot inbound to a destination airport could easily tell from the range signal whether he was east or west of course. To home in on the range station, he turned to intercept the desired inbound "leg" or beam (1 and 2) and flew his intercept heading until the dah-dit or dit-dah signal gradually merged into a solid, continuous tone, indicating he was "on the beam" (3). Turning to the designated inbound heading, he continued to track the beam all the way to the station (4). Station passage was indicated by a steady buildup in signal volume, then an abrupt drop-off as the aircraft entered the inverted "cone of silence" extending skyward from the transmitter beacons. Upon reporting station passage, the pilot might be told to set up a racetrack-shaped holding pattern (not shown) at an assigned altitude. When cleared for final approach, the pilot picked up the outbound reciprocal leg of the station for a minute or two, then executed a "procedure turn" (5) to reverse course and reintercept the same leg, inbound. Back on the beam, he slowed his plane to final approach speed, extended his landing gear, and started his let-down. Reporting station passage at the prescribed thousand-foot minimum (6), and cleared by the control tower for final approach, he continued his timed, 500-feet-per minute descent outbound along the range leg beamed toward the airport, being careful not to descend below safe minimum altitude until he had the field in sight (7). If he failed to spot the airport within the prescribed time/distance from the station, he immediately pulled up and executed the standard missed approach procedure for that particular airport.

180-degree turn and intercepted the northeast leg of the Chicago range once again. He was just about over the station for the second time when the CAA broke in to report Chicago-*Omaha* weather. At this point, Benny decided he'd had enough milling around for one evening. Still on instruments, he flipped the TriMotor into an almost vertical bank, wracked it through a gut-sucking 360-degree turn, hit the range just as the signal came back on, and completed his final approach. Mr. Patterson was waiting for him when Benny got off the plane. Before Patterson could utter a word, Benny walked up and said, "Pat, if a pilot of mine gave me a ride like that, I'd fire him."

Patterson didn't fire Benny. Instead, he became one of Howard's most ardent admirers. After the 1936 Bendix Race crack-up in which Benny and his wife, Mike, were almost killed, Patterson looked after the two of them. When Benny was able to fly again with the aid of an artificial limb, Patterson put him back to work as a test pilot.

Compass Rose

The modern compass rose is divided into 360 degrees of arc. In a 360-degree turn, an aircraft describes a full circle. A 180-degree turn is a half circle. When a pilot says "I did a 180," he means he reversed direction or turned back from his original destination. In aerial navigation, points of the compass are expressed in degrees, and always in three digits: North is 360 degrees, east 090, south 180, and west 270.

World without Horizon

At last Braznell was ready to make the plunge into that "all white world without horizon" as yet known only to a handful of aviation pioneers:

A few weeks after my new Scheduled Air Transport Rating came through, I was northbound from St. Louis to Chicago in a single-engine Hornet Pilgrim with two passengers—a man and a woman. It was snowing when we left St. Louis, and I had to fly low to keep contact with the ground. The Pilgrim's two-way radio was working perfectly, but my only navigational aid was the Chicago range, still too far away to be of much use.

North of Springfield we were flying in the tree tops with no forward visibility. A call to Chicago confirmed that the weather there and to the west was improving. Chicago was reporting a 3,000-foot ceiling and four miles visibility. This was the moment I'd been anticipating for nearly a year. I increased rpm, eased the stick back, and began to climb.

Immediately we were in an all-white world without horizon. My first reaction was a sigh of relief to be gaining separation from the trees. By the time we passed through 4,000 feet, my super-attentiveness to the instruments dissolved, and I settled back with a relaxed smile. I will never forget the sense of well-being that flooded over me. I felt I could do anything with that ship. Let the Chicago weather go to pot—who cared? I had already worked out and rehearsed every detail of the flight, right down to the instrument approach and landing. Nothing to worry about now.

Meanwhile, I began to sense that the mood in the passenger compartment was less ecstatic. There was a small window to the Pilgrim's cabin right behind my head, and through it I heard the man shouting, "What's happening? Where are we? Get down! Get down! You're going to kill us!" I tried to calm him, but didn't have much luck. He started to plead—first with me, then with the woman passenger. Perhaps she could bring me to my senses.

"Pilot, is everything all right?" she asked, in a voice as smooth as whipped cream.

"Couldn't be better," I replied.

About fifty miles out of Chicago we broke out of the clouds, and everything was peaceful for the remainder of the trip. After we landed, the man came up to me and apologized. I tried to act blasé—to leave him with the impression that our little adventure was (yawn) entirely routine. But it wasn't. It was the beginning of an era as far as I was concerned.

One particular passenger flight in the early days of all-weather airline operation sticks in my mind. It was a trip from St. Louis to Memphis in a Ford TriMotor, about a year after the incident I just described. Charlie Dolson, who later became president and chairman of Delta Airlines, was my copilot, and Diddy, my son Bill, and my infant daughter Carole were our only passengers. Diddy and the kids were returning to our new home in Memphis after a visit with her parents.

Before leaving St. Louis I learned that the north-bound ship from Memphis had turned back due to low ceilings and icing conditions. Having flown in from Chicago just a short time earlier, I knew there was a temperature inversion (warmer air aloft) over St. Louis, and the cloud tops as far south as I could see were no higher than 6,000 feet. So, shortly after taking off from St. Louis, I climbed through the clouds, leveled at 6,000 feet, and set course for Memphis.

I think this was Charlie's first experience in flying under actual instrument conditions. As we climbed through the overcast, he asked whether my wife approved of my flying in "weather like this." In answer, I pointed back at the cabin. Diddy was reading a magazine. Carole was asleep on her lap. Bill was running up and down the aisle, carefree as a colt. To my way of thinking, they were far safer and more comfortable up there above the clouds than they would be bumping along over the hills and tree tops below.

Memphis was still overcast, with rain, when we arrived over our destination. We hit the Memphis range station on the nose and made an instrument approach I had worked out in advance. (We had no "standard" instrument approach charts in those days; each pilot developed his own).

Breaking out of the clouds at about 1,000 feet, with the landing strip dead ahead, I was feeling pretty full of myself—maybe a bit too full of myself to pay proper attention to the film of red clay silt that had washed onto the rain-slickened runway. As soon as we touched down, the Ford's wheels lost their traction and we began sliding. My brakes were useless, so I used right throttle and opposing rudder pressure to throw the plane into a 180-degree ground loop. Then I gunned all three engines. With engines wide open and the nose of the Ford pointing back the way we'd come, we slid tail-first off the end of runway, through a shallow ditch, and into a pasture, barely missing a herd of startled cattle.

Later, as we were driving home, Diddy remarked, "I can't understand why they let cows graze on the Memphis Airport." Foolishly, I admitted those cows were not, strictly speaking, *on* the Memphis Airport. Now you know why the incident sticks in my mind. Diddy has never let me forget it.

The Shape of Things to Come

By 1934 the lumbering trimotors and boxy single-engine cabin planes the airlines had acquired only four or five years earlier were already history. The death of famed Notre Dame football coach Knute Rockne in the crash of a Fokker F-10—a crash blamed on the structural failure of one of the Fokker's plywood wings—pushed that estimable aircraft into early retirement. Ford stopped building planes in 1932, and though scores of its indestructible TriMotors remained in limited service for years afterward, they were no match for the sleek new airships Boeing, Lockheed, Vultee, and Douglas had begun to produce.

As every would-be aviator learns in his first hour of ground school, the flight of an aircraft is a function of four opposing forces—*lift, thrust, gravity,* and *drag* or wind resistance. Up to this point in the evolution of flight, aeronautical engineers had succeeded in creating wings sturdy enough to lift airships weighing upwards of seven tons and engines powerful enough to thrust those blunt-nosed, box-shaped vessels through the air at 100 to 110 miles per hour. Now, for the first time, young American aircraft designers such as Jack Northrop, Donald Douglas, and Jerry Vultee were systematically attacking the drag factor, learning in wind tunnel studies and demonstrating in actual flight how streamlining a ship's silhouette could produce astounding increases in air speed, payload carrying capacity, and fuel efficiency.[2]

An early success was the NACA engine cowl—so called because it was developed by the National Advisory Committee for Aeronautics, NASA's predecessor, in a wind tunnel developed for that purpose. In tests conducted over a three-year period, NACA engineers demonstrated that a streamlined hood or cowl, properly installed over the cylinders of a standard air-cooled engine such as the Wright Whirlwind, could actually

improve engine cooling while increasing air speeds by as much as 20 miles per hour. Further wind tunnel tests demonstrated that the best location for wing-mounted engine housings or *nacelles* was *in* the wing, directly in line with and projecting outward from the wing's leading edge, rather than suspended below the wing or between wings as had been standard practice in the past. Streamlined cowls and embedded, forward-mounted engine nacelles became standard features in nearly all airliners introduced after 1928, the year the NACA studies were published.

Aircraft landing gear were another major source of wind resistance. Aeronautical engineers first tried streamlining these appendages with airfoil-shaped *pants* and teardrop-shaped wheel covers or *spats.* Then, in 1931, Lockheed introduced the Orion, a six-passenger plane with fully retractable landing gear and a top cruising speed of close to 200 miles per hour. That was the end of pants and spats. After the Orion, retractable gear was de riguer for every new aircraft built for the airlines.

The sporty Lockheed Orion and Northrop Alpha (1930), the brilliant but short-lived Boeing 247 and Vultee V-1 (1933), the Douglas DC-2

2. Streamlining is a coinage of the late 1920s. By the mid-1930s, everything was "streamlined," even such non-aerodynamic structures as radios, clocks, and refrigerators.

(1934) and DC-3 (1936), and every commercial aircraft built thereafter owed its gleaming, silvery finish and bullet-like streamlining to a *stressed skin* engineering concept pioneered in the mid-1920s by German designer Adolph Rohrbach. Rohrbach discovered that a thin skin of rolled duralumin alloy stretched tightly over an aircraft's wood or metal frame could be made to bear a portion of the weight and dynamic stress which, in earlier ships, had to be supported entirely by bulky internal spars and wing bracing. The result was not just a pretty face, but an airframe that was much stronger, pound for pound, than the plywood, linen, and corrugated aluminum-sheathed clunkers of that day. A comparison of wing sections of the Ford TriMotor and Douglas DC-2 reveals another major advantage of the stressed skin technology: the slimmer, externally stressed DC-2 wing offered far less wind resistance than the internally braced TriMotor wing. The result: greater aerodynamic efficiency—more speed for less fuel.

The Condor and the Owl

In any assemblage of airliners of the 1930s, the Curtiss Condor sticks out like an ostrich in an aviary. It was a throwback, an anachronism, a clumsy bi-winged Rube Goldberg of an aircraft in an era of Flash Gordon modernism. The earliest commercial versions of the aircraft, introduced around 1932, had twin tails, old-fashioned fixed-pitch props, and twin Curtiss Conqueror twelve-cylinder water-cooled engines. With the enormous parasitic drag created by that great laundry line of struts, guy-wires, and flapping, canvas-covered wings, the early Condors could scarcely make it off the ground on hot summer days. In the winter they attracted ice like cows attract flies, and the piercing scream of a slip-

stream flowing over their ice-shrouded rigging made strong men quail. Even though Curtiss improved the performance of later models by fitting them with 710-horsepower Wright Cyclone engines and variable pitch propellers, the Condors remained an object of affectionate ridicule among the pilots who flew these Edsels of the airways.

The Condor's main attraction, if not its only virtue, was a wonderfully roomy passenger cabin—roomy enough, in fact, to provide Pullman-type sleeping accommodations for twelve overnight guests. *Sleeper planes!* Just what American Airways' marketing people figured they needed to draw passengers away from United's faster Boeing 247s and TWA's more direct transcontinental route. Despite strenuous objections from American's engineers and pilots, ten Condor sleepers were ordered and put in service.

Braznell, recently transferred from Memphis to Chicago, was among the pilots assigned to American's new "Owl" flight between Chicago and Newark:

On its first few runs, everyone would turn out to see if the Condor would make it over the telephone lines at the end of Chicago Airport's 3,500-foot cinder runway. Standard procedure was to open the engines to full takeoff power as the aircraft rolled onto the runway, accelerate to about midfield—the point of no return—retract the landing gear (airborne or not) and hoist her over the wires with all the back pressure pilot and copilot could muster. This spectacle was repeated every twenty-four hours.

After the Condors were modified and their takeoff performance improved, we began regular "Owl" service, with late night departures from Chicago to Detroit, Buffalo, and Newark. The Owl was kept in the hangar before flight, and Sleeper passengers were permitted to board and retire to their berths any time after 10 P.M. As soon as the first passenger came aboard, total silence prevailed in the hangar. Even in the adjoining operations office everyone spoke in whispers. A few minutes before midnight the plane was gently pushed onto the ramp and the crew tiptoed aboard. Pilot and copilot went noiselessly through their preflight procedures, right up to the moment we hit the engine starter switches. At this point the number one engine would usually let fly with a series of backfires loud enough to shatter window panes. As the second engine caught, the Condor's wings would start flopping up and down in synch with the firing and repeated backfiring of each cylinder. This flopping and belching and backfiring would continue until our poor, pop-eyed passengers were practically climbing the curtains of their "sleeper" compartments. Every night we put on this tippy-toe routine, not just once, but three times— Chicago, Detroit, and Buffalo—and always with the same glorious finale. It was the craziest show I've ever seen.

Coddling the Customers

Cabin service was much improved by the advent of trained stewardesses, or flight attendants, beginning in 1933 with the first Condor sleeper flights. (For many years, American hired only young women for these jobs, and they all were required to have nursing degrees.) On the Condors, hot meals, served from the planes' well-equipped galleys, replaced the old, familiar box lunch.

Actually, those old pre-Condor box lunches— typically featuring one or two pieces of cold fried chicken, a ham or roast beef sandwich, Waldorf salad, and maybe a Dixie cup of ice cream—were heaven compared to today's tourist-class airline food.

Cold fried chicken was such a regular item on the early airline menu that American came to be known as "The Chicken Airline." Pilots, who shared the same fare as their passengers, would

customarily dispense with their chicken bones by holding them near an open cockpit window and letting the venturi effect of the slipstream suck them out. "We left a trail of chicken bones strewn across the land from Newark to Chicago," Braznell recalls.

Blackout

During the winter of 1934–1935 Braznell flew most of his scheduled flights in one of the company's hot new Vultees, a low-wing, single-engine plane equipped with all the latest gadgets: retractable gear and flaps, variable pitch props, artificial horizon, rate of climb indicator, and two-way radio. The Vultee carried up to eight passengers, but on two memorable occasions that winter, Braznell's manifest listed just one name:

Arriving at Chicago, my new home base, one evening just about dark, I was greeted by our station manager on the flight ramp before I could step out of the cockpit. "We have an emergency," he said. Some VIP friend of American's chairman, E. L. Cord, needed a lift to Mayo Clinic in Rochester, Minnesota, to be with a dying brother at his deathbed. Mr. Cord had volunteered the company's services. "It won't take a minute to refuel your aircraft," the manager assured me. "Why don't you stay aboard, and we'll radio you your flight plan."

I thanked him for the offer, but having never been north of Chicago in my life, with night coming on and a light snow already beginning to fall, I decided I needed a few minutes to look at a route map and check the Rochester weather. In the operations office I found a map of the Chicago-Rochester sector and laid out my course, vectoring in a heading based on forecast winds aloft. The forecast was for snow all the way, with low ceilings and reduced visibility.

Dinosaurs at Rest

The ungainly looking Curtiss Condor was the last biplane to enter commercial service in the United States. It was also the first airliner to offer Pullman-type sleeper accommodations, the first American Airways ship to carry flight attendants, and the first with variable pitch props. Like most airplanes of its era, the Condor was weak on fundamentals: load-carrying capacity (6,000 pounds), range (560 miles), cruising speed (around 145 miles per hour), and takeoff power (every day a new thrill).

The building in the background is the original St. Louis Municipal Airport Terminal, erected in 1932–1933. The neo-classic architecture is fairly typical of hundreds of air terminals, post offices, libraries, and other public buildings built by the federal Works Progress Administration in the early years of the New Deal. The WPA gave a tremendous shot in the arm to commercial aviation during the Great Depression, investing more than $112 million in some 320 airport development projects between 1933 and 1939. *Photo courtesy of American Airlines*

An American stewardess welcomes passengers aboard the airline's new Condor Sleeper. In 1934 American inaugurated overnight service between Chicago and Newark, with inter-mediate stops in Detroit and Buffalo. The "sleeper" designation was largely illusory—one would have to have been deaf, drugged, or comatose to get much rest in a Condor berth.

One thing pilots liked about the Condor was its spacious "greenhouse" flight deck. *Photos courtesy of American Airlines*

Braznell spent most of the winter of 1934–1935 flying the hot new Vultee V-1A out of Chicago, his new home base. With its low-wing, stressed aluminum construction, retractable gear, and fully cowled 710-horsepower Wright Cyclone engine, the Vultee was on the leading edge of commercial aircraft design when introduced in 1933. The last single-engined, single-pilot ship American put into service, the Vultee carried up to eight passengers. It had a top speed of well over 200 miles per hour, cruised at 180 miles per hour, and had a range of about 1,000 miles.

BOEING 247: With its 30- to 40-miles-per-hour advantage over competing trimotors and biplanes, the ten-passenger Boeing 247 was clearly in a class by itself when United put it into service in early 1933. United's competitive advantage didn't last very long, however. Within a year, TWA and American would counter by introducing the Douglas DC-2, a ship that outclassed the 247 in every respect. *Photo courtesy of Jesse Davidson Aviation Archives*

DOUGLAS DC-2: Remembered primarily as the forerunner of the famous DC-3, the DC-2 was a winner in its own right—a considerable advance in aircraft design, load carrying capacity (fourteen passengers) and cruising speed (170 miles per hour) relative to its contemporaries. Donald Douglas thought so highly of it that he almost refused C. R. Smith's request for the wider-bodied twenty-one-passenger"modification," the DC-3, that would make his company world-famous. The building in the background is the original Chicago Municipal Airport passenger terminal, circa 1935. *Photo courtesy of American Airlines*

Viewed from Newark Airport tower during a snowstorm in the winter of 1935–1936, five species of aerial dinosaurs huddle together in the cold. In the foreground, left to right, are a Ford Tri-Motor, a Curtiss Condor, and a Douglas DC-2. In the background, left, is a clutch of Stinsons—two SM 6000 models (far background) and one "A" model (the one immediately behind the Condor). Another DC-2 fills out the picture. The Douglas DC-3 will soon make all of them not just obsolete, but extinct. *Photo courtesy of American Airlines*

By the time we were twenty minutes out of Chicago, I was flying on instruments in moderate to heavy snow. As I was about to call Chicago operations for the latest en route weather, my radio went dead and, simultaneously, my cockpit lights went out. After checking what I could with my flashlight, I called my passenger to the cockpit and explained the situation. As far as I could tell, we had suffered a complete electrical failure. Our options were to return to Chicago and get another plane or try to hit Rochester by pilotage and dead reckoning. We would be landing at a strange field, without lights, but I was willing to keep going if he was game. He said, "Let's go."

Those few minutes of preflight planning made all the difference. With a flashlight between my knees lighting the instrument panel and a suction-driven directional gyro as my primary compass, I was able to hold my precomputed heading without much trouble. Right on schedule we spotted the lights of La Crosse, Wisconsin, glowing through light clouds and falling snow. Over La Crosse, I dropped down through a break in the undercast, picked up the Mississippi River and the bridge crossing over into Minnesota, and followed the lights of cars heading down the highway toward Rochester. We located the Rochester Airport beacon easily, hand-cranked the gear and flaps into position, and landed without any further problems. After shutting down, I hurried into the airport office to call my boss and let him know what had happened since we lost radio contact. I didn't see my passenger again, but I was told he made it to the hospital in time to say good-bye to his brother.

The Tycoon

The first decade of commercial flight, 1926 to 1936, witnessed a gradual shift in the ownership and control of the nation's airlines, from aviation pioneers such as the Robertson brothers to industrialists and financiers such as North American Aviation's Clement Keys and AVCO's E. L. Cord—men to whom buying and selling airlines was just one of many ways to make a fortune.

Errett Lobban Cord was a particularly interesting study—a self-made multimillionaire who worked as a bus driver and car salesman before striking it rich in the automobile manufacturing business. His company built the swank Auburn and Cord motor cars. By 1931 Cord had successfully ventured into the aviation industry, both as an aircraft manufacturer (Stinson aircraft, Lycoming engines, etc.) and as the founder of two upstart air carriers—Chicago-based Century Air Lines and California-based Century Pacific Lines, Ltd. In 1932 he swapped his controlling interest in the two airlines for a major stake in AVCO. Later that year, after waging a successful fight for control of its board, he elected himself chairman of AVCO and its largest subsidiary, American Airways.

Cord brought to American a reputation as a fare slasher and cost cutter. At Century he had provoked a pilot strike by threatening to cut salaries, already the lowest in the industry, to roughly half the industry average. Although something of a pilot himself, he made no bones about his contempt for professional airmen, whom he referred to at various times as "glorified bus drivers" and "overpaid chauffeurs."

Braznell:

Mr. Cord had a special version of the Vultee equipped for his personal use. Unlike the usual single-pilot line ships, this one was fitted with dual controls. I was about to discover why.

It was in the spring of 1935, soon after I'd begun flying the Chicago-Buffalo-Newark run in the new Douglas DC-2s. I had just returned to Chicago after a rough flight, when my boss, Gage Mace, called me into his office and told me Mr. Cord wanted a pilot to "accompany" him to Newark. It appeared that I had been nominated for the job, seconded, and duly elected.

When I boarded the ship, Cord was already strapped into the pilot seat. He glanced at me impatiently and without a word motioned me into the copilot seat. I tuned in the Chicago range, gave him the bearing for the first leg of the trip, and off we went.

Everything went very smoothly at first. But approaching Goshen, Indiana, the sky grew dark and I could see we were heading into a granddaddy of a thunderstorm. As soon as we plunged into the clouds, Mr. C. began to perspire. After a few good bumps his knees started shaking and bucking uncontrollably. But his hands remained gripped on the wheel, and I wasn't going to force my attentions on him. I just sat there like a vacationing bus driver, enjoying the ride. Soon we were in the middle of the storm—torrential rain, lightning, violent turbulence. Cord's eyes grew round and fixed, his body rigid. Sweat rolled down his face. Feeling sure I could get us out of whatever jam he could get into, I had made up my mind not to touch the controls unless he asked for help. But now we were clearly in trouble. The turn indicator was deflected fully to the right, the ball pressed against the opposite corner of its race, the altimeter unwinding like a yo-yo. We were in a deadly spin, and there sat the great tycoon, speechless, paralyzed.

I gave him a sharp poke in the ribs—just hard enough to loosen his death-grip on the controls. After recovering from the spin, I got the plane squared away, resumed course, and climbed back up to our assigned altitude. Near Cleveland we broke out on top, into a clear blue sky. I kept the controls until we reached Youngstown, then Cord took over and flew the rest of the trip. We spoke hardly a word to each other. It was as if nothing had happened.

Black Days

In 1933, soon after Franklin Delano Roosevelt began his first term as president, the Democrat-controlled U.S. Senate launched an investigation of alleged conspiracy and collusion in the awarding of air mail contracts under the Hoover administration. Senator Hugo L. Black, later appointed by Roosevelt to the Supreme Court, headed the inquiry, which focused on Postmaster General Brown's so-called Airline Spoils Conference of 1930. Although it was widely viewed as a political hatchet job on the former Republican administration, Black's investigation provided enough evidence of profiteering and excessive influence on the part of the major aviation holding companies to raise a public cry for reform.

What the public got, instead, was a classic example of political overkill. Acting on Black's advice, Roosevelt issued an executive order on February 9, 1934, summarily canceling all air mail contracts and ordering the U.S. Army Air Corps to commence flying the mail, effective February 20. The cancellation of the mail contracts raised a firestorm of protest. Charles Lindbergh, still revered throughout the world as the patron saint of aviation, decried the act, claiming the airlines had been "condemned without just trial." Newspapers that had headlined the scandal and echoed Black's call for reform now protested the administration's "vendetta" against the airlines. Eastern Airlines' Eddie Rickenbacker characterized the decision to turn over the air mail service to a bunch of green Air Corps pilots as "legalized murder."

As Rickenbacker had warned, the Air Corps' ill-equipped and inexperienced pilots were no match for the task pressed upon them. Ten airmen died in air mail–related crashes between February 20 and March 10, at which time all air mail operations were suspended. On March 19 operations were resumed on a reduced scale, with flights restricted to daylight hours. Even so, two more Air Corps pilots were killed. Finally, the Army, the Roosevelt administration, and Congress had all had enough. Hastily enacted legislation paved the way for resumption of commercial air mail service on May 7, 1934.

Pilot's Log: Walter Braznell, 1930–1935

1930 January	Flying Boeing 40B-4 mail runs between St. Louis and Chicago—plus an occasional Sunday sightseeing flight in one of the company's new Ford TriMotors.
February	Time off to get married, honeymoon.
May	F-10 Trimotor passenger runs, St. Louis–Tulsa—St. Louis–Chicago.
December 1930– September 1931	Boeing and Fokker Super Universal runs, St. Louis–Chicago.

1931

September 1931– December 1933	Flying passengers, Pilgrim 100, St. Louis–Chicago. First two-way radio trip on CAM 2, Oct. 1931. Record 1 hour, 32 minute flight from St. Louis to Chicago, November 1931. First reference to American Airways, Inc., Universal Division. New Chicago terminal inaugurated. At year-end:

      Total hours, 1931: 985

      Total flight time, career to date: 2,960

Total instrument time, career to date: 4 hours 40 minutes.

1932

January– October	Logging "blind" practice time in company trainer. Twenty-two hours on instruments in first nine months of 1932. SATR check ride (commercial pilot instrument rating) October 20, 1932.
December	First trip with Kollsman Altimeter and Sperry Gyro Compass. 1,080 hours logged in 4,040 hours, total at year end.

1933

August	Last big National Guard encampment—Fort Riley, Kansas. Squadron cross-country flight to Chicago World Fair.
December	Temporary move to Memphis, flying Ford TriMotors from Memphis to St. Louis and Chicago and back. First trip with stewardess, Miss Ruth Lorenz.

1934

January	Ground-looped TriMotor at Memphis with Diddy and kids aboard. Outlaw John Dillinger and guards transported from Memphis to Chicago.
February	Army starts flying mail on Feb. 19. Eleven airmen killed in 20 days.
May	Move to Chicago, check out in Curtiss Condor. Assigned to Chicago-Newark run.
July	First trip in Condor equipped with variable pitch props. First Sleeper runs. Flying under hood when not on actual instruments.
August	Flying Vultee V1 on St. Louis–Chicago run.
November	Night flight to Mayo Clinic—Complete electrical failure 20 minutes out.

1935

January	Flying Condors, Chicago–St. Louis. Lots of hood time.
March	Several Condor flights to Detroit. Check out in Douglas DC-2, flying Chicago-Newark route.
December	898 hours logged in 1935. Total time to date: 6,863 hours.

The Air Mail Act of 1934 prohibited any carrier that had participated in improper bidding in the past from holding commercial mail contracts. The alleged wrongdoers got around that provision simply by adopting slightly different names. Far more important was the provision of the act intended to break up the aviation "trusts" by denying bidding rights to any airline affiliated with an aircraft manufacturer. The prohibition hooked all of the major domestic carriers—American, United, TWA, and Eastern—and forced an immediate, wholesale restructuring of the aviation industry.

In April 1934, American Airways was spun off by AVCO and reincorporated as American Airlines, Inc. When the new air mail contracts were awarded, American emerged with a much improved route system connecting such hub cities as Los Angeles, Dallas–Fort Worth, Newark (New York), Boston, Philadelphia, Washington, D.C., Chicago, St. Louis, Tulsa, Cleveland, Cincinnati, Nashville, and Memphis.

With a new name, a better route structure, and a dynamic young Texan named Cyrus Rowlett Smith at the controls, American Airlines was ready to fly.

Book Two

Chief Pilot

The Flagship Fleet

ive months after American Airways was re-organized as American Airlines, Inc., Chairman E. L. Cord fired the airline's president, Lester D. Seymour, and elevated the thirty-six-year-old general manager of its Southern Division, C. R. Smith, to take his place. Soon afterward Cord moved to England—some say to duck a Securities and Exchange Commission investigation into some non-airline stock deal—leaving Smith in sole command.[1] Though Cord remained one of the company's largest shareholders until his death in 1974, he was never again active in the company's affairs.

Aside from putting Smith in charge, Cord left one other enduring legacy to American Airlines before sailing off into the sunrise: a route system that actually went somewhere. In the wholesale restructuring and rebidding of air mail contracts following passage of the 1934 act, his political savvy and close ties to the Roosevelt administration unquestionably weighed in the balance,

helping to secure the routes and route extensions needed to transform American Airways' crazy-quilt route structure into an air *line* providing truly competitive single-carrier service from coast to coast. In the bidding process American not only retained all of its preexisting routes but also picked up eight lucrative new commercial air mail contracts: Fort Worth–Los Angeles, Newark-Chicago, Boston-Newark, Boston-Cleveland, Cleveland-Nashville, Newark–Fort Worth, Washington-Chicago, and Chicago–Fort Worth.

Besides shaking up the nation's airlines and air mail route structure, the Roosevelt administration used its powers under the new Civil Aviation Act to recast air mail rates for the second time in four years. Still determined to teach the airlines a lesson, the Post Office slashed rates an average of 15.8 cents per mile, from 42.6 to 26.8 cents, effective January 1, 1934. Despite its recent route awards, American lost nearly $1.8 million in annual mail revenues as a result of these cuts. United and TWA suffered even greater losses. If there had been any question

1. Robert Serling, *Eagle: The Story of American Airlines.*

A Queen's Coronation

America's air travel industry came of age on June 25, 1936, the day American Airlines inaugurated service between Chicago and Newark aboard its new "flagship," the Douglas Sleeper Transport, or DC-3. Though based on the successful model of the Douglas DC-2, the DC-3 carried twenty-one passengers—a 50 percent increase in payload over the DC-2—while the Sleeper version provided comfortable Pullman-style berths for fourteen passengers on overnight flights. In other respects—speed, range, reliability, safety features, passenger comfort—the DC-3 so far outclassed the competition, including her illustrious sire, that she made every commercial air carrier then in service instantly obsolete. For nearly ten years, until the end of World War II, she would reign unchallenged, the queen of the airways.

American's C. R. Smith introduced the DST with the flourish of a veteran showman. In the presence of Chicago celebrities, a contingent of officers from the nearby Glenview Naval Air Station, and a squad of newspaper reporters, photographers, and publicists—with bands playing, pennants streaming, and champagne bottles bursting—Douglas Sleeper Transport N16002 was officially rechristened the Flagship Illinois. As the Flagship Fleet grew, the reams of publicity generated by similar christenings and launchings in city after city served by the American system gave ticket sales a tremendous boost.

The DST's inaugural flight from Chicago to Newark on that watershed day in 1936 was flown by Walt Braznell and W. A. "Little Bill" Miller. The flight covered the 724-mile route in just under four hours. That's Braznell in the dark cap, standing half hidden at the back of the christening platform. Mrs. Lincoln Harris, wife of a prominent Chicago banker, does the honors. Pioneer aviator Merrill C. Meigs stands directly behind her. In the foreground stand (left to right), Vice President–Operations Ralph Damon, Vice President–Marketing Charlie Speers, Operations Manager Hugh Smith, and C. R. Smith. *Photo courtesy of American Airlines C. R. Smith Museum*

Center of the Action

In May 1934, soon after the airlines resumed flying the mail, American transferred Pilot Walt Braznell from Memphis to Chicago and put him to work flying Curtiss Condors on the new Chicago-Newark run. Braznell was twenty-seven, married, and the father of two young children. With five and a half years experience on the line and 5,300 hours of commercial flying time, he was beginning to feel like a veteran—and with reason: Despite his youth, there were only eleven AA pilots senior to him in years of service with the company.

With a maximum cruising range of 550 miles and a normal cruising speed of about 140 miles per hour, the luxurious but lumbering Condor hadn't a chance of making it all the way from Chicago to Newark nonstop, even if there had been enough Chicago/Newark passengers to justify a direct flight. Typically, Braznell's runs included intermediate stops at Detroit or Buffalo, or both, with occasional detours into Albany, Elmira, and Syracuse to onload or offload passengers and mail—six to six and a half hours flying time, much of it at night and often under widow-making weather conditions. Within a year, American would begin nonstop service between Chicago and Newark aboard the faster, longer-range Douglas DC-2s, cutting average transit time to four and a half hours eastbound, five hours westbound. But even then, pilots who flew the Chicago-Newark run earned their pay.

The transfer to Chicago put Walt in the center of the action. Chicago was not only headquarters for the recently rechristened American Airlines but also the hub of the airline's expanding route system. And despite fierce head-to-head competition from United and TWA, the Chicago-Newark run was, or would soon become, American's top revenue producer.

that the airlines' future lay in hauling passengers rather than lobbying for mail subsidies, this unkindest cut of all put an end to the discussion.

Survival, Pride, and Prospects

In 1930, when Walter Folger Brown first conceived and then proceeded to ram through his plan for consolidating the nation's weak and undercapitalized air transport system, the United States boasted forty-three domestic airlines. By January 1934, when Congress enacted the Civil Aviation Act, the list had shrunk to twenty-four. The air mail rate reductions that followed led to further mergers and failures of the weaker lines, narrowing the field to just sixteen operational domestic carriers by 1938.

As air mail subsidies shrank, passenger travel soared. The annual volume of airline passenger miles flown tripled between 1933 and 1937, to 477 million. By the time the United States entered World War II, domestic carriers were flying nearly a billion and a half passenger miles per year, with the three leading carriers accounting for the lion's share of the volume. Thus, within the span of a decade, Walter Brown's vision of a passenger-oriented airline industry dominated by three strong and highly competitive transcontinental carriers had come to pass.

From the mid-1930s onward, the Big Three airlines seemed to set their respective sights on outgunning the other two lines in an all-out contest to become the biggest, fastest, and most luxurious coast-to-coast carrier. Never mind that the demand for transcontinental travel was, to

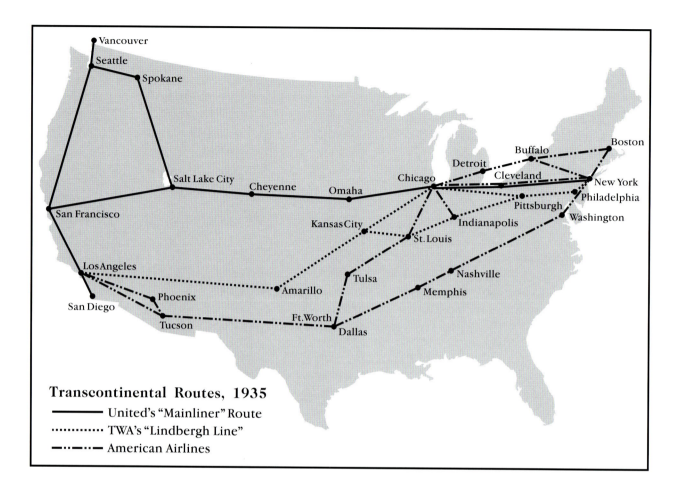

Transcontinental Routes, 1935

——————   United's "Mainliner" Route

············   TWA's "Lindbergh Line"

—·—··—   American Airlines

put the best possible light on it, "developmental"; never mind that the chief West Coast cities in those days were still a far cry from the tourist meccas, trade centers, and financial-industrial powerhouses they are today; never mind that the average transcontinental traveler wouldn't have been caught dead in an airplane, much less trust one to transport him safely over 2,500 miles of mountains, desert, and fruited plains. Indeed, the airlines' preoccupation with transcontinental air travel seems to have had nothing to do with economics and everything to do with pride and prospects. But then, that's what the airline business was all about in those days—pride and prospects.

Four Titans

The Air Mail Act of 1934 effectively barred anyone who was even suspected of having colluded in the 1930 Spoils Conference from working for a commercial airline. All at once a generation of aviation pioneers disappeared and a new generation took its place at the head of the nation's major domestic airlines—men such as United's Pat Patterson, TWA's Jack Frye, Eastern's Eddie Rickenbacker, and American's C. R. Smith.

However severe and unjust, the top-management purge proved to be the right medicine for an industry struggling to survive in the depths of the Great Depression. These young leaders—

Rickenbacker was the only one over forty—brought a youthful vitality, venturousness, and breadth of vision that had been lacking in the past. More than any modern corporate CEO who comes to mind, Patterson, Frye, Rickenbacker, and Smith personified their companies—personified them to the extent that it was often difficult to distinguish the organization from the individual, or the individual from the organization.

United's Pat Patterson

Born in Honolulu in 1899, the son of a sugar plantation superintendent who died when he was a boy, William A. Patterson went to sea as a teenager and later got a job as an office boy with Wells Fargo Bank in San Francisco, where, after a long apprenticeship, he rose to the exalted rank of junior loan officer. A loan he arranged for Vern Gorst, president of Pacific Air Transport, led to increasing involvement in that company's affairs, including acting as financial adviser in the 1928 merger of Pacific into Boeing Air Transport. After the merger, BAT President Phil Johnson persuaded the young banker to throw in his lot with the airline, hiring Patterson as his personal assistant. When Johnson was forced out of the airline because of his presumed involvement in the 1930 Spoils Conference, Patterson, then just thirty-four, was chosen to run the restructured, renamed, and newly independent United Airlines.

In its first few years under Patterson, United lost ground to American and TWA. This was partly due to a disastrous decision by his predecessors to saddle the airline with a huge fleet of soon-to-be-obsolete Boeing 247s. But Patterson himself seriously erred in pursuing a quixotic suit against the government for wrongfully terminating United's air mail contracts. United

eventually won its case, and a token settlement, but by the time the suit was settled, many of its choicest routes had been taken away or opened to competition from other airlines by a vindictive Bureau of Air Commerce.

Under Patterson's gentle, paternalistic leadership, United "operated like a well run utility" according to aviation historian Charles Kelly.[2] In the later years of his administration, however, his increasing caution and conservatism proved costly—notably, and ironically, when United let slip the opportunity to lead American and TWA into the Jet Age after negotiating and then declining first crack at another Boeing aircraft, the 707.

Eastern's Eddie Rickenbacker

Eastern's predecessor airline, Pitcairn Aviation, was founded by Harold F. Pitcairn, veteran barnstormer and designer-manufacturer of the famous line of Pitcairn Mailwing biplanes. In 1929 Pitcairn sold the airline (later renamed Eastern Air Transport) along with its lucrative air mail contracts connecting New York, Atlanta, and Miami, to Clement Keys's giant North American Aviation. During the Depression, Pitcairn spent most of the fortune he had garnered from the sale of the airline developing and promoting the autogyro, a combination fixed- and rotary-wing aircraft, similar in some respects to helicopters.

Kelly notes, "Of all the domestic lines, Eastern was for years the most consistent money-maker." He credits Eastern's early success to a virtual monopoly over the New York–Miami travel market—and to Eddie Rickenbacker. Rickenbacker, a successful race car driver before World War I,

2. Charles J. Kelly, Jr., *The Sky's the Limit: The History of the Airlines.*

applied for a commission in the Army Air Service in 1917, but was rejected as too old. After serving for a time as General Pershing's chauffeur, he wangled a transfer to an Air Service fighter unit in the waning months of the war and, as they say, the rest is history. From March 1, 1918, to Armistice Day, November 11, 1918, Rickenbacker scored a record twenty-six confirmed victories and led his squadron, the famous "Hat in Ring" 94th Pursuit Squadron, to sixty-nine total kills, a feat for which he was awarded the Congressional Medal of Honor. Following the war, an unsuccessful venture in automobile manufacturing led to a job with General Motors' LaSalle Division, then with the company's General Aviation subsidiary. In 1932, after a brief stint with American Airways (he left shortly after E. L. Cord won control of the company) he was instrumental in arranging the merger of North American Aviation into his former employer, General Motors. Following the forced reorganization of the airline industry in 1934, Eastern Air Transport was spun off of North American, made a separate subsidiary of GM, and renamed Eastern Airlines. Rickenbacker was appointed general manager. In 1938, when General Motors decided to get out of the airline business, Rickenbacker once again played matchmaker and, with the help of Laurance Rockefeller and a few of Rockefeller's Wall Street friends, helped arrange a corporate buyout that made Eastern an independent corporation, with Rickenbacker at last in sole command.

Independent and strong-willed, Rickenbacker ran a tight ship during his twenty-seven years at the helm of EAL. No one ever accused Rickenbacker's Eastern Airlines of coddling its customers or employees. Its reputation for labor problems, poor service, flight cancellations, and late arrivals was unsurpassed. But for a time it was a money machine.

TWA's Jack Frye

Jack Frye also learned to fly in the Air Service during World War I. After the war he moved to southern California, did a bit of stunt flying for the silent movies, and set up a flying school and a passenger service specializing in chauffeuring movie stars to their high desert retreats. Frye sold his flying business to Western Air Express in 1930, a year before WEA and Transcontinental Air Transport merged to form Transcontinental and Western Air (TWA). He was appointed vice president of operations for TWA in January 1934, one month before the Post Office's ill-fated cancellation of commercial air mail contracts. On the night the mail contracts expired, he and Eastern's Eddie Rickenbacker teamed up in one of the most effective publicity stunts in airline history, the record-shattering "Last Mail Flight" across the nation aboard one of TWA's brand-new DC-2s. Later the same year, in yet another government-mandated reorganization, Frye was named president of TWA.

A pilot first and last, Jack Frye maintained his air transport license for many years after assuming executive office and often took the controls on flights around the TWA system. He appears to have been a far better judge of aircraft than of business associates. As a plane-picker he was instrumental in TWA's introduction of the DC-2, the Boeing 307 Stratoliner (the first pressurized four-engine transport in domestic service), and the Lockheed Constellation—inspired choices that, in their time, gave TWA a clear, if short-lived, edge over its larger competitors, United and American. On the other hand, it was at Frye's urging that his sometime friend and fellow air-racing enthusiast, multimillionaire Howard Hughes, bought control of TWA in 1939—a mistake Frye had frequent cause to regret during the nine years he served under Hughes. Frye was forced out in 1948. His ultimate replacement, the estimable Ralph Damon, died of a heart attack in 1955, no doubt induced by the constant frustration of dealing with one of the aviation industry's supreme eccentrics.

American's C. R. Smith

Cyrus Rowlett Smith was born in Minerva, Texas, in 1899. Like Patterson, he lost his father at an early age and was raised by a tough, resourceful, and independent-minded mother who somehow managed to inculcate those same virtues in all seven of her offspring. Young C. R. worked as part-time bookkeeper, bank examiner, and advertising agent (he had his own agency) while earning a degree in business administration at the University of Texas. In 1928, two years after Smith joined A. P. Barrett's Texas-Louisiana Power Company as assistant treasurer, Barrett acquired a small airline, Texas Air Transport, and appointed Smith general manager. Immediately Smith and Barrett set out to expand the line's route system through mergers and contract awards. In 1929, TAT, recently renamed Southern Air Transport, was acquired by AVCO and subsequently merged into the holding company's newly formed American Airways. Smith served as general manager of American's Southern Division from 1932 to 1934, when he was chosen by Chairman E. L. Cord to replace Lester Seymour, an earlier Cord appointee. Under Smith, American rapidly overtook United as the nation's largest airline, a distinction it retained through most of his thirty-one years as acting chief executive. Following a military leave of absence from 1942 to 1945, during which he served as deputy commander of the Air Transport Command, C. R.

returned to American Airlines as chairman and chief executive officer. Ralph Damon, who carried the title of vice president and general manager through most of the war, and actually ran the company in C. R.'s absence, continued as president from 1945 until 1949.

Smith retired from American in 1968 to accept an appointment as secretary of commerce in the Johnson administration, choosing as his successor the company's general counsel, George A. Spater. Following Spater's forced resignation in 1973, C. R. returned briefly to guide the company through a difficult and messy transition in management. He re-retired in 1974, after turning over the reins to Albert Casey.

In business as in private life, Smith was known as a fearless poker player—a master of the calculated risk. Few airline executives have come close to matching his record as a business manager or his stature as an industry leader. But, for all that, his enduring fame—his legend—rests in the sense of camaraderie and loyalty he instilled in his people during his stewardship of American Airlines. To longtime AA employees, regardless of rank, he was always "C. R." or "Mr. C. R.," never "Mr. Smith." He knew most of them by their first name, obviously enjoyed their company, took a personal interest in their welfare and that of their families, and seldom failed to acknowledge an achievement or remember an important anniversary with a note personally inscribed on his beat-up Woodstock typewriter.

Table Stakes

In the first few years of his presidency, Smith put together an outstanding management group, including Ralph Damon, former president of Curtiss Aeroplane & Motor Company, as vice president–operations, Charlie Speers as vice president–marketing, Charlie Rheinstrom as vice president–sales, and Bill Littlewood as vice president–engineering. One of the first orders of business for Smith and his new team was to replace the ragtag collection of Stinsons, Vultees, Fairchilds, Ford TriMotors, and Curtiss Condors acquired from American Airways with equipment that would allow American Airlines to compete head-to-head with United's Boeings and TWA's new Douglas DC-2s.

United's Boeing 247—no other major airline ever flew the plane—deserves recognition as the forerunner of a generation of sleek propeller-driven American-built aircraft that would dominate commercial aviation, worldwide, for the better part of three decades. Introduced in 1933, the ten-passenger, twin-engine monoplane was basically a modification of a high-speed bomber, the B-9, Boeing had been producing for the Army Air Corps since 1931—same streamlined, stressed-aluminum body, same 550-horsepower Pratt & Whitney Wasp engines, same distinctive, long-nosed profile. With a cruising speed of 155 miles per hour, the 247 was nearly half again as fast as the trimotors TWA and American had been flying over competing routes. It was also a good 15 miles per hour faster than the biwinged Curtiss Condors American introduced about the same time United unveiled its new Boeings. American's single-engine Vultees were considerably faster than the 247, but they lacked the 247's range, payload capacity, and, most important, the safety and peace of mind afforded by those twin engines.

The 247 covered the transcontinental flight from San Francisco to New York in twenty hours, requiring only seven refueling stops. By contrast, TWA's Ford and Fokker trimotors needed twenty-eight hours and eleven stops to

lumber from Los Angeles to New York via Albuquerque, Kansas City, and Chicago. American's Condors took roughly the same amount of time to cover the longer southern transcontinental route from Los Angeles to New York, via Dallas and Atlanta. With this clear-cut advantage, and a contract with Boeing that essentially guaranteed no other airline would fly the 247 for a year or more, United was prepared to mop up the competition.

United and Boeing were, at the time, subsidiaries of the same holding company, United Aircraft and Transport. The sweetheart deal that allowed United to co-opt the first sixty 247s Boeing produced—roughly two years' output—may have seemed a brilliant coup at the time, but it proved to be a near-fatal miscalculation for both companies.

Locked out by the Boeing-United pact, TWA's Jack Frye looked to a relative newcomer, Douglas Aircraft, for a plane capable of competing with the 247. Originally Frye wanted a trimotor, and he specified that it must carry at least twelve passengers, have sufficient range to fly nonstop from Chicago to New York, and be able to take off with a full load from any airport served by TWA *after* losing one engine. Douglas responded with a design for a twin-engine, low-wing monoplane, the DC-1, and despite some initial misgivings about whether two 710-horsepower Wright Cyclone engines could handle the load, TWA agreed to underwrite the production of a test model. The DC-1's proving flights, including the critical engine-out takeoff, were so successful that Douglas decided to stretch the fuselage and add two more seats, upping the payload to fourteen passengers, plus mail. Even in its new, stretched configuration the Douglas ship, redesignated the DC-2, flew rings around the 247. Not only was the Boeing fully 15 miles per hour slower, but it also required a refueling stop on flights between Chicago and New York, whereas under normal wind conditions the DC-2 could make the run nonstop in either direction, knocking about an hour and a half off of United's schedule each way.

Frye placed an order for twenty-five DC-2s. The first of these ships went into service in July 1934, less than two years after TWA and Donald Douglas reached agreement on the specifications for the DC-1. American came aboard six months later, inaugurating DC-2 nonstop service from Chicago to Newark in December 1934. United, which had gambled heavily on the 247 and could neither afford to break its contract with Boeing nor buy additional planes from Douglas, now found itself in the competitive bind it had hoped to inflict on TWA and American. Attempts to boost the 247's performance with bigger engines and more efficient variable pitch props only prolonged the agony. By the end of 1935 United, still by far the nation's biggest airline in terms of passenger revenues, was hemorrhaging market share on every run in which its Boeings competed with the Douglas aircraft. Unfortunately for United's Patterson, the poker game had just started, and American's Smith was about to raise the stakes.

Sleeper Play

Despite its obvious advantages over the 247, the Condor, and every other plane then in commercial service, Smith and his chief engineer Bill Littlewood were not overly impressed with the DC-2. It was so unstable in flight that even veteran fliers like Smith became air-sick. In rainstorms its cockpit windshield leaked like a rusty bucket. Its flaps and gear had to be raised and

lowered with a hand pump—a job copilots learned to loathe. Its wheel struts were stiff as the springs on a pogo stick, and produced roughly the same effect on landings. Its wing and prop de-icing systems constantly malfunctioned, and even the primitive cabin heater wouldn't start without a few swift kicks.

Most important, the Douglas plane's body was too narrow. Smith, still entranced with the vision of a coast-to-coast sleeper service that would rival the railroad Pullman cars in luxury and style, and convinced that transcontinental airline passengers would pay a hefty premium to sleep lying down, directed Littlewood to develop plans and specifications for a wide-bodied sleeper version of the DC-2 that would accommodate up to fourteen berths or—almost as an afterthought—seven extra passenger seats in its normal daytime configuration.

Doomed to Failure

"American ordered fifteen DC-2s and then began thinking about a modified version *to replace the Condor sleeper.*" (Emphasis added)

—C. R. Smith, address to the Newcomen Society, San Francisco, June 16, 1954

"There was a lot of eyebrow-lifting throughout the industry when word got out that American was working with Douglas on a plane that would carry twenty-one passengers behind two engines. United Airlines authorities said our investment was improper and doomed to failure; the airplane couldn't possibly perform with that kind of load."

—Walt Braznell

In a marathon two-hour telephone call, Smith laid out his proposal to a skeptical Donald Douglas. He secured Douglas's acquiescence to Littlewood's "modifications" only after committing American to a firm order for twenty aircraft.

Calling the new Douglas Sleeper Transport a modification of the DC-2 was a bit of a stretch, literally and figuratively, even at the outset of the project. By December 1935, when the first prototype DST rolled off Douglas's assembly line in Santa Monica, California, it bore only a superficial family resemblance to the DC-2. In the first place, it was substantially wider in the body and weighed 24,000 pounds fully loaded—6,000 pounds more than the DC-2. To support its

increased gross weight, Douglas had added ten feet to the aircraft's wingspan and replaced the DC-2's 700-horsepower Wright Cyclone engines with 1,000-horsepower Wright G-102 engines. The more powerful engines also boosted the DST's normal cruise speed 5 miles per hour, to 180 mph, and gave it a maximum ceiling of more than 20,000 feet—far higher than passenger planes could operate without cabin pressurization. A redesigned tail, with a ventral fin extending forward nearly one-third the length of the fuselage, solved the stability and lateral control problems that had plagued DC-2 pilots and passengers. Electrically actuated hydraulic systems replaced the old hand-operated landing

Shifting Gears

The DST/DC-3 was the first commercial airplane with constant speed, variable pitch propellers—props that could be set to whatever rpm or pitch setting the pilot wished. Variable pitch propellers perform roughly the same function as gearing in automobiles: Both are designed to deliver maximum rotary power or torque for rapid acceleration, then shift to a slower engine speed and higher gearing ratio for fuel-efficient long-range cruising. In a propeller-driven aircraft, the "shifting" is accomplished by simultaneously adjusting prop speed and pitch (angle of the airfoil relative to the direction in which the propeller spins) as indicated in the schematic drawing: Low pitch/high rpm for takeoff and climb (lower blade) and high pitch/low rpm for cruise (upper blade). The DC-3's Hamilton Standard props could also be "feathered" when an engine failed in flight—that is, the stationary blades could be rotated so that their leading edges pointed directly into the aircraft's slipstream (middle blade). In this configuration they offered less wind resistance than a windmilling flat-pitched propeller. The difference in air speed and maneuverability could mean life or death, particularly if an engine failed immediately after takeoff.

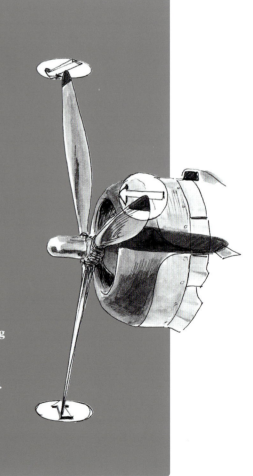

Fair Lady

From its snub-nose to its equally distinctive dorsal fin, from raked-back wing tip to wing tip, the DC-3 (DST model shown here) was a masterpiece whose classic lines influence aircraft design to this day. Spit and polish were fetishes with C. R. Smith. No fancy all-over paint jobs for his beauties—he liked them clean and nude. *Photo courtesy of American Airlines*

gear and flap controls. And, along with its sleeper berths, the new DST offered passengers such luxurious refinements as functional, easily controlled heating and ventilating systems, comfortable seating,[3] wide aisles, and well equipped galleys from which winsome young stewardesses—all single, all trained nurses—dispensed rather passable hot meals and beverages.

Best of all, the daytime version of the DST, the DC-3, carried twenty-one passengers. Even if his original fascination with Sleepers was

slightly off the mark, it didn't take a man of C. R's intelligence long to recognize the Douglas plane's strong suit: Here was a craft that cost no more to operate than the DC-2, but carried half again as much payload. *Bingo!*

When Ducks Walked

In the early 1930s, particularly in the winter months, an airline passenger's chances of flying from coast to coast without encountering weather-related flight cancellations or delays were practically nil. But by the time the DC-3 came along, improvements in weather forecasting and reporting, flight instrumentation, and radio navigation equipment had substantially improved the odds of getting where one was going more or less on schedule, even, as they

---

3. The DC-3 typically carried seven rows of seats, with two twenty-one-inch seats on one side of the nineteen-inch aisle and one on the other. By contrast, the average wide-body jet today offers eight- to ten-across seating in economy class, with an almost irreducible 18 inches of sit-space per passenger.

used to say, when ducks were walking. American's new DC-3s were themselves far better equipped for foul-weather flying than any airliner of their time. They were, for example, among the first commercial aircraft with static-free loop radio antennas, direction-finding radio compasses, and the new Sperry automatic pilot. Their wing and prop de-icing systems were much improved over the Condor's and DC-2's—

Walt and Slonnie

Captain Walt Braznell, Captain E. L. Sloniger, and an unidentified stewardess pose for a publicity shot beside the doorway of one of American's new Douglas Sleeper Transports (identifiable from the DC-3 by the small slot "ceiling window" in the upper right of the photo). "Slonnie," American's number one pilot in terms of seniority, served in World War I and had a colorful career as a barnstormer and itinerant commercial pilot (Mexico, China, Hawaii, etc.) before joining Robertson Aircraft in October 1927.

a point which may strike some old-timers as faint praise. And their flight instrument panels were studded with state-of-the-art gyro instruments and pressure gauges. But the factor mainly responsible for the DC-3's superior all-weather reliability was its remarkable range. Capped off with 822 gallons of fuel, it could stay aloft for eight hours and fly nearly 1,400 miles nonstop—enough to travel from New York to Chicago and back. By contrast, the DC-2 carried 540 gallons, or roughly six hours of fuel. On transcontinental flights the DC-3s could easily fly coast to coast with only three intermediate stops. DC-2s required four, and Boeing 247s needed seven.

To Walt Braznell and his fellow line pilots that extra range was like a prepaid insurance policy:

Before the DC-2s and 3s, our maximum cruising range had been about four hours. Try to imagine clearing Buffalo to Newark in winter snows and storm winds on a three-and-a-half-hour flight plan, with just four hours of fuel. On eastbound trips our last safe harbor before hitting the New York metropolitan area was the emergency field at Elmira, New York, 175 miles west of Newark. Once beyond Elmira, we were committed to land at Newark—which was then the only commercial airport serving New York City. An unexpected windshift, a bank of fog rolling in from the Atlantic, and a pilot could easily find himself out of fuel with nowhere to go.[4]

With the DC-3's extended flight range—its ability to hold over a destination airport or detour to an alternate when weather conditions made it unsafe to attempt a landing—the airlines' schedule reliability improved dramatically. Fewer en route fueling

4. In 1938 the newly created Civil Aeronautics Authority adopted a rule requiring airliners to carry fuel reserves sufficient to fly to their destination, then proceed to their alternate and land with at least forty-five minutes of fuel remaining. Such a rule would have made air travel all but impossible before the advent of the DC-2s and 3s, since none of the earlier aircraft could carry that much fuel.

stops also meant fewer weather-related delays in takeoff and landing clearances. As schedules became more reliable, air travel lost its novelty, and business travelers became regular customers. For the first time, passenger transportation became a paying proposition and, with the help of air mail and air cargo revenues, American and a few of the other major carriers started to generate profits for their shareholders.

Summing up, the DC-3's reliability and comfort made air travel popular; its extra seating capacity and low cost per seat mile made air transportation profitable;[5] and Smith's gamble on converting his hodgepodge collection of aircraft into the nation's first all–DC-3 "Flagship Fleet" made American Airlines. American put its first DC-3 into service in June 1936. That year it earned its first profit—$4,600. By the end of 1937 it had breezed past United and TWA to become the nation's leading airline in both revenues and revenue passenger miles, a distinction it would retain for nearly a quarter century.

"You and Your . . . Sleepers!"

American inaugurated overnight transcontinental service aboard its new DSTs in September 1936. Westbound American Mercury flights departed Newark in the late afternoon, stopped at Memphis, Dallas, and Tucson, and arrived at Glendale Airport in Los Angeles around breakfast-time the following morning, covering the 2,600-mile journey in approximately eighteen hours. The return flight took sixteen hours. With its double-occupancy Sky Room (also known as the Honeymoon Suite), free-flowing cocktail service, and aura of "pure glamour,"[6] the Mercury was an immediate success with the Hollywood set. Flights were routinely sold out weeks in advance. But despite the heavy bookings and a

hefty sleeper surcharge, the overnighter was not as profitable to operate as the twenty-one-seat DC-3s. The daily Mercury flights were discontinued during World War II and all of American's DSTs were turned over to the Air Corps, to be stripped of their luxurious seats and sleeper berths and converted into warhorse C-49s.[7]

United and TWA, which eventually queued up to order DC-3s, also experimented with sleepers, but quickly soured on the idea. Aside from the DST's relatively high cost per seat mile, there was a small problem with the overnight sleeper concept that no one seemed to have foreseen: passengers had to be wakened at every stop en route so they could clear their ears before landing.

Every pilot who flew the DSTs had his favorite tales about them. Walt's story about an incident involving the legendary Duke Ledbetter might be considered the last word on the subject:

> After reaching cruising altitude one night, Duke turned over the controls to his copilot, left the flight deck, and was tiptoeing down the narrow, dimly-lit aisle toward the lavatory, when he was arrested by the sound of violent struggle in one of the sleeper berths. As he paused outside the drawn curtain, worried about his passenger's safety, but not quite sure what a captain's duties were in a situation like this, a woman's girdle flew out of the lower berth and plopped at his feet. Always the gentleman, Duke instinctively stooped to pick it up, only to find himself eyeball-to-eyeball with the berth's infuriated occupant. Snatching the garment out of his hands, she stared at the red-faced captain and growled "You and your damned sleeper planes."

5. The DC-3 cost 3.4 cents per seat mile, versus 4.8 for the DC-2 and 8 cents for the trimotors.
6. Serling, *Eagle: The Story of American Airlines.*
7. As distinguished from the far more numerous military version of the DC-3, which carried the military designation C-47.

Airline Fatalities, 1934–1941

	Passengers	Pax. Miles (in millions)	Fatalities /100 MM Pax. Miles *
1934	461,743	187.8	9.05
1935	746,946	313.9	4.78
1936	1,020,931	435.7	10.10
1937	1,102,707	476.6	8.39
1938	1,343,427	557.7	4.48
1939	1,876,051	749.8	1.20
1940	2,959,480	1,147.4	3.05
1941	3,551,833	1,481.9	2.33

* Fatalities per 100 million passenger miles
Source: Air Transport Association

Dark Side of the Boom

The boom in airline travel during the mid-1930s had its dark side: an alarming increase in passenger fatalities. From 1928 through 1936, the first nine years in which airline fatalities were officially recorded, there were 55 accidents involving passenger fatalities and a total of 181 passenger deaths—slightly more than three deaths per incident, or one death for every two million passenger miles flown. While the incidence of fatal accidents remained at about the same level from 1930 through 1937, total passenger fatalities rose sharply toward the end of the period, mainly because the airlines were flying bigger planes and carrying more passengers per flight. In 1936 eight scheduled airline crashes took the lives of 44 passengers and 17 crew members. The following year eight more crashes killed 40 people. As the death toll rose and the scare headlines rumbled off the nation's presses, airline officials and civil aeronautics regulators discovered they had a crisis on their hands. United Airlines, with five crashes and 38 passenger fatalities from 1936 through 1938, suffered most from the public's

heightened concerns about air safety. TWA experienced three fatal accidents, with a loss of 25 passengers during the same period. American lost a DC-2 with 14 passengers and a crew of three in January 1936 after the plane, en route from Memphis to Little Rock, mysteriously veered off course and plunged into a swamp about 40 miles from its destination. The cause of the crash was never determined. From that point on, however, American's safety record over the balance of the decade was exemplary—nearly a billion passenger miles flown without a fatality.[8] Or perhaps, it was just luckier than its competitors. In any event, American felt the public backlash just as sharply as United and TWA did.

Afraid to Fly?

Flight safety has always been a subject airline advertising and publicity departments broach with the greatest delicacy, if they mention it at all. In the industry's Old Boy's Club, publicly bragging about safety records was and still is taboo, as is any suggestion, however vague and indirect, that "our airline is safer to fly than their airline." There are, of course, exceptions to every rule. Early on, United's Patterson stopped speaking to C. R. Smith for a time because Smith had permitted his advertising agency to run an ad promoting American's "low level route through southern sunshine to California." In Patterson's view, "low level" and "sunshine" were clearly code words for "safer"—a claim United's wordsmiths vigorously disputed, counterclaiming that American flew over more mountains than did their airline.

8. In May 1941 the National Safety Council recognized this achievement by presenting American Airlines with its highest airline safety award.

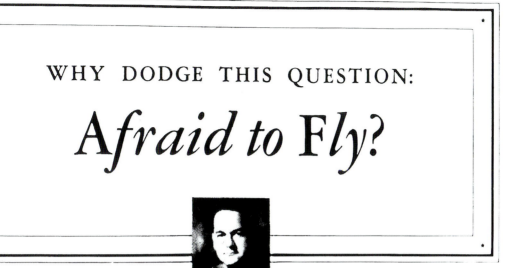

WHY DODGE THIS QUESTION:

Afraid to Fly?

WE know that fear keeps many people from enjoying the advantages of air transportation. *So why should we be silent on this subject?* Regrettable as it is, the records show there *have been* accidents and fatalities in *every* form of transportation. What we do not understand, is why some people associate danger with a transport plane more than they do with a train, a boat, a motor car, an interurban, or a bus. Is it because airline accidents have received more publicity?

The fact is, there *are* risks involved in *all* kinds of travel.

It is also a fact that the *air transportation industry has shown greater progress and achieved a much higher standard of efficiency in a shorter span of years than any other form of transportation the world has ever known.*

Why quote statistics? They are not always conclusive. They are often only controversial. I could show you figures to prove that you would have to fly around the world 425 times — or make approximately 14,165 flights back and forth between New York and Chicago—before you would be liable to meet with an accident. Do these statistics overcome your fear of flying? I think not. There is only one way to overcome that fear—and that is, to fly.

Many of our regular passengers, who now prefer air travel to any other form of transportation, admit they were very timid about their *first* flight. Perhaps you say: "It is my business if I want to go on being afraid and confine myself to

C. R. Smith

PRESIDENT
AMERICAN AIRLINES, INC.

slower forms of transportation." No one questions that. The question is: "Is it good business?" Maybe your competitor is flying. Many people lived and died who never rode on a train because *they* were afraid. Today we smile at those old-fashioned fears. And today, to the more than a million airline passengers of last year, the fear of air travel is just as old-fashioned.

American Airlines, Inc. has carried more than a million passengers. These people travel by air for the same reason they use the telephone, send telegrams, and ride in elevators. It is a quicker, more modern, more efficient way to accomplish what they want to do.

Are airlines safer than railroads? You can find intelligent people to take both sides of the argument.

Whether you fly or not, does not alter the fact that *every* form of transportation has *one* thing in common—risk! No form of transportation—on the ground, on the water, or in the air—can guarantee its passengers absolute immunity from danger.

This whole subject of fear about flying can be summed up as follows. PEOPLE ARE AFRAID OF THE THINGS THEY DO NOT KNOW ABOUT. You would be equally afraid of trains if you had never ridden on one.

As soon as you become acquainted with air transportation your fear will be replaced by your *enjoyment of the many advantages of air travel.*

Reprint courtesy of American Airlines' C. R. Smith Museum

The "sunshine" flap was nothing compared to the brouhaha over American's famous *Afraid to Fly?* ad, published under Smith's signature in February 1937. Here, for the first time in aviation history (and possibly the last), an airline spokesman dared to confront head-on a legitimate public concern about safety. Smith handled the job brilliantly. The ad's impact was immediate and enormous, if the amount of controversy it stirred within the industry is any measure. It may even have caused a few prospective customers to swallow their fears and give the airlines a try, which was the ad's main intent. But Smith would have been the first to admit that words alone were not going to resolve the crisis of confidence enveloping the airline industry. First, the individual airlines had to clean up their acts and, as he and his second-in-command Ralph Damon were discovering, American had a lot of cleaning up to do.

Looking back on the early days of the DC-3 era from the perspective of forty years in the airline industry, Walt Braznell remembered the years 1936 and 1937 as a low-water mark in the evolution of commercial flight.

Before the DC-2s and 3s, passenger safety had not been a big issue—not as big as it should have been, certainly. Our pilots were all veterans of thousands of hours on the line, and the prevailing wisdom—a holdover from the open-cockpit air mail days—was, if we got to our destination in one piece, so would our passengers. Consequently, every pilot flew exactly as he saw fit. No one in management felt the need for formal training programs, flight manuals, or standard operating procedures. New planes were delivered, never more than two or three at a time, and it was largely up to the individual pilots to learn how to fly them.

But the Douglas ships were far more sophisticated than any we had previously flown, and there were a lot more of them. When the company dumped this huge fleet of DC-3s and DSTs in our

laps, we were totally unprepared. We had at least a hundred pilots by this time, and every one of them had his own ideas about how to fly the aircraft—power settings, flap settings, approach speeds, two point vs. three point landings, and so on. Every time a copilot flew with a different pilot he had to adapt to a whole new set of cockpit protocols and flight procedures. It was chaos.

Fortunately no one was killed. American did not lose a single aircraft due to pilot error during the transition into DC-3s. But the cost of neglected crew training in non-fatal accidents, downtime, and loss of public confidence eventually convinced our management we needed higher standards of flight supervision and training. Our mistakes in phasing in the DC-3 would never be repeated.

The primitive state of the art of instrument flying was another factor weighting the risks of air travel. There were no radar centers to monitor airborne traffic and vector aircraft to their destinations; no ground-controlled radar approaches; no operational VHF instrument approach systems; no autopilot-coupled landing devices. In fact, there were no standard instrument approach procedures at all; every pilot made up his own, often extemporizing as he went along.

Consider, as well, that it had been only three years since the Bureau of Air Commerce had begun requiring airline pilots to be instrument-qualified. The skills required for the bureau's Scheduled Airline Transport Rating were not quickly or easily learned, and genuine proficiency in making precision instrument approaches under severe weather conditions required not only hundreds of hours of practice but also years of experience. Nevertheless, line pilots with no more than fifty or sixty hours of actual instrument flight time were routinely committed to land their aircraft under miserable weather conditions, with nothing to guide them to the runway but the faint and often unreliable hum of a low-frequency radio beam. Years later Braznell would write,

"It's a wonder—and a tribute to the professionalism of our pilots—that the airline industry did not lose more ships than it did back in those dark days."

An Accident in Progress

The following fictional but true-to-life episode, condensed from an article called "The Air Is How Safe?" in the April 1937 issue of *Fortune,* illustrates one of the supreme ironies of commercial aviation. The pilot, like scores of real airline pilots facing similar emergencies, exhibited a degree of skill, judgment, and courage that might have been considered worthy of a medal in a field where such virtues were less common. Yet, given the extreme circumstances, it is not difficult to imagine how the same expert pilot might have failed. A twist of luck, the smallest miscalculation, a single miscue during his long, grueling ordeal might just as easily have led to a tragic accident—one that would almost certainly have been blamed on "pilot error":

Allied Airlines Flight Ten out of Chicago, a DC-2 with 14 passengers aboard, was approximately 40 minutes out of Newark, flying in a solid overcast at 9,000 feet and estimating arrival over Newark at 9:45 P.M. The aircraft, captained by veteran pilot Phil Adams, with copilot Frank Hemings at the controls, had just passed the intersection of the north leg of the Harrisburg range with the eastern leg of the Bellefonte range, on which it was flying. This gave Adams an exact fix on his location. With a few quick twirls of his circular slide rule, he calculated the aircraft's average ground speed since his last fix at 190 miles per hour. At this rate, Flight Ten would hit the Newark beacon a few minutes ahead of schedule.

At the time Flight Ten departed Chicago, a storm was reported approaching the Atlantic Coast from the southwest, but the company's weatherman concurred with the U.S. Weather Bureau in predicting that it would not reach Newark until nearly midnight. He forecast a 2,000-foot ceiling with three miles visibility at the flight's estimated time of arrival. A half hour out of Newark, however, the flight dispatcher in the company's Newark office called Adams to warn him that the ceiling was down to 1,000 feet and lowering. A few minutes later, dispatch called again, reporting 900 feet and a mile and a half visibility in light snow and fog. Crossing the Martin's Creek range, eighteen minutes out, Adams contacted the Newark control tower and was told to descend to 2,000 feet and report over Summit, New Jersey. Newark tower reported an 800-foot ceiling, with one mile visibility in moderate snow. Over Summit, Flight Ten was cleared to 1,000 feet and told to report over the Newark beacon. Tower was now reporting a 400-foot ceiling with heavy snow, fog, and a mile visibility.

Adams saw that he was trapped in one of the sudden turns of weather that characterize the Atlantic seaboard. The storm that was supposed to hit two hours later was already on top of him. As he mulled over his options, the Newark range signal surged and then vanished, indicating he was in the cone of silence directly above the station. Taking the controls, Adams instructed Hemings to report station passage, then throttled back and turned to track the southwest leg of the Newark range outbound, allowing his air speed to drop to 100 miles per hour. After four minutes he reversed course to track the beam inbound, ordered gear down, and descended to 800 feet. At station passage, Adams called for half flaps and began a steady 500-foot-per-minute rate of descent. Now it was simply a matter of holding the ship on the outbound beam that intersected Newark Airport until they had the field in sight. A minute and ten seconds later, 300 feet above the terrain and still no runway lights visible, Adams `took it around,' pushing his throttles forward and starting a smooth climb-out. Immediately, he called his dispatcher to report the missed approach. Dispatch advised him the ceiling was "variable" and that he might break out on another pass. Adams decided to give it another try, but asked the dispatcher to check out weather conditions at every suitable alternate landing field within the aircraft's remaining range, "just in case."

The second attempted approach failed. Adams climbed to 3,000 feet, throttled back to conserve fuel, and once more called for advisories on available alternates. The company's station manager came on the line, and he had nothing but bad news. One of Flight Ten's original alternates, Camden, was now closed by the storm; the other, Albany, was likely to sock in before Adams could reach it. A quick check of every other airport within range, from Boston to Washington, revealed the same pattern. All stations were reporting weather barely at or below minimums. After more consultation with weathermen, the station manager reported that the squall hitting the airport at the moment was expected to raise before long. He advised Adams to hold over Newark.

After shuttling back and forth through the soup for what seemed an eternity, Adams concluded this was no squall, but rather the full brunt of the storm. Furthermore, he could see he had run out of options, having burned up more than an hour's worth of fuel in futile efforts to land at Newark. Now his fuel tanks were running low and his escape routes to the north, south, and west were

blocked. One way or another, Flight Ten would have to land in Newark.

Coolly and with utmost precision, Adams went through the identical maneuvers he had used in the preceding two passes. This time, however, he was prepared to fly the aircraft on instruments all the way to the ground, if necessary. From "low cone" on in, his eyes would be on his flight instruments only. Heming was to keep his eyes out of the cockpit and sing out when he had the runway in sight. Inbound from the Newark range, Adams watched the altimeter slowly unwind —300 feet, 200, 150. Meanwhile, Hemings, who had taken his instructions literally, was leaning out his side window, staring into the gloom. Suddenly he shouted, "There—dead ahead!" Instantly, Adams pushed the nose down, and as he did, he got his first glimpse of Newark's runway lights rushing up to meet him. At 50 feet the runway's cinder surface was clearly visible in the beam of the plane's landing lights, despite the whirl of snowflakes and blowing drifts. Adams retarded his throttles and without rotating the plane's nose above the horizontal, drove the ship onto the runway. As it cruised slowly to a stop, a gruff voice barked over the tower channel, *Take your time clearing the runway, Flight Ten. No one else will be using it this evening.*

"Without rotating the plane's nose above the horizontal, he drove the ship onto the runway."

Chief Pilot

In January 1937 Walt Braznell was appointed chief pilot for American Airline's Chicago-based pilot group. American was getting serious about beefing up its crew training and supervisory staff, and despite his relative youth—he had just turned twenty-nine—Braznell was an obvious candidate for one of four new regional chief pilot slots. In terms of service with AA, he was among the most senior pilots stationed in Chicago. His flying record was flawless. Just six months earlier he had been chosen to fly American's inaugural DC-3 flight from Chicago to Newark. And if he had fewer total flying hours than some of the veteran Chicago pilots, he was unquestionably among the most proficient in instrument flight and radio navigation, the pilot skills American's management considered to be most in need of attention. Nevertheless, Braznell always felt his move into management was largely a matter of fortune—the luck of the draw. And to the end of his career, he remained ambivalent about whether, in exchanging his line flying job for an administrative slot, he had drawn the right straw.

One winter afternoon in 1935, while I was flying the Condor run between Chicago and St. Louis, American's chief engineering pilot, Dan Beard, came aboard in St. Louis and asked whether he could ride in the cockpit as an observer on the return trip.[9] I knew Dan was on a special assignment from man-

agement, and assumed it had something to do with the new sleeper planes the company had recently ordered from Douglas. Certainly, he was welcome to ride up front.

After takeoff, I rigged up my homemade flying hood, removed my earphones, and, with my copilot flying lookout, proceeded to fly on instruments to Springfield, then Peoria, and finally Chicago, using dead reckoning to judge when to begin my letdown to each field. I'd been practicing this on and off for months, but it was a new experience to Dan. Apparently he liked what he saw, and made some favorable comments to my boss. I didn't hear about this until much later.

A few weeks after Dan's ride, our new operations manager, Hugh Smith, was my passenger on the same trip—my old air mail milk run. Even in the lumbering Condor, I was accustomed to flying the route in typical air mail style—that is, without wasted time or motion. We flew direct to Springfield, landed straight ahead, taxied up to the loading pad and chopped one engine while the ground crew off-loaded and on-loaded mail bags. My left prop was turning the moment the door slammed shut. After a quick mag check we started our takeoff from the loading pad, heading straight for Peoria. Same routine at Peoria Airport. Then we were off and running to Chicago. After we landed at Chicago Airport, "Mr. Hugh" asked me if I had any idea what our total ground time had been on the run from St. Louis. No, I hadn't thought about it. "One minute and forty seconds," he said. I wasn't sure whether to take this as a compliment. The pilots in Texas, where Mr. Hugh had last been stationed, were apparently accustomed to taking life at a more leisurely pace.

On a layover in Newark on New Year's Eve that year I had dinner with a friend from Colonial Airlines, Jim Townsend. Later we walked up to the Essex House where a bunch of other pilots were staying. We had a couple of drinks with them and returned to our hotel a little after midnight, none the worse for a little socializing. Both of us had early flights the following morning.

A few hours after I got home on New Year's Day, Hugh Smith called. He wanted to know if I

9. Dan Beard, along with his boss, Bill Littlewood, played a major role in the development of plans for the enlarged version of the DC-2 that ultimately became the DST/DC-3. Dan also served as company engineering rep, project manager, and test pilot during the months that the first DSTs were being built and flight-tested at the Douglas plant in Santa Monica. Over the next twenty-five years, this talented and extraordinarily dedicated pilot/engineer would act as midwife at the birth of every aircraft model American ordered, from the DC-4s to the Boeing 707.

had been at the Essex House "party" the night before. I said yes, and he brusquely ordered me to be in his office at 8 A.M. the following day. We had a rule against drinking the day before flying a trip. Violators of the rule were subject to dismissal. I lay awake most of the night thinking what a wretched way this was to end my flying career.

When I arrived at operations the next morning, a half dozen other pilots were waiting outside Smith's office. They told me the party had gotten pretty rough at the Essex after Jim and I left. Several hundred dollars worth of damage had been done to hotel property. One by one the other pilots filed silently into and out of the boss's office. When my turn came, I felt like I was walking the plank. Smith greeted me dourly and again asked if I'd been at the Essex House party. Yes. Then he asked the killer question: Had I been drinking? I said Yes. It was New Year's Eve. I had been with friends. I joined them in a few drinks, but left the party at a reasonable time and was fit for duty the following morning. I hadn't had any part in damaging hotel property.

Mr. Hugh waved me to the door and said I could expect to hear from him.

The next few days were pure hell. Not a word from the boss. Then, late one night, as I walked into Chicago operations after a trip from Newark, I saw Smith sitting in his half-darkened inner office. He beckoned to me, and I went in. The first thing he said to me was, "You know, Braznell, it's absolutely amazing. Of all the pilots at the Essex House New Year's Eve, you were apparently the only one who took a drink." Then he smiled one of his rare smiles and motioned for me to sit down.

I don't remember the rest of the conversation clearly. I know he asked if I would like to be the chief pilot for Chicago, and I said yes, if I could have the authority to make some changes. We talked about them, he nodded, and we shook hands.

It's funny how all this came about. I think it might have been the combination of Dan Beard's favorable comments, my first trip with our new operations officer, and the fact that I told him the truth about that night at the Essex that saved my job and headed my career in a new direction.

Before accepting the chief pilot's job, I had neglected to ask what it paid. When I cornered Mr. Hugh the next day, he mentioned a figure that was about ten percent less than I'd been earning as a line pilot, but he assured me the decrease would be "only temporary." I said I'd consider the pay loss a year's tuition in management. As it turned out, it was only the down-payment. Flying, to me, has always been a privilege—something I would gladly do for nothing if I had other means of supporting my family. Now I was about to learn what it was like to work for a living.

Standardization

Although he missed flying the line, Braznell would later remember his years as Chicago's chief pilot, January 1937 to June 1942, as the most fascinating and challenging in his career. As we've already noted, these prewar years were an important transition period for the airlines and for airline pilots. With the advent of passenger travel, a generation of aviation pioneers who had literally taught themselves how to fly, and had flown just about any way they chose, were expected to adapt to new standards—new uniform procedures designed to ensure a greater margin of safety than ever before. As a chief pilot, Braznell had a central role in developing the new procedures and teaching his pilots to use them.

As the primary link between management and line pilots, airline chief pilots of Braznell's generation had a foot in both camps. (The good ones, in his opinion, were "part manager and all pilot.") Typically, their duties included checking out new or newly assigned pilots and giving them their semi-annual proficiency checks, mediating disputes over route assignments and the like, and administering nearly all aspects of flight crew management—hiring, training, scheduling, disciplining, and termination.

For someone who so admired the rugged individualists and eccentrics of the open-cockpit era—someone who was himself as independent and opinionated as they come—it is ironic that Braznell would choose, or was chosen, to become an instrument of conformity. But in his time, standardization was anything but an arbitrary procedure. It evolved through a continuous process of experimentation and selection, with plenty of give and take among pilots and supervisors. One simply didn't dictate to pilots of Walt's generation. On the contrary, it was often necessary to *prove* that a new SOP (standard operating procedure) worked better than whatever they were accustomed to doing. A case in point:

The DC-2s and 3s were among the first widely used commercial aircraft with retractable flaps. Some of our older pilots would have nothing to do with the new gadgets. Others, like my old friend Duke Ledbetter, had some remarkable theories

Duke Ledbetter.

about how to use them. One day, just after I'd made chief pilot, C. R. Smith came aboard one of Duke's flights and decided to ride up front in the cockpit jump seat.

"How do you like the new DC-3s?" said C. R.

"Great," said Duke, ". . . now that I've learned to land the buggers." "Stay up front," he added, "and I'll show you how it's done."

Approaching Newark, Duke called for full flaps and made a normal approach and pre-landing rotation. Then, with the wheels still about ten feet off the ground—a slight miscalculation, as he later put it—Duke ordered the flaps retracted. The ship immediately fell out of the sky, hit the runway like a pile-driver, and bounced three or four times, before Duke finally got it under control. Duke had reasoned that the best way to keep a lightly loaded DC-3 on the ground after touch-down—to prevent it from skipping and ballooning—was to spill the added lift created by the flaps. It wasn't a bad idea; he just neglected to land the plane first.

Anyway, C. R. was not amused. That afternoon, I got a call from Mr. Hugh informing me that the boss wanted "someone to show Duke how to land a DC-3." Here I was, a brand-new chief pilot, and my first assignment was to teach one of our most senior pilots, and a good friend at that, how to fly.

Ledbetter wasn't the only one having trouble with the new DC-3. Even though it was considerably more forgiving than the stiff-shanked DC-2, it was still considered a tricky plane to land, especially in a crosswind. Like Duke, every American pilot had, by this time, developed his own preferred method for bringing it in—half flaps, full flaps, no flaps, two-point, three-point, you name it.

Fred Bailey and I went to work on the problem, experimenting with different techniques.[10] The procedure that consistently worked best for us was to make our approach with full flaps, taking maximum advantage of the added lift and lower landing speed they provided. Over the runway, we would make a gentle flare-out and basically fly the plane

10. Fred Bailey was Braznell's assistant chief pilot— later, and for many years, chief pilot–Chicago.

Two-Point vs. Three-Point Landings

In a three-point landing, the pilot flares or rotates his aircraft into a slightly nose-high attitude a few feet off the ground and gradually increases back pressure on the yoke until the plane loses air speed and mushes into the ground, landing on the front wheels and tail wheel simultaneously. Air mail pilots were all three-point landers, as were nearly all Navy- and Air Corps–trained pilots of the pre–tricycle landing gear era.

In a two-point landing, the plane's approach angle is slightly shallower and the landing rotation less severe. As Braznell explains, the aircraft is literally flown onto the runway, touching down on the two front wheels. The tail wheel is held off the ground with neutral or slight forward yoke pressure for a few seconds to ensure that the ship does not accidentally become airborne again.

onto the ground, touching down in a two-point, tail-high attitude. This attitude gave us better lateral and directional control through rotation, touch-down, and initial landing roll than was possible in a nose-high three-point landing attitude. Raising the flaps and slowly lowering the tail wheel after the aircraft was safely grounded helped overcome the DC-3's annoying tendency to keep on flying as long as it was in motion. The technique worked well, and we had no trouble getting the Chicago pilots to adopt it as standard procedure.

American's Fort Worth–based pilots were all three-point landers, and to hear them talk, only sissies needed flaps to land an airplane. So Fred and I challenged them to send their best three-pointers to Chicago for a little landing competition. The competition was to determine which technique, Texas- or Chicago-style, produced the shortest, smoothest, and most accurate (spot) landings.

The day chosen for the contest couldn't have been more ideal from our standpoint. Fine dry snow, whipped by a 25- to 30-mile-per-hour quartering wind, was swirling over the runway surface as Fred and I and the boys from Texas took our turns. The issue was decided almost immediately. In that gusting crosswind, the Texans' nose-high three-point landers could barely keep their planes under control, much less execute precision landings. We made several converts to the Chicago-style that day, and two-point, flaps-

down landings quickly became the standard, system-wide.

The landing seminar Fred and I conducted that winter of 1937 was the first of many experiences in attempting to rationalize what had always been a highly individualistic approach to flying the line. Most of the systems and procedures we introduced during those pre-war years would probably strike the young men and women graduating from our flight academies today as "no brainers." Yet to the pilots of that period they were revolutionary—in every sense of the word. Take flight plans, for example. When we started requiring Chicago pilots to file flight plans before every trip, some of our senior pilots threatened an open revolt. We were burying them in paperwork; abridging their author-ity. The exercise was demeaning, a waste of time: "Who needs a written plan? I've been flying this trip so long I could do it in my sleep," etc., etc. Well, of course they could. But we figured that the planning process would condition them to antici-pate all those variables that can sneak up and grab the overconfident pilot—wind, weather, time, fuel consumption, reserves. Anyway, the revolt didn't last very long or amount to much. Soon all Ameri-can stations were requiring flight plans, and within a year or two the civil aeronautics authorities had made them mandatory throughout the industry.

Before 1937 we had no published route maps or approach charts. The first I ever saw were those that Fred Bailey and I sketched out for the various

Aeronautical Charts

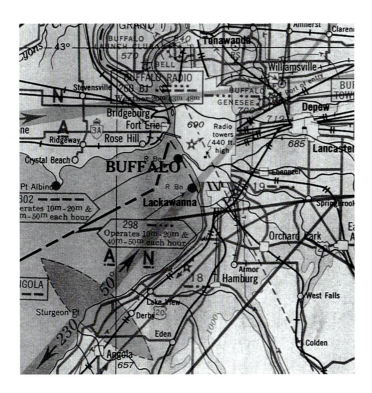

Sectional charts published by the Commerce Department's U.S. Coast and Geodetic Survey were ideal for pilotage (visual navigation) and low-frequency radio navigation in the 1930s and 1940s. Although the scale—1:500,000, or eight miles to the inch—makes them impractical for modern high-speed cross-country navigation, they are still standard equipment in the cockpits of thousands of light aircraft.

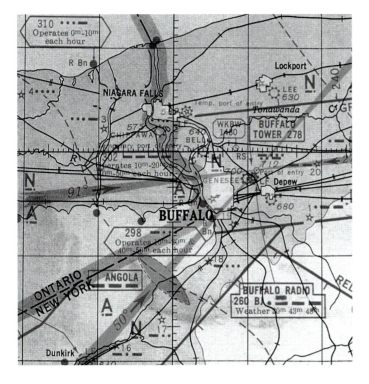

WAC charts scaled sixteen miles to an inch were developed for the Air Force during World War II and are still used in civil as well as military aviation. The "WA" stands for "World Aeronautical."

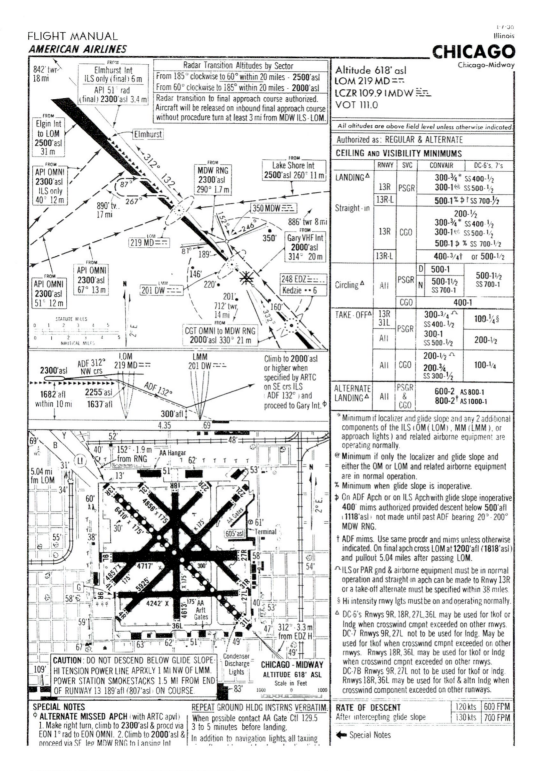

AMERICAN AIRLINES FLIGHT MANUAL: Route and destination approach charts developed by American Airlines and produced by its own cartography department were standard fixtures in AA flight kits of the 1940s and 1950s. The manual business was later sold to former United Airlines pilot Carl Jeppeson and merged into his own highly successful flight manual publishing enterprise.

runs our Chicago pilots flew. They were crude little pen and ink diagrams—not exactly models of the cartographer's art. But they covered the basics. We mimeographed and distributed them to our own pilots and anyone else who asked for a set. Other stations soon began issuing their own route and approach charts. Eventually management decided to centralize all this ad hoc chart making and hired a professional draftsman to do the work. This was the genesis of those thick, muscle-building route manuals American Airlines published and American pilots lugged around in their flight kits for many years.

Copilot School

Since the days of the trimotors, the first transport aircraft designed to be flown by two pilots, airline crew training had largely consisted of apprenticing new copilots to senior pilots and allowing them to marinate in the right seat of the cockpit for several years—observing, performing routine and often menial tasks, occasionally being permitted to make a takeoff or landing—until they were deemed sufficiently seasoned to command their own ships. It was a slow and dreadfully inefficient process, at best; one not at all suited to an airline facing an immediate need for large numbers of DC-3–qualified flight crews.

One of Braznell's first assignments when he took over as chief pilot of American's Chicago division was to set up an accelerated training program for the swarms of young pilots the company was in the midst of hiring. American's new centralized pilot school at Chicago Airport was not for beginners. Trainees were expected to have a minimum of a thousand hours flying time and possess a working knowledge of instrument flying and radio navigation techniques. From this raw material, instructors Bill Lester and Colin McIntosh produced airline pilots qualified not only to perform the routine tasks nor-

mally assigned to neophyte copilots, but more important, to assume the in-flight duties of their captains when necessary.

The Chicago school was Spartan in the extreme compared to modern-day airline flight academies. Its facilities consisted of a single classroom equipped with rows of one-armed desk-chairs, a blackboard, and a brace of clanky steam radiators; a single Link instrument trainer, looking for all the world like a carnival kiddy-ride; and a single-engine Stinson cabin plane with dual controls for in-flight instrument procedure training.

Lester, a former American pilot barely recovered from a near-fatal crash in a Stinson trimotor a few years earlier, ran his charges through an intensive six-week cram course in meteorology, instrument flight, radio navigation, aircraft systems (hydraulics, electrical systems, engine carburation and ignition systems, etc.), company procedures, routes, manuals, forms, flight planning, and civil aviation flight safety regulations.

McIntosh had the task of teaching them to master the Link trainer. One of his former students, the famous aviation writer and novelist Ernie Gann, vividly recalls the experience:[11]

To the uninitiated, this machine can rival the Chinese water torture. It is a box set on a pedestal and cleverly designed to resemble a real airplane. On the inside the deception is quite complete, even to the sound of slip stream and engines. All of the usual controls and instruments are duplicated within the cockpit, and once under way the sensation of actual flight becomes so genuine that it is often a surprise to open the top of the box and discover you are in the same locality.

11. Ernest K. Gann, *Fate is the Hunter.* Gann flew for American from 1939 to 1946, with time off for Air Transport Command service during World War II and an occasional peacetime leave of absence to finish a book or satisfy his wanderlust.

Lester's "School of Knowledge." *Photo courtesy of American Airlines*

The device is master-minded by an instructor who sits at a special control table. He can make the student's flight an ordeal. Godlike, he can create head winds, tail winds, cross winds, rough air, fire, and engine or radio failure. He can, if he is feeling sadistic, combine several of these curses at the same time. McIntosh, our usual instructor, is ever partial to such fiendish manipulations . . . Some of us soon learn to hate McIntosh.

Colin McIntosh and Walt Braznell went back a long way. They met in 1928 when Braznell was giving flying lessons at Robertson Aircraft's pilot school at Lambert Field, St. Louis. McIntosh, a re-cent graduate of Williams College, was one of his first students. McIntosh went on to Air Corps flight school at Brooks Field, Texas, washed out on medical grounds, and soon afterward ac-cepted a position on the faculty of a small mid-western college teaching, among other things, the theory and practice of celestial navigation. Through the intervening years the two men had remained in touch. When American's manage-ment dumped the Copilot School program in his lap, Braznell contacted McIntosh and invited him to come aboard as an instructor. Later, as head of American's Long Range Navigation School,

McIntosh would spend most of the war years teaching Air Transport Command flight crews how to keep their feet dry flying across the Atlantic, Pacific, and Indian Oceans—a contribution to the war effort for which many pilots, including Gann, would have cause to bless the dour Scot of Copilot School days.

Upon completing Lester's course and successfully passing the required written examination and instrument flight tests, the trainees, still on probationary status, would be turned over to Walt or Fred Bailey, or sent off to Newark, Memphis, Fort Worth, or Los Angeles, where they would be checked out in the DC-2s and DC-3s by one of the company's regional chief pilots. Up to this point, none of the neophytes had touched the controls of a real airliner. But before being assigned to a regular commercial run, they had to demonstrate they could find their way around their ship's cockpit blindfolded (literally) and land the brute without compacting its landing gear or frightening the instructor.

Of course, all this was just the beginning of their education as airline pilots. They would spend from eighteen months to several years studying and honing their art under a long succession of masters before being given command of their own ships. And for the rest of their flying careers they would endure an endless routine of semiannual, annual, and biannual company and civil aeronautics examinations—physicals, proficiency checks, route checks, aircraft ratings, federal certification exams, and so on.

In scarcely a decade, flying for the airlines had progressed from being a vocation for free-spirited adventurers like the young Slim Lindbergh to a profession demanding as much discipline and training as medicine or law. And rightly so. As a veteran Civil Aeronautics Administration inspector once remarked, "Even the most incompetent doctor or lawyer seldom kills more than one customer at a time. A single pilot error in an otherwise exemplary career can destroy millions of dollars worth of property and wipe out hundreds of lives."

"Watch Your Attitude"

American's new chief pilot–Chicago quickly discovered that his copilot trainees were not the only ones needing to brush up on their instrument technique. Although civil air regulations required scheduled airline pilots to pass periodic examinations demonstrating proficiency in all phases of instrument flying, and despite the efforts of the Bureau of Air Commerce's overworked flight examiners to enforce the rules, Braznell and Bailey witnessed some stunningly nonstandard procedures and techniques in their first round of check rides with the station's line pilots.

One pilot tried to convince me that the best way to make a blind approach to Chicago Airport was to spiral down the cone of silence directly over the radio range station until he broke out of the clouds, then head off in the general direction of the runway. He didn't convince me.

On a check ride with another pilot, we were inbound to the station from Lansing. At station passage, he turned west and started letting down. Around 1,000 feet, we're still descending, the pilot under the hood, and I'm looking at some very imposing smoke stacks a mile or two dead ahead of us. "What are you doing?" I asked politely. "Letting down," he replied. "I can see that," I said, "but you're flying in the wrong direction. Go back to the station and make your procedure turn and let down according to the book." "But I always let down like this," he said. "Not any more. On my word of honor, we will either follow the let-down procedure precisely as it's written, or you've flown your last flight with American." Harsh words for a brand-new chief pilot, I suppose. On the other hand, I wouldn't have been doing him or his widow a favor if I had treated the situation lightly.

The instrument skill levels we encountered on that first series of check rides ranged from silky to scary. The pilots who seemed to be having the most trouble were those who chased the highly sensitive rate of climb or vertical speed indicator. If the plane in level flight hit a down-draft and the indicator suddenly registered a 300 or 400 feet per minute rate of descent, the pilot would raise the nose of the aircraft. Immediately, the indicator needle would bounce up and show a 300 to 400 foot rate of climb. Down would go the nose. Push, pull—up, down. All this unnecessary motion was making me sick; I could imagine what it would do to a plane-load of first-time airline passengers.

The technique was not only ugly and uncomfortable; it was dangerous, as well. In a thunderstorm or clear air turbulence, where you might expect sudden up- and down-drafts to register changes of thousands of feet per minute on this delicate pressure gauge, a pilot who attempts to chase the vertical speed needle by making abrupt changes in attitude or power setting can cause severe structural damage to his aircraft.

One day, after taking this kind of punishment from a particularly dedicated needle-chaser for as long as I could stand it, I took a piece of cardboard and taped it over his vertical speed indicator. That meant he had to rely on his gyro-operated attitude indicator (artificial horizon) and much slower-moving altimeter to maintain level flight. Immediately, the ride became less bumpy. After a few minutes the pilot was able to execute steady, smooth 500-foot-per-minute climbs and descents at constant air speeds simply by making normal adjustments in power settings and raising or lowering the aircraft's nose a few degrees, relative to the artificial horizon.

I began working on this approach systematically, charting the exact power settings and attitude changes necessary to maintain level flight, or climb or descend at given rates of speed under any given aircraft configuration—wheels up, wheels down,

50 percent flaps, and so on. It was a simple formula: Configuration + Power + Attitude = Air Speed and/or Vertical Speed—and it worked.

When I wrote up my notes on "Attitude Instrument Flying" and circulated them among the Chicago pilots, they immediately bought the idea. Before long I was getting inquiries and requests for copies from pilots at other American Airlines stations, from chief pilots at other airlines, and even from the armed services. Eventually, all three services—the Army Air Corps, Navy, and Marine Corps—incorporated the concept of attitude instrument flying in their training manuals.

For years afterward, Fred Bailey and I used the technique in training Chicago pilots. During instrument check rides, we would routinely cover the pilots' vertical speed and air speed indicators and have them execute precision climb-outs and approaches with reference only to their directional gyro, artificial horizon, and memorized power settings. After the war, when we began flying pressurized aircraft at high altitudes, the training American Airlines pilots received in attitude instrument flying would prove to be a life-saver. But that's another story.

Home On The Range

As air travel gained momentum in the mid and late 1930s, a situation that had long been apparent to pilots, airline executives, and civil aviation authorities became increasingly obvious to the public as well: The nation's air mail–era airways navigation and control systems were dangerously obsolete. The agencies primarily responsible for promoting air safety were hamstrung by horse-and-buggy budgets and bureaucratic confusion. Radio technology had advanced considerably since the first low-frequency radio range stations were built in the mid-1920s, yet pilots were still risking their necks, and those of their passengers, making low passes at airport runways with nothing better to guide them than the wandering, static-filled signals from those antique LF radio stations. Better technologies existed, but the U.S. economy was still in recession, and Congress was not of a mind to allocate millions of dollars to tear out the old radio network and start all over again. Federal funding for civil aviation–related programs would remain tight throughout the Depression and would cease entirely once the United States entered World War II. The big-ticket items would just have to wait until the war was over.

Even so, pressure from all sides produced a few notable advances in aeronautics and air safety regulation during the latter half of the decade:

1. Unified Air Traffic Control. Before 1938, federal laws ceded control over air traffic in the immediate vicinity of civil airports to the individual municipalities. Cleveland's municipal airport was the first in the United States to establish a system for keeping track of in- and outbound flights via radio. This was in 1931, about the time airlines began equipping their fleets with functional two-way radios. Within a few years, dozens of other cities had established similar radio control facilities.

The airlines themselves were among the first to develop *regional* airway control and flight monitoring services. In 1934 American Airlines' Chicago dispatcher Glen Gilbert designed a system for tracking the position of company planes operating within one hundred miles of his station. Other commercial carriers operating in the Chicago area were invited to participate in this voluntary flight monitoring and control program, and before long American, operating under a temporary license from the Bureau of Air Commerce, was directing traffic, assigning takeoff and landing sequences, and radioing in-flight weather advisories to most of the carriers operating in the Chicago sector. The system was gradually ex-

panded to encompass the entire air corridor between Chicago, Cleveland, and Newark, with regional traffic control centers at each station. In July 1936 American agreed to turn its three air traffic control centers over to the Bureau of Air Commerce, which went on to establish additional centers in Detroit, Pittsburgh, Los Angeles, Oakland, and Washington by the end of 1937.

Before 1938 regulatory authority over the airline business was divided among the Interstate Commerce Commission, which regulated air mail rates and passenger tariffs; the Commerce Department's Bureau of Air Commerce, which controlled airways, licensed pilots, and certified aircraft; and the Post Office, which handled the bidding and awarding of air mail routes. Then Congress enacted the Civil Aeronautics Act of 1938, replacing the clumsy tripartite regulatory system with a single Civil Aeronautics Authority.[12] The new agency assumed jurisdiction over practically all aspects of civil aviation, including the regulation of airports, which had formerly been under the control of municipal and state authorities. This expanded authority provided the legal underpinning upon which our modern system of seamless, runway-to-runway air traffic controls was created. Among other things, the newly constituted CAA was authorized to establish minimum altitudes for instrument approaches, provide for vertical and horizontal separation of all flights operating under instrument flight rules, establish rules governing the filing of flight plans, and mandate flight clearance and in-flight reporting procedures for aircraft operating within air traffic control areas. Far from resisting this concentration and extension of regulatory authority, the airlines eagerly welcomed it: The 1938 act became their Magna Carta—a compact

12. Reorganized and renamed Civil Aeronautics Administration in 1940.

Why I Never Got Any Business from Eastern

Bill Lear, the irrepressible genius whose many contributions to the aviation industry included the development of one of the first automatic direction finding radios (ADF), tells a story that may explain some of the foot-dragging that preceded the broadscale acceptance of these handy devices.

I knew Eddie Rickenbacker real well. He sent me down to Miami to see Charlie Frantz, Eastern's operations manager. When I tried to sell Charlie on the idea (of the Lear ADF) he asked what it weighed. When I replied, "55 pounds," he balked saying, "That's 55 pounds of payload I could be carrying Miami to New York and New York to Miami." That, he indicated, he couldn't afford.

I countered with, "Wouldn't you like to have a backup in case one of your pilots gets confused on the radio ranges?" I guess it was the wrong thing to say. He immediately got his nose out of joint. "Are you inferring that an Eastern Airlines pilot would get lost?" he challenged. "You mean they don't get lost?" I said. "No, sir!" he bristled.

About two weeks later, an Eastern Air Lines plane got lost on a southbound flight. At that time the company frequency was 4,000 to 5,000 kilocycles—good for long distance communications. You could hear what was going on from Maine to Rio. Everyone was calling him, trying to help out. Plus, he was getting a lot of precipitation static. He was just about ready to run out of fuel after tooling about for four and a half hours when he called in saying he knew where he was and was landing at Charleston. When he landed he called saying he was just outside the Charleston administration building.

Now remember, everyone could hear this. The Charleston operator told him there was no one outside. "I'm right outside," he said, "I'll come right in and talk with you." Now everyone was hanging on their receivers, all over the East Coast, waiting for the next chapter in this mix-up. The pilot finally came back on the air. He had found he was at Tallahassee, not Charleston. The whole thing became a subject for the Congress and was written up in the Congressional Record to demonstrate the need for better navigation capabilities. I couldn't resist the urge to send Charlie Frantz a telegram. I said, "Dear Charlie, It was a good thing your pilot wasn't lost."

Of course, this was the reason I never got any business from Eastern.

(From *Stormy Genius: The Life of Aviation's Maverick, Bill Lear*)

between civil authorities and regulated air carriers to ensure the safety of the nation's airways.

2. Direction-Finding Radios. One of the few significant advances in aerial navigation in prewar years was a simple device called a *loop antenna*. The antenna, coiled inside a doughnut-shaped aluminum shield, provided virtually static-free reception of low-frequency range signals, even in severe snow or rain. More important, the antenna could be rotated from within the cockpit to pinpoint the direction to or from any low-frequency "homing" station within range of its radio receiver. The range station had to be equipped with a homing transmitter, but by 1938 most stations were so equipped. Loop/direction finders also worked on standard broadcast channels.

To get a bearing on a station, a pilot had to crank the antenna turning mechanism until signal volume peaked, indicating the loop was facing directly toward its target. (In later models, this search function was performed automatically, from the instant the radio was tuned to the desired station frequency.) The position of the loop was represented by an indicator needle mounted on a compass card. To home in on the station, the pilot simply turned his aircraft in whichever direction the needle pointed, made a few adjustments for windage, and maintained course until a swing of the needle indicated station passage.[13] The pilot could also pinpoint his plane's exact location by taking simultaneous bearings on two stations and triangulating them on his route chart.

Direction-finding radios, originally developed for ship-to-shore marine navigation, were first adapted for aerial navigation around 1932. But the airline industry of the Depression era was slow to adopt the technology. While a few carriers such as American Airlines began installing them in their planes as early as 1935, others held off until 1938, when the CAA began requiring loop antennas and DF receivers on all scheduled airliners. Amazingly, even after DFs became standard equipment, many veteran pilots refused to use them, preferring to navigate exclusively by means of low-frequency aural signals.

Ultimately, direction-finding radios proved their worth. DF homing devices of one sort or another were used extensively by the Allied air forces during World War II. For many years following the war, automatic direction finders (ADFs) were considered indispensable adjuncts to radio range navigation and instrument approaches. Long after very high frequency omnidirectional range systems (VOR) supplanted the old low-frequency airways, ADFs remained the

principle backup navigation equipment on most commercial and military aircraft.

3. Instrument Approach and Landing Systems. If the United States failed to produce an instrument landing system superior to the old LF radio beam approach before the war, it was not for lack of trying. In a special report on the status of airline safety, the June 1938 issue of *Fortune* wryly observed that, in aviation circles, "You can't throw away an empty whiskey bottle without hitting somebody who has just invented a blind landing system." At the time, at least ten operable systems existed, of which six had been flight-tested in the United States.

U.S. National Bureau of Standards physicists Harry Diamond and F. W. Dunmore are credited with having developed the first "blind" landing technology to incorporate the three essential elements of a modern instrument landing system (ILS): a *glide path* transmitter for vertical guidance; a *localizer* beam for directional guidance, and two *marker beacons,* poetically described as "curtains of radio energy running athwart the landing path,"[14] to signal the aircraft's distance from the runway. On September 5, 1931, at College Park, Maryland, Bureau of Standards pilot M. S. Boggs had the honor of making the first landing using the new approach system.

The following year the Diamond/Dunmore project was transferred to the Bureau of Air Commerce, which soon afterward shelved it in favor of a cheaper and far less sophisticated system developed under Air Corps sponsorship. The Air Corps project proved to be a deadend,

13. It wasn't quite that easy: First the pilot had to figure out whether the loop was pointed directly at the station or directly away from it. Both positions produced exactly the same peak signal.
14. From Samuel B. Fishbein, *Flight Management Systems.*

but not so the original Bureau of Standards model. Several commercial versions of the bureau's experimental ILS were built and tested over the next ten years by private-sector research groups. By 1938 an adaptation developed by the Washington Institute of Technology was reported to be "to a point of immediate commercial importance."[15]

Another offshoot of the old Bureau of Standard system, this one developed by Lorenz-AG of Berlin, a subsidiary of International Telephone and Telegraph, had, by this time, been in widespread operation in Europe for several years. The Lorenz Low Approach system employed ultrahigh-frequency (UHF) radio beams for localizer and glide slope instead of the VHF frequencies used in the original Bureau of Standards model. One advantage of the Lorenz system was that it eliminated the distinct upward curvature in the ILS's glide slope beam that had been driving American engineers and test pilots nuts.

In May 1937 the Bureau of Air Commerce and ITT set up a test facility at Indianapolis Municipal Airport and arranged to demonstrate the Lorenz system to a delegation of congressmen, "high officials of federal and commercial aviation,"[16] and newspaper reporters. American Airlines agreed to provide a flight crew and a Lorenz-equipped DC-2 to perform the demonstration landings. Chicago Chief Pilot Walt Braznell and Chief Engineering Pilot Dan Beard were assigned to fly the mission. Braznell continues:

> Dan and I had a few days to familiarize ourselves with the Lorenz systems and equipment. The demonstration itself proved to be much more

realistic than we had anticipated. During the morning, a weather front moved into the area, and the ceiling and visibility at Indianapolis Airport dropped below our published low-frequency approach minimums soon after takeoff. From that point on, neither we nor our distinguished guests saw the ground until we were a few hundred feet off the approach end of the runway. We made three takeoffs and landings under these conditions without the slightest problem.

The demonstration was a success in all but one respect: Nothing happened. Congress failed to appropriate the $9 million in funds Bureau of Air Commerce officials had hoped to obtain for additional Lorenz system installations. The Indianapolis installation was dismantled, crated, and put in storage. American Airlines eventually bought it and shipped it to Fort Worth, where it was used for pilot training.

When the Bureau of Air Commerce discontinued work on the Diamond/Dunsmore ILS in 1934, its Newark installation was appropriated and carted off to Oakland, California, by United Airlines' H. M. Hucke. Hucke, who had been party to the Bureau of Standards' earlier experiments, continued working on the system with the aid of his radio staff, researchers from Bendix Aviation, and other interested groups. By 1938 the United team had developed an exciting new wrinkle of its own. It was a device that linked shipboard ILS localizer and glidepath receivers directly to the aircraft's autopilot—in short, an *automatic* instrument landing system. Braznell's old friend Benny Howard, now a United Airlines test pilot, was in charge of the flight-test phase of the R&D program. When Howard heard of Braznell's participation in the Lorenz demonstrations, he called him and extended an invitation to check out United's new system.

15. *Fortune,* June 1938.
16. Newspaper article datelined Indianapolis, May 14, 1937.

After Indianapolis I was hooked on the subject of instrument landings. So, when Benny and his associate R. T. Freng invited me to come to Oakland and participate in their test program, I jumped at the opportunity.

I flew with Benny for a week. It was a great experience and one that left a lasting impression on me. I was flying a strange airplane, a Boeing 247, and my head was under the hood continually, including takeoffs and landings. On my last day, Benny took down the hood and said, "For six days you've been flying on autopilot and landing blind within fifty feet of that smoke pot. Now let's see you do it all by yourself." For the next half hour I had my hands full, trying to land a strange airplane with any degree of professional polish. My landings were a good deal rougher than they had been under the hood, and I never came close to the touchdown spot I'd been nailing all week. From that day forward I became a staunch advocate of autopilot-coupled approaches and landings, and the longer I remained in management, the more outspoken I became.

A Matter of Degrees

Since man first took to the sky, the vast ocean of air and water vapor enveloping the earth has only slowly and begrudgingly yielded the secrets of its moods and movement, its complex geography and dynamics. In the mid-1930s, the science of meteorology was still in its infancy. Weathermen were only beginning to learn about air masses and cyclones and the forces that cause them to swirl about the globe. Jet streams were unknown, and stories told by high-flying airmen of 100-miles-per-hour winds and clear air turbulence strong enough to flip a twelve-ton aircraft onto its back were deeply discounted. Most people, aviators included, were as ignorant of aerodynamics and the physics of propulsion as

the birds and bees. High school textbooks explained that aircraft propellers "screw" or "paddle" their way through the air.[17] Distinguished scientists theorized that manned aircraft would never fly beyond the speed of sound. And while experienced airmen knew that planes tended to behave a bit livelier in cold air than in warm, few ventured to ask why. Certainly, no one had ever attempted to measure the effects of temperature, altitude, and other atmospheric variables on aircraft and engine performance.

This business of atmospheric variables was, or should have been, of more than academic interest. Pilots and passengers were getting killed on hot summer afternoons because aircraft that should have cleared a gas tank or power line on takeoff didn't. Walt Braznell remembers an early attempt to unravel the mystery of atmospheric variables:

In the spring of 1937, about a year after American started flying the DC-3s, our Chicago maintenance crews found themselves swamped with complaints from pilots that their ships were losing power—barely staggering off the ground with payloads the same aircraft carried with ease during the winter.

I can't explain why it took so long to identify the cause of the problem. After all, internal combustion engines are basically air pumps, and variations in air density due to thermal expansion had to effect their performance, as well as the efficiency of propellers and wing surfaces. But air

17. Propellers, like wings and sails, are airfoils. As air flows over the curved upper surface of a spinning propeller blade the air stream forms a partial vacuum that literally sucks the propeller forward—that is, forward relative to the aircraft's direction. The combination of the partial vacuum on one side and the pressure of the air stream pushing on the opposing side of the rotating airfoil gives the prop its thrust.

density hadn't been a problem up to then. Before the DC-3, most commercial planes carried such a light load, relative to the area of their wing surfaces, that losses in engine efficiency or lift caused by changes in altitude or air temperature went unnoticed. The DC-3s, however, were comparatively heavy planes. Their wings were designed to carry nearly twice the load—24 pounds per square foot—supported by their predecessors. When the weather got hot, the change in their takeoff and climb performance could be dramatic.

After a while, Fred Bailey and I grew tired of hearing complaints about engine problems. We were sure air temperature was a factor, but how much of a factor? We decided to find out. Through the summer, fall, and following winter, whenever we flew a check ride, we carefully noted the air temperature, wind speed, approximate gross weight, and runway lift-off point on every takeoff. By the following spring we had compiled and charted data on scores of takeoffs under all sorts of weather conditions. As crude and incomplete as it was, the evidence left no doubt in our minds that air temperature had a measurable effect on takeoff performance. With additional data based on takeoffs performed under more controlled conditions, we knew it would be possible to precompute the takeoff roll for any given type of aircraft under any combination of gross weight, temperature, altitude, and effective wind velocity.

In 1939, soon after American moved its headquarters to La Guardia, Fred and I took our findings to New York and presented them to the company's senior operations people. We told them our maintenance crews were chasing a will o' the wisp, running down pilot complaints of low power on hot-weather takeoffs. We showed them our charts correlating temperatures and takeoff rolls under various wind and load conditions. To compensate for changes in these critical variables, we recommended replacing the existing 24,000-pound gross weight limit with a sliding scale based on our proposed density/wind speed/lift-off formula. To make this proposal work, we added, pilots would have to compute their takeoff roll and adjusted maximum gross weight before every flight. And

they would have to be given the authority to off-load fuel or payload, if necessary, to stay within their weight limitations. We concluded with the prediction that it would be just a matter of time before the CAA required these safety measures.

Our proposal did not go over well, to put it mildly. American's new senior operations officer,[18] a former politician whose previous airline experience consisted of a brief career as chief pilot of an air taxi service back in the 1920s, said the whole idea was crazy—"a bunch of horse feathers," or words to that effect. He suggested I get back to my pilot training duties and let New York worry about the airline's payloads.

I was right about it being "just a matter of time" before the authorities took action—a long time, unfortunately. The first civil air safety regs requiring the sort of preflight calculations Fred and I outlined to American's management in 1939 were adopted by the CAA around 1949, as I recall. Anyway, our experiments put an end to pilot complaints about sluggish engine performance.

Disaster

If the aerial disasters of 1936 and 1937 came close to destroying the public's tenuous faith in the future of air travel, another terrible calamity in the autumn of 1938 did more to restore that faith than any amount of airline advertising and self-promotion could have achieved.

In late September 1938 a savage hurricane swept out of the Caribbean and crashed into New England with tides and tempests driven by winds of up to 100 miles per hour. The storm blacked out cities, washed out roads and rail lines, ripped

---

18. Although he did not mention him by name, Braznell was obviously referring to Oral M. "Red" Mosier, who joined American as vice president of operations in 1938. Walt never got along with Mosier, but then, few people did. By all accounts the fiery-tempered Mr. Mosier reserved his considerable charm for special occasions.

down telephone lines, and inundated harbors and inland ports in masses of seaborne wreckage. Hundreds of New Englanders were killed or seriously injured; thousands were left homeless. With all forms of surface transportation at a standstill, and a stranded population already badly in need of fresh food and medical supplies, the airlines were pressed into service.

American Airlines, the only major carrier operating between New York and Boston at the time, was the first to respond. On the day following the hurricane, it put all available East Coast–based aircraft and crews to work airlifting medical supplies and personnel into the stricken area. The next day, additional ships and pilots were rushed in from other parts of the system to assist in the relief effort. United, TWA, and Eastern joined in almost immediately, operating dozens of flights on American's routes under emergency government authority.

In a week's time this airline task force flew more than a hundred round-trips, airlifted an estimated sixty tons of supplies, and shuttled thousands of rescue workers, doctors, nurses, and medical evacuees into and out of Boston Airport. For seven days, until normal surface transportation was restored, New England's aerial lifeline held.

The import of this first major airlift in aviation history—a spontaneous affair at that—was not lost on the American public. The airlines earned a nation's gratitude for the way they responded to the crisis. And the almost effortless efficiency with which they conducted the relief mission surely raised a few eyebrows in government and military circles. Without really trying to prove anything, the commercial air carriers jointly demonstrated their ability to mobilize very large, very complex aerial resupply missions in times of national emergency, and to do it without a hitch. In less than three years the United States

would be at war, and the lessons of the New England airlift would be applied on a vastly larger scale by the combined airline and military contingents of the Air Transport Command.

Pretenders and Successors

American Airlines had scarcely had time to launch its new Flagship Fleet before its archrivals United and TWA separately began laying plans for a new generation of super transports that they hoped would leave American and its vaunted DC-3s in the dust. This time United cut its familial ties with Boeing and, instead, began negotiating with Douglas for the development of a long-range, four-engine craft to be known as the DC-4. But even though United agreed to underwrite half of the research and development costs, Douglas insisted it could not afford to take on the project without orders for more planes than United could commit to buying. Reluctantly, United turned to the other leading U.S. lines—American, TWA, Eastern, and Pan American—each of which agreed to co-sponsor the DC-4.

The DC-4E (E for "experimental") was doomed from the start. Even the concept was uninspired. Although the original specifications called for a ship that could haul more than twice as many passengers as the DC-3s, the added cost of operating and maintaining those two extra engines largely offset the increase in payload. In other critical areas—cruise speed, range, and ceiling—the newer, vastly more expensive aircraft would offer little advantage, if any, over the DC-3s. On top of that, the engineering departments of the five co-sponsors were running amok with demands for design changes and systems modifications.

The "E" proved to be an even worse disaster than the project's early critics had expected. By

Douglas DC-4E and DC-4 (C-54)

Although the original triple-tail proto-type of the DC-4 (DC-4E) was a flying fiasco, it incorporated advanced features such as tricycle gear, flush riveting, power-boosted controls, an AC electric system, and an auxiliary electric power unit (APU).

The later version of the DC-4, first flown in February 1942, was considerably smaller than DC-4E. It carried forty-two passengers, weighed 37,250 pounds empty, and was designed to carry a payload of up to 28,000 pounds—though during the war and, notably, the postwar Berlin Airlift, the

military version (C-54) often carried far greater loads. Its twin Pratt & Whitney R-2000 radial engines, rated at 1,350 horsepower, gave the DC-4 a cruising speed of 190 to 200 miles per hour, depending on the load. Like its noble ancestor, the DC-3, it was sturdy, dependable, and clean-lined—a pleasure to fly. Its major drawback was the lack of cabin pressurization, which limited its operating ceiling to the same bumpy, crud-filled altitudes cohabited by most prewar aircraft. After the war, when stratospheric cruising levels became the norm for passenger airliners, the DC-4's scheduled airline duties were largely confined to cargo hauling, a job at which the aircraft excelled. *Photos courtesy of National Archives*

the time it was officially unveiled in 1938, TWA and Pan Am had already pulled out of the consortium. United, American, and Eastern took a good look at the triple-tailed turkey and called it quits. Douglas's engineers retreated to their drawing boards and eventually produced an altogether different and superior aircraft. Douglas recouped its development costs, if not its face, by selling its original and only "E" model to the Japanese government.[19]

By mid-1942, when the first production models of the new DC-4 were ready for service, the United States was at war, and the airlines were no longer in the market for aircraft. The Army Air Corps and Air Transport Command put them to good use, however. More than eleven hundred C-54s, as the military version was called, saw duty as long-haul cargo, personnel, and air-evac transports during the war. Another seventy-nine DC-4s were produced for the airlines after the war.

While American, Eastern, and United stuck with their bets on the eventual success of the DC-4 program, TWA had begun spreading its money around the table early in the game. Even before it agreed to participate in the ill-fated E-model consortium, TWA had signed a contract with Boeing for the construction of a new pressurized, long-range airplane called the *Stratoliner*—so named because it would be the first commercial transport designed to operate in the upper altitudes or stratosphere. When TWA's board balked at putting up $2 million for the six Stratoliners he had ordered, Jack Frye turned to his old flying buddy Howard Hughes for help. Hughes agreed to bankroll the pur-

chase. Then, on second thought, he decided to buy the airline as well.

The first production models of the Boeing 307 Stratoliner were delivered and placed in service in 1940, two years after Hughes gained control of TWA. Thus, Boeing and TWA shared the honor of introducing the first and only four-engine, land-based airliner to see service in the United States before the war. As far as honors go, that was about it, however. In 1941 Boeing halted production of the 307 to concentrate on building B-17 Flying Fortress bombers. The handful of Stratoliners built for TWA and Pan Am before the war were conscripted into the service, where, as C-75s, they compiled an outstanding safety record flying Army brass back and forth across the Atlantic—20 million passenger miles without a crash or splash.

Howard's Little Secret

Hughes used the ballyhoo associated with the Stratoliner's development as a smoke screen to conceal his real intentions. Almost from the moment he took command of TWA, he and Frye began secretly drawing up plans for an aircraft so advanced relative to the 307 and DC-4 that it would blow the competition away. A few months later Hughes took his rough designs to Kelly Johnson of Lockheed, and swearing Johnson to secrecy, set Lockheed to work on Project Constellation, the name he had selected for his new super airliner. Hughes wanted exclusive rights to the aircraft and was prepared to write a check for $18 million—an unheard of figure in the airline industry—for the first forty Constellations Lockheed produced.

The aircraft that took shape over the next three years bore the mark of Hughes's eccentric genius. Like the prototype DC-4E it had a triple

19. During a test flight shortly after the sale was complete, it crashed into Tokyo Bay. All aboard were killed. The reasons for the crash remain a mystery.

tail and tricycle gear. Unlike the production model of the DC-4, its cabin was fully pressurized for high-altitude flight, and in contrast to the DC-4's utilitarian, tube-shaped fuselage, the Constellation sported the gracefully swooping, slightly humpbacked line of a breaching porpoise. Even at rest it looked like it was flying.

The Constellation development project was nearing completion in the fall of 1941 before anyone in the industry besides TWA and Lockheed knew of the plane's existence. Then came the war, and the Air Corps decided to give priority to the production of Douglas transports—twin-engine C-47s (alias DC-3s) and four-engine C-54s (DC-4s). For the next few years, Lockheed's plant in Burbank, California, was occupied with orders for its P-38 fighters. When at last the Air Corps authorized the production of a few C-69s, the military version of the Constellation, the war was more than half over. Hughes himself delivered the first C-69 to the Army in April 1944, flying the plane nonstop from Burbank to Washington, D.C., in under seven hours. The aircraft probably needed an engine change after Hughes's record flight, but the performance, 360 miles an hour, coast to coast, put American and United on notice that they would have their work cut out for them when the war ended—as indeed they did.

Long Live the Queen

So, while her successors waited in the wings and the few pretenders to her crown fell by the wayside, that dauntless old dame, the DC-3, remained mistress of the domestic skyways until well into the 1940s.

By the beginning of World War II, Douglas had produced 579 DC-3s and DSTs. But that was just the beginning. Some ten thousand military versions of the DC-3—Air Corps C-47s, Navy R4Ds, and RCAF and RAF Dakotas—were built by Douglas during the war. In addition, the Russians built several thousand DC-3 clones, the Russian Lisunov Li-2, under a wartime licensing agreement. Even Japan had its own pirated version of the DC-3, the L2D "Tabby," of which more than four hundred copies were built.[20]

The last of American Airlines' DC-3s was retired in 1949, thirteen years after the first Flagship entered service. Thirteen years is not a particularly long service life by today's standards; a large percentage of commercial jet aircraft in operation today are more than twice as old. But in the 1930s and 1940s, it was a remarkable achievement. Moreover, hundreds of the old birds went on to long and productive second careers as commercial transports, private executive aircraft, fire fighters, and the like after being retired by the airlines. It is estimated that nearly two thousand DC-3s, DSTs, and C-47 Gooney Birds are still in flying condition, if not in active service, throughout the world.[21]

In sheer numbers of aircraft produced for the commercial market, the DC-3 ranks far behind those Jet Age classics, the Boeing 727, 737, and 747. But neither the Boeing ships' commercial success nor their extraordinary longevity diminish the DC-3 legend. Airlines these days fly dozens of makes and models of jet aircraft, most of them indistinguishable to all but the most sophisticated air traveler. No passenger ever mistook a DC-3 for any other plane. In its prewar heyday it stood alone, dominating the airways in a way that seems almost inconceiv-

20. Aviation historian Ed Davies.
21. McDonnell Douglas Corporation, via Laurence Zuckerman, *New York Times*, March 22, 1999.

able today. A single figure serves to illustrate the point: During the three-year period from 1939 to 1941, DC-3s accounted for well over 90 percent of the commercial passenger miles flown in the United States.

Pathfinders and Pioneers

Those young American Airlines acolytes who earned their airline pilot's wings at Bill Lester's School of Knowledge are long since retired. A few old-timers who flew "The Threes" are still around, and when they make an appearance at a gathering of American's Grey Eagles, younger retirees attend them with the same reverence and listen to their hoary stories with the same rapt attention that pilots of their generation once bestowed on the grizzled air mail veterans of the 1920s.

And deservedly so. The veterans of the 1920s were the airline industry's pathfinders, blazing trails through a vaulted wilderness. The young men who came up through the copilot ranks in the late 1930s era were its colonizers—its yeoman pioneers. With their sturdy workhorses, the DC-3s, they tamed the wilderness and made it bloom.

The New Breed

A recent graduate of American's copilot school, Class of '39, First Officer William "Kelly" Owen proudly displays his new AA wings, and his new home office, AA Flagship Pennsylvania. In his first few months on the line, Copilot Owen's chief duty will be to lower the AA pennant (barely visible on the right side of the DC-3's cockpit) just before takeoff and hoist it again after landing.

Owen joined American Airlines in 1939 with seven years as a licensed pilot and just under a thousand hours of flying time. During his thirty-seven-year career with the company (with credit for

three years of active duty in the Air Force during World War II), he served as an engineering test pilot, line captain, and assistant chief pilot, and participated in both the Korean and Vietnam airlifts. Captain Owen retired in 1975 with more than 30,000 military and civilian hours on his log book, a pristine flight safety record, and a reputation as a walking encyclopedia of aircraft and aviation lore. *Photo courtesy of W. K. Owen*

We Call Them Captains Now

A gallery of pilot—forgive us, "captain"—photos from American Airlines' *Horizons* magazine, January 1938. This was the first public recognition of the field promotions of the company's flight officers, from "pilot" and "copilot" to "captain" and "first officer." The practice was introduced by Pan American Airways some years earlier. The *Horizons* editor committed two grievous errors here: one, the curious omission of several of the company's most senior pilots—Doc Ator, Ray Fortner, E. L. Sloniger, and others; and, two, ranking the captains according to total flying hours, rather than their company *seniority*. In a pilot heirarchy where seniority is rank (and don't you forget it!) this was an unforgivable gaffe.

HORIZONS   JANUARY   1938

WE CALL THEM

☆

1. C. F. Pedley—12,764:41 hours—AM 4 *Base: Dallas*
2. R. L. Mitchell—12,417:04 hours—*Assistant to the Operation Manager: Ft. Worth*
3. J. H. Burns—9,611:04 hours—AM 22 *Base: Cleveland*
4. U. E. Rousch—9,604:47 hours—AM 7 *Base: Chicago*
5. C. L. Goldtrap—9,580:15 hours—AM 4 *Base: Dallas*
6. O. J. O'Connor—9,527:48 hours—AM 18 *Base: Boston*
7. A. H. DeWitt—9,526:04 hours—AM 7 *Base: Chicago*
8. C. W. Maris—9,440:51 hours—AM 4 *Base: Glendale*
9. T. O. Hardin—9,294:07 hours—AM 23 *Base: Dallas*
10. S. P. Bittner—9,116:40 hours—AM 22 *Base: Cleveland*
11. B. C. Moore—8,983:37 hours—AM 7 *Base: Chicago*
12. J. G. Ingram—8,961:12 hours—AM 4 *Base: Glendale*
13. T. J. Haire—8,945:29 hours—AM 30 *Base: Ft. Worth*
14. J. H. Walker—8,800:10 hours—AM 30 *Base: Ft. Worth*
15. T. R. Howe—8,874:52 hours—AM 7 *Base: Chicago*

PTAINS NOW

16. T. J. Hill—8,866:21 hours—AM 7 *Base: Chicago*
17. W. S. Shannon—8,760:01 hours—AM 18 *Base: Newark*
18. W. A. Brooke—8,749:37 hours—AM 21-23 *Base: Newark*
19. W. W. Braznell—8,644:28 hours—*Chief Pilot: Chicago*
20. R. J. Rentz—8,579:40 hours—AM 30 *Base: Ft. Worth*
21. W. H. Moore—8,525:15 hours—AM 23 *Base: Nashville*
22. L. Claude—8,482:33 hours—AM 7 *Base: Chicago*
23. L. W. Bryant—8,420:10 hours—AM 25 *Base: Chicago*
24. R. C. Maguire—8,400:50 hours—AM 7 *Base: Newark*
25. W. B. McFail—8,360:00 hours—AM 23 *Base: Memphis*
26. T. J. Lee—8,349:15 hours—AM 23 *Base: Nashville*
27. B. W. Robinson—8,311:13 hours—AM 22 *Base: Cleveland*
28. E. S. Swanson—8,219:34 hours—AM 7 *Base: Chicago*
29. E. Petteway—8,193:51 hours—AM 30 *Base: Ft. Worth*
30. M. M. Kay—8,186:32 hours—AM 23 *Base: Memphis*
31. S. D. Page—8,026:59 hours—AM 30 *Base: Ft. Worth*

War Years

AIR RAID, PEARL HARBOR—THIS IS NO DRILL

—Rear Admiral Bellinger, USN, 7:58 A.M., December 7, 1941

Yesterday, December 7, 1941—a date which will live in infamy—
the United States of America was suddenly and deliberately attacked
by naval and air forces of the Empire of Japan . . .

—President Franklin D. Roosevelt

On December 8, 1941, Congress declared war on Japan—Japan not having bothered with such formalities before launching its strike on Pearl Harbor. Three days later, Germany and Italy, honoring a fourteen-month-old Tripartite Pact with Japan, declared war on the United States, thus bringing to its inevitable conclusion the long, slow drift from strict neutrality, to non-belligerent status, to open hostilities between the United States and the Axis powers. We were now committed to a two-ocean, three-continent war against the superpowers of Europe and the Far East—a conflict that would clearly call for the rapid deployment of troops and war materiel by sea and air, far beyond our borders. Our State, Navy, and War Departments had not months, but years to anticipate and prepare for such a war. But when at last the balloon went up, where were the air resources—the planes; the flight crews, engineers, and mechanics; the administrators and staff personnel; the training schools and maintenance centers—needed to build and sustain a global air transport system?

At the time the United States entered World War II, the U.S. Navy and Marine Corps had no long-range air transport or air evacuation capability whatever. The Army Air Force (AAF) operated fewer than 250 transport aircraft,[1] mostly short-range passenger carriers. Its transport arm, the Air Service Command, was essentially a non-scheduled military airline set up to fly Army brass and priority cargo from one stateside air base to another. Another service, the Ferrying Command, was established in June 1941, when

1. "Driven by an urgent need for fighters and bombers, and influenced by a belief that transports could always be bought 'off the shelf,' the Air Corps placed almost no new orders for such craft in 1939 or in the first half of 1940. In June 1940, this policy was abruptly changed, and by the middle of 1942, no less than 11,802 medium transports were on order. However, it had not been possible to buy thousands of ready-made transport planes; exactly five were delivered in the last half of 1940. By the end of the year the Air Corps had a total of 122 transports, and most of those were obsolete. Only 133 more were delivered in 1941." Colonel Charles H. Young, *Into the Valley: The Untold Story of USAAF Troop Carrier in World War II*, 3.

the United States was still a nonbelligerent, to ferry Lend-Lease aircraft to Canada for trans-shipment to Great Britain. It had few if any aircraft of its own, and thus was not a factor in the Army's logistical planning until mid-1942, when it acquired a new commander, General Harold George; a new name, Air Transport Command; and a new mission—to airlift military cargo and personnel wherever needed, anywhere in the world. All the ATC lacked at that point was the men, planes, and know-how to accomplish its mission.

Which brings us back to our original question: *Where were the resources?*

Command Performance

The nation was still reeling from the most stunning military disaster in its history when, on December 12, 1941, the Washington office of the Air Transport Association received a call from the White House summoning its president, Edgar Gorrell, to a conference the following morning with President Roosevelt and the commanding general of the U.S. Army Air Force,[2] H. H. "Hap" Arnold. The purpose of the conference was to establish the role of the domestic airlines in "supporting the national war effort."

Despite the short notice, Gorrell was perfectly prepared. As he waited outside the Oval Office, he carried in his briefcase three inch-thick copies of an airline industry emergency mobilization plan that his staff, together with operations experts from various member carriers, had been fine-tuning for months. The basic plan, calling for a massive conversion of airline equipment and personnel to military air carrier operations in the event of a national emergency, had been ratified by the ATA's executive committee several weeks earlier and was already working its way

through the War Department chain of command. All that was needed to put it into effect was President Roosevelt's stamp of approval.

As aviation historian Robert Serling describes it,[3] Roosevelt began the conference by announcing he had just signed an executive order authorizing the War Department to "take possession of, or assume control" of the airlines for the duration of the national emergency. Roosevelt then pushed a copy of the order across his desk for Gorrell and Arnold to read. In Serling's words:

> The stunned Gorrell protested. The War Department was already putting ATA's plan into effect. Airline planes and their crews at that very moment were being diverted to emergency military missions. What purpose would it serve to nationalize an industry fully prepared to go all-out in the war effort?

Arnold, who apparently had not seen or heard of the executive order until that moment, immediately took Gorrell's side.

> Only the airlines, Arnold pointed out, had the equipment and skilled manpower to run a global air transportation system as a civil adjunct to the military, but under military orders. He had studied the ATA plan, he added, and noted that it included immediate requisitioning of a sizable proportion of airline flight equipment by the military, to be flown by civilian crews as military aircraft until the Air Corps got more of its own transports. The whole . . . plan, Arnold emphasized, offered solid proof of the industry's good faith and capability. [Roosevelt listened, smiled, then] picked up the executive order and tore it up.

2. The name was changed from Army Air Corps to Army Air Force in June 1941.

3. Robert J. Serling, *When the Airlines Went to War*, 19–20. See also Serling's *Eagle: The Story of American Airlines*, 161.

Thus, Serling concludes, the airlines were "saved from total seizure by Gorrell's impassioned plea and Arnold's stalwart support."

Well, maybe so. But, with due respect, the scene Serling describes sounds suspiciously like a set-up, a bluff—a bit of political theater scripted by one of the wiliest practitioners of the art ever to occupy the White House. Is it conceivable that Roosevelt would take the extreme measure of nationalizing the airlines without prior consultation with his own Air Force chief of staff? Had the president forgotten the calamity he brought down upon his head in 1934, the last time he ordered the Army to take over the domestic airways? Or was this naked display of power just FDR's way of getting the airlines' attention and assuring their full cooperation "for the duration"? We shall never know. But if it was a bluff, it certainly had the desired effect. Between March and June 1942 the Army requisitioned 183 planes—mainly Douglas DC-3s, DSTs, and DC-2s—out of the domestic airlines' total fleet of 359 aircraft. Most were purchased outright or leased for the duration of the war. In addition, the Army preempted all standing orders for DC-3s and DC-4s at the Douglas plant in Santa Monica, California. Production of Lockheed's new Constellations, Boeing's Stratoliners, and other aircraft deemed nonessential to the war effort was halted. Within a few more months, hundreds of airline pilots and mechanics—roughly half of the carriers' available manpower—would be reassigned to military contract operations with the War Department.

Meanwhile, the airlines were being swamped with reservations by high-ranking military officers, government officials, and war-related indus-

The Home Front

Braznell writes:

War does strange things to people. After Pearl Harbor, paranoia and imbecility seemed to go hand in hand on the home front. For a while we had National Guardsmen with fixed bayonets at the entrance to all passenger terminals. God knows what they were supposed to be protecting. Airline crews had to run a gauntlet of security guards before they were admitted on the flight line. New security regulations required that we close the window curtains on all passenger planes during takeoffs and landings. This was so spies and saboteurs, posing as ordinary passengers, could not observe and secretly photograph what was going on around the nation's air fields. Of course, there was nothing to prevent spies and saboteurs from hiring private planes for a few bucks and flying practically anywhere they chose to go. My first experience with this war hysteria almost led to an international incident. Early in 1942 my boss Roy Mitchell and I flew up to Canada to inspect our navigation radio facilities at Strathburn and Jarvis, two stations on American's route between Detroit and Buffalo. Roy had arranged the proper clearances, but something went wrong—the usual wartime SNAFU. When we landed at Toronto, our first stop, we were surrounded by military police and informed we were under arrest for violating Canadian airspace. Denials, explanations, and apologies were useless. After cooling our heels for several hours, we were marched into the office of the station commander, who informed us we were not only being detained until the matter was cleared up, but it was also possible that our plane, an ancient relic of the American Airways era, would be *confiscated!* At that Roy exploded, "That piece of crap? Serve you right if our government made you keep it for the duration."

try leaders, all claiming the highest travel priority. Practically the entire load-carrying capacity of the domestic airline industry was absorbed in the war effort. Yet, despite the strain, not a peep of complaint was heard from the airlines' top managements: After all, there was a *war* on.

The Air Transport Command

Brigadier General Harold George was a career Air Corps officer, a bomber pilot and strategic air power theorist who, by his own admission, knew absolutely nothing about the air transport business. Army Air Force Commanding General Hap Arnold had taken this deficiency into account when he summoned George to assume command of the Air Force Ferrying Command, soon to be reborn as the Air Transport Command (ATC). Arnold immediately proposed as George's second-in-command a man who knew nothing about the military and practically everything about running an air transport business—American Airlines' Cyrus R. Smith.

With his reputation for bluntness and his legendary disdain for brass hats and red tape, Smith hardly fit the image of an Army staff officer. But he willingly accepted the job and, with the full support of Generals Arnold and George, immediately set out to convert the Air Force's paper transport command into the world's largest air carrier.

Characteristically, Smith's first act as deputy commander was to fire off telegrams to a hand-picked list of airline executives and their employers (including American Airlines) informing them that their services would be required by their country—and General George—for the duration. Realizing that his own authority as a newly commissioned bird colonel might not swing enough weight, Smith signed Arnold's

name to the telegrams.[4] Smith got his men, and the equally pragmatic Arnold quickly forgave him for this minor breach of military protocol.

The Air Transport Command that George and Smith began assembling in mid-1942 was essentially the organization outlined in the mobilization plan ATA had submitted to the War Department nearly a year earlier. The new service was to be under the Air Force's chain of command and staffed by Air Force officers. It would operate Air Force–owned or leased aircraft, and employ a combination of Air Force and civilian flight crews, engineers, and mechanics. That's how the general orders read. In fact, the ATC was largely an airline show during the early years of the war. Like Smith, most of the ATC's cadre of Air Force officers were airline people—reservists who had been recalled to active duty from their civilian jobs as airline pilots and administrators. All of the command's early transoceanic survey flights and the bulk of the transport missions flown in 1942 and 1943 were manned by airline crews operating under contracts with the War or Navy Departments. The planes they flew were mostly DC-3s that had been leased or purchased from the airlines, stripped down, repainted, and reassigned to the airlines as C-53s. Even these aircraft conversions were performed under contract by the airlines, as were most of the aircraft and engine overhauls performed on the ATC fleet throughout the war. The airlines also set up and operated training schools for mechanics and flight crews, including the navigators and radio operators required on transoceanic flights. As the war progressed, these airline-trained mechanics and crew members, more than 47,000 in total, supplanted airline contract personnel to some extent. But the

4. Serling, *When the Airlines Went to War*, 40, 41.

A DC-3 by Any Other Name

C-53s were stripped-down DC-3s. A number of DSTs (the sleeper version of the DC-3) saw military service as C-49s. The far more familiar C-47 designation applied to DC-3–type aircraft built specifically for the USAAF and incorporating distinctly military features such as large cargo doors and beefed-up cargo compartment flooring. Air Transport Command models were typically equipped with internal fuel tanks for added range, a navigator's station, and a Plexiglas overhead bubble for celestial navigation. The Naval equivalents of the C-47 were known as R-4Ds. The RAF and RCAF called them Dakotas. But airmen and GIs all over the world affectionately dubbed them Gooney Birds. Douglas built nearly twelve thousand of these rugged, versatile, and supremely dependable aircraft during the war. The Soviet Union and other Allied licensees built thousands more; no one knows precisely how many.

airlines continued to fly most of ATC's long-haul transoceanic missions throughout the war.

From start to finish, ATC was a remarkable success, an example of cooperation between the armed services and private sector that has few parallels in the history of modern warfare. What began with a handful of Air Force personnel and civilian conscripts grew, by the end of the war, to an organization of more than 200,000 personnel and 3,000 aircraft, with operations ranging from the Arctic to the jungles of South America and equatorial Africa, from the Sahara to the ice-capped peaks of the Himalayas.

An Urgent Message

Of course, conflicts among ATC's military and civilian components were inevitable. Throughout the war, but particularly in the early going, there were clashes between the government bureaucracy and the airline contractors, between career Air Corps officers and the more laid-back airline conscripts, even among the airline contractors themselves. Braznell tells of one such incident:

A few days after Pearl Harbor, American Airlines got an urgent call from the War Department for immediate deployment of twelve DC-3s to the U.S. Marine air station at Quantico, Virginia. Aircraft were to be stripped of redundant radio equipment, galleys—all but the bare essentials. Crew members were to bring rugged civilian clothing—enough for a couple of weeks—and pack their government-issue .38 automatics.[5] Fresh ammunition would be provided at their intermediate destination. Further sealed orders were to follow.

The American dispatcher in New York rounded up all the standby crews available, and after coming up short, tapped a couple of Boston- and Chicago-based crews that happened to be passing through or laying over for the night. That's how my crew got involved. I understand New York

dispatch even contacted one or two crews in flight and ordered them to return to LaGuardia and discharge their passengers. It was, apparently, that serious an emergency.

At Quantico our stripped-down ships were loaded with Marines in full battle gear and dispatched in flights of three to Miami, where we were to refuel and pick up the complement of Pan Am navigators who were to guide us to our destination—still unknown to all but one or two of our top operations people.

When we arrived in Miami, we learned that our orders had been changed: We were to offload the troops and supplies immediately. Pan Am's president Juan Trippe had refused to allow his navigators to accompany our crews. The War Department had apparently acquiesced to his demands: Only Pan Am crews and aircraft were authorized to proceed beyond that point. Wartime emergency or not, nobody was going to play on Pan Am's side of the street if Mr. Trippe could help it.

We never discovered the aborted mission's exact destination. Its purpose, we were told, was to secure one or two Latin American air bases the War Department considered important to the Allied war effort and which it feared might fall into the hands of Nazi fifth columnists. Whether or not it came off as planned also remains a mystery.[6]

From the beginning, Pan American's Juan Trippe let it be known he didn't appreciate having a bunch of domestic airlines mucking around in his territory—his territory being loosely defined as everywhere east of Boston, west of San Francisco, and south of Miami. Nor was Trippe particularly pleased about the selection of an Air

5. In those days Post Office regulations required that airline pilots be armed with government-issued sidearms.

6. Braznell's story differs significantly from previously published accounts of this episode. All we can say is, he was there. Further, we were able to confirm the main points of his narrative with American Airlines Captain Kelly Owen, another American Airlines pilot who participated in the mission.

Corps bomber pilot and an American Airlines executive to run the new Air Transport Command. In his view, it made far more sense for the Air Force and the Navy to turn over their worldwide air transport missions to Pan Am, then the nation's sole overseas carrier, and put Trippe in command of the combined ATC/NATS/Pan Am operations.[7] The War and Navy Departments politely declined this magnanimous offer, but continued to avail themselves of Pan Am's transport services and considerable international expertise on the same contractual terms available to other carriers.

Alaska's Airborne Minute Men

The war mobilization plan developed by Gorrell's Air Transport Association and adopted by the War Department called for each of the major airline contractors to be assigned a particular territory, route, or theater of operations. The approach was similar to the way air mail routes were awarded in the 1920s and 1930s, but on a global scale. American and Northeastern Airlines, for example, were to operate primarily over the North Atlantic Great Circle route from the eastern seaboard to Great Britain by way of Newfoundland, Greenland, and Iceland—weather permitting. TWA conducted an intercontinental shuttle between Washington, D.C., and North Africa throughout the war. Pan Am and Eastern drew Central and South America as well as the South Atlantic route to North Africa by way of Natal and Ascension Island; Northwest and Western Airlines covered Alaska; United criss-crossed the Pacific from San Francisco and Seattle to Alaska, Hawaii, and the South Pacific. This division of labor made sense, in principle. Ordinarily it worked in practice as well. But when emergencies arose, as they often did in the early going,

it was all hands on deck, and the devil take the hindmost.

Such was the case in June 1942, when a Japanese naval task force launched a surprise carrier-based attack on the U.S. air base at Dutch Harbor, Alaska, occupied two small, undefended islands on the western tip of the Aleutians, and appeared to be poised for an invasion of the Alaskan mainland.

On Saturday afternoon, June 13, 1942, a call went out from the Air Force's Air Services Command for help in organizing a massive airlift of troops and supplies to the defenders. Several Northwest Airlines crews were already on the scene. The other airlines' response was immediate. By Sunday morning, scores of converted DC-3 transports (C-53s) operated by crews from ten airlines were in the air,[8] heading for the airlift's supply depot and base camp in Edmonton, Alberta. From Edmonton, the armada fanned out to the north and west—some to provision the garrison at Dutch Harbor, others to reinforce remote outposts in the Aleutians, and others to shuttle military cargo and personnel to and from air bases in Anchorage, Fairbanks, and Nome.

Shortly after the airlift began, the Japanese fleet withdrew from Alaskan waters, abandoning the troops dug in on the islands of Attu and Kiska and removing any immediate threat of invasion. The crisis over, Alaska's airborne Minute Men were, presumably, free to go home. But the Army decided that, as long as they were there, it

7. Serling, *When the Airlines Went to War.*
8. The ten were American, Braniff, Chicago & Southern (Delta), Eastern, Northwest, Pan American, Penn Central (Capital), TWA, United, and Western. American Airlines crews manned twelve of the fifty-odd aircraft that participated in the Alaska airlift. American also contributed a disproportionately large number of engineers and mechanics to the pooled maintenance team that kept the Alaska fleet running practically around the clock throughout the month-long campaign.

would make the most of the airline crews' valuable services. At the time, the Army Corps of Engineers was rushing to complete a system of roads, airfields, and refueling stations through fifteen hundred miles of wilderness, from Dawson Creek in northern British Columbia to Fairbanks, Alaska. The project was vital, not only to Alaska's defense, but to a plan to ferry thousands of Lend-Lease fighters and bombers from American factories to our new ally, the Soviet Union, by way of Canada, Alaska, and Siberia. With the first Lend-Lease aircraft scheduled to begin streaming northward within weeks, and the highway system still several months from completion, the airline armada was pressed into service airlifting aviation fuel, construction workers, equipment, and supplies into a dozen hastily cleared dirt airstrips paralleling the highway's proposed route.

Flying the Alaskan airlift was an experience most of the airline Minute Men would never forget—or wish to repeat. From the perpetually fog-shrouded Aleutians to the craggy desolation of its inland mountain ranges, Alaska is one huge hazard to navigation, as inhospitable to airmen and groundlings alike as any land mass on the face of the planet. During the long summer days the armada was stationed in northern Canada and Alaska, temperatures inland ranged from low broil (100-plus degrees) in lowlands to below zero in the snow-capped mountain passes. Low overcasts, blowing dust and smoke from scores of construction sites, severe icing, and thunderstorms with "hail stones as big as hens' eggs" added excitement to the airmen's daily flight routine.[9] Sorties through mountainous territory were restricted to visual flight rules because of the

sparseness and unreliability of radio navigation aids. Vast ferrous mineral deposits caused radio beams to bend miles off course and magnetic compasses to swing like bird dogs on the hunt.

As for radio communications, once out of range of home base, Edmonton-based airlift crews were on their own. There were no air traffic or weather advisories, no instructions from their companies' station dispatcher, no ground crews standing by at landing strips to "fill 'er up" or attend to minor maintenance problems—no one, in short, to tell them what to do, or do it for them.

While the good weather and extended summer daylight hours lasted, flight crews and mechanics grew accustomed to eighteen-hour workdays. A typical shift might include three or four shuttle flights from Edmonton to Fort St. John, then to Fort Nelson, and back—twelve to sixteen hours flying time in total. Crews slept on air mattresses in their planes during short breaks between missions and took turns spelling one another or drowsing at their crew stations during flights. Every fifth day they were allowed to stand down, take a hot shower, sleep in a real bed, and tie into a moose-steak dinner at the old Canadian Pacific Hotel in Edmonton.

Their aircraft got even less rest. When one crew took a day off, another would take its place. Routine maintenance tasks, even complete engine overhauls, were performed swiftly and at odd hours of the night, so that during all the time the airlift was in progress, rarely was one of the armada's fifty ships out of commission for more than six hours at a time.

The Alaskan armada departed Edmonton on August 14, 1942, its mission completed. The first American-built fighters consigned to the Soviet Union arrived in Fairbanks, via the Alcan air/land bridge, before they left. The Alcan Highway and its network of semi-permanent steel airstrips was

9. American Airlines *Flagship News*, March 1944.

Author's Aside: The Summer of '42

We moved to New York in the summer of 1942, a month before the author's eleventh birthday. After six years as American's chief pilot–Chicago, Walt had been promoted to a new, senior administrative position in the company's New York–based Operations Department. He still had his reserve commission in the Army Air Force, courtesy of the Missouri National Guard, and was subject to recall, either voluntary or otherwise. I suppose, like most of his contemporaries, he was feeling the contrary gravitational tugs of family responsibilities on the one hand—a third child was on the way—and a desire to "do his part," "get in on the action," or whatever one chooses to call that perverse male instinct to put oneself in harm's way. As it turned out, the choice of a military or civilian role in the war effort was not his to make. Both the Air Force and American Airlines had decided that Walt Braznell's services were needed in New York, at LaGuardia Airport, behind a desk, and that's how it was to be.

We didn't see much of him that summer, or for the balance of the war, for that matter. With C. R. gone and half the airline's personnel called away to military duty, everyone left was pulling double or triple duty, trying to keep the airline running while servicing the continuous, ever urgent demands of the armed forces. When Walt wasn't working nights and weekends at LaGuardia, he would be away on an ATC contract mission somewhere —Newfoundland, Greenland, Brazil, India, New Guinea. I'm embarrassed to say that my sharpest recollections of him during that period in our lives were of the trinkets he brought home from his travels—ivory statuettes, an authentic British pith helmet, a jeweled knife, a carved ebony tiger, and a large assortment of inlaid sandalwood boxes. The smell of sandalwood still evokes memories of Walt, the war years and, particularly, those long, wet, lonely summers of 1942 and 1943.

That first summer was a rough time for my mother, what with caring for a newborn baby, settling into our new house and surroundings, and coping with two rambunctious older children, largely on her own. Perhaps the hardest part for her—for all of us—was cutting the umbilical cord that linked us to the Midwest and my mother's and father's families back in St. Louis. None of us, excepting Walt, had ever been east of Indiana before we moved to New York. The Midwest was home. Here we were strangers in a strange land.

Of course, we were outrageously fortunate. We were as safe from the war as anyone on the planet could be. We had Walt with us much of the time. Mother had her baby and a host of friends—mostly transplanted American Airlines wives like herself—to keep her company while he was away. And my sister and I had a new house, new neighborhood, new playmates, and all that lush Long Island countryside and coastline to explore.

But as an eleven-year-old, I took our family's wartime dislocations personally. Only much later did it occur to me that our experiences that summer of '42—the long separations, the uprootings and resettlement, the challenge of accommodating to a strange new environment and way of life—were not at all unique. What we experienced was but a pale facsimile of what was happening to millions of American families. For those of us at home, and doubtless for those who survived the blood-letting and devastation of the real war, World War II was a watershed, or more accurately, a deep cleft in our lives. We were thus before the war and *so* afterward—rarely the same, often quite different people—and our world, henceforth, would be both smaller and infinitely larger than the one we left behind.

completed in November 1942. The Japanese invasion of the American and Canadian northland never materialized. And the last of the Japanese forces occupying the islands of Attu and Kiska in the Aleutians were driven out or killed in fierce hand-to-hand fighting in the summer of 1943. Regarded as a serious threat to national security at the time it occurred, the Japanese occupation of those two small, windswept rocks seems, in the light of history, utterly feckless. As Roy Mitchell might have put it, *"Serve 'em right if our government made 'em keep 'em!"*

A Matter of Survival

For months after the United States entered World War II the Army Air Force's highest mortality rates were experienced not by the fighter or bomber groups—their turn would come later—but by the Ferrying Command. Young pilots fresh out of flight school, with limited instrument training and no experience whatever in transoceanic navigation or long-range cruise control, were being assigned to ferry aircraft with which they were barely familiar across the raging North Atlantic in the dead of winter. It was no contest. One after another, planes would take off from Bangor or Presque Isle, Maine, refuel in Newfoundland or Labrador, if they got that far, and then disappear without a trace.

Veteran American Airlines pilot William "Big Bill" Keasler remembers flying a planeload of green ferry pilots to Bangor early in 1942. Later that evening, as he sat around an Army barracks for hours coaching the young airmen and answering their endless and hopelessly naive questions, he felt his heart sink. Later, Keasler learned that just one of the twenty-one pilots he had flown to Maine made it to England. The rest were lost at sea.

To its credit, the Air Force was quick to recognize the terrible error of its ways. Early in the war it contracted with TWA, American, Northeast, and other airlines and private aviation schools to provide AAF flight school graduates destined for the Ferrying Command or Air Transport Command with a modicum of training in all-weather flying and long-range navigation. Under the ATC's General George, this patchwork of private schools grew and coalesced into a virtual university, with scores of campuses all over the country, thousands of students, and a single high standard of training. Countless airline pilots of the postwar era owed their careers, and not a few, their lives, to the education they received in those wartime contract schools.

Oh God, It's Friday

One of Walt Braznell's responsibilities as American's new chief of flying was to arrange and oversee the training of hundreds of Army and Navy transport pilots at the company's contract schools in Chicago, Burbank, Fort Worth, and elsewhere. It was a job after his own heart, or would have been, except for the services' habitually blasé attitude toward scheduling.

On a Friday afternoon soon after my transfer to LaGuardia, I got a call from Washington. We were about to receive a fresh shipment of flight school graduates—about four hundred in all—each with roughly 130 hours flying time. How long would it take to give them sufficient training to pass their commercial and instrument ratings?

I had no idea. In fact, I had no idea where we were going to put them. Our existing flight schools were already jam-packed with fledgling pilots undergoing similar training. That, my caller reminded me, was my problem. The trainees would be arriving Monday morning. Good luck, old man, and don't forget *theresawaron!*

As soon as my Washington contact hung up I phoned Diddy and told her I wouldn't be home for a couple of days. Then I made a few long-distance calls and headed down to the hangar with my overnight bag and a handful of blank contracts. By Monday afternoon I was back in New York, and our four hundred new trainees were heading for hastily arranged subcontract schools in Indianapolis, Chicago, Niagara Falls, and Wilmington. This sort of thing went on all through the early months of the war. Fridays just weren't Fridays without an urgent call from Washington.

One of American Airline's principal wartime assignments was to airlift military personnel, equipment, and supplies across the North Atlantic under contract to the Air Transport Command. This posed a problem, initially, since up to mid-1942, few American pilots had any experience flying over bodies of water larger than Lake Michigan, and hardly anyone possessed the requisite skills in long-range navigation.

The notable exception was Colin McIntosh, Braznell's old friend from Robertson Aircraft days and one of the guiding spirits of American's Chicago-based Pilot School. Not only was McIntosh thoroughly proficient in the arcane arts of celestial navigation, but he had, as well, recently gained invaluable experience as a pathfinder-navigator, guiding Catalina flying boats across the Pacific, from San Diego to the Philippines, under contract to Consolidated Aircraft.

Braznell and Johnny Davidson, American's chief pilot for the North Atlantic, decided to bring McIntosh to New York and have him set up a night school to teach Davidson's pilots the essentials of celestial navigation. Accordingly, a classroom was set up at LaGuardia, with access to a rooftop "observatory." There—three nights a week, weather permitting—McIntosh patiently guided his part-time charges through the mysteries of the heavens.

Ernie Gann, one of the pilots under McIntosh's tutelage, remembers the experience well:[10]

Once having learned the principal navigation stars—Arcturus, Spica, Sirius, Dubhe, Polaris—we were supplied with octants (the aerial version of the sextant), and began practicing the measurement of various celestial bodies above the horizon. The sun was easy to bring into place and fix in the small bubble which floated somewhat nervously inside the viewfinder. Stars and planets were ill-behaved at first, dodging and disappearing from my field of view when most needed. There were times when I mistook one star for another, leading to the embarrassment of fixing my position in Zanzibar when I knew very well I was on the shores of Flushing Bay.

Gann was not the only member of the class having trouble fixing his position. After several weeks, Braznell and Davidson reluctantly concluded that, at the rate the class was progressing, the war would be over before their part-time students were fit to navigate the Atlantic. Meanwhile, regular transatlantic flights were scheduled to begin within a month or two. Back to the drawing board.

McIntosh returned to Chicago with orders to organize a crash course for navigator trainees. Within two weeks he and Personnel Manager John Deater had hired two more instructors, scrounged an obsolete Lockheed Hudson bomber from the Air Force to serve as an in-flight laboratory, and turned an empty hangar into a classroom complete with desks, manuals, training aids, and celestial navigation equipment.

Not the least of the problems facing the new Navigator School was a critical shortage of prospective students. Every pilot and pilot trainee,

10. Ernest K. Gann, *A Hostage to Fortune.*

every engineer and mechanic not subject to recall or draft was needed on the line. But fortunately, American's management discovered a rich
pool of potential navigator talent in the hundreds
of underemployed ticket agents remaining on
the payroll. Most of these agents, their jobs made
redundant by wartime travel restrictions, were
only too happy to volunteer. Braznell writes:

> I was on hand to welcome the first class when
> it arrived. Mac's arrangements had been made so
> quickly that the varnish on the seats of our refur-
> bished desks was still tacky and stuck to the pants
> of our erstwhile ticket salesmen. Within a few
> weeks, these bright young men would be guiding
> aircraft across thousands of miles of the North and
> South Atlantic by means of dead reckoning and
> precise celestial navigation. And this would con-
> tinue throughout thousands of wartime missions
> without the loss of a single aircraft due to naviga-
> tional error. Quite a tribute to Professor McIntosh
> and his pupils.

The North Atlantic

In October 1942 American began flying regularly scheduled flights for the Air Transport Command across the North Atlantic between New
York and Prestwick, Scotland. For the benefit
of our younger readers, to whom transatlantic
flights via Concorde or jumbo jet may be as routine as having one's hair cut, perhaps we should
put this event in historic perspective. In the fifteen years since Charles Lindbergh's first nonstop
flight from New York to Paris, the Great Circle
transatlantic route had been flown hundreds of
times. But seldom on a regular schedule. And
rarely in winter. And *almost never* westbound in
the dead of winter with a load of passengers.[11]
In accepting the North Atlantic mission American
was, therefore, biting off a very large chunk of

the proverbial cookie—and everyone from ATC's
General George to the greenest American crew
member had cause to wonder how well it could
chew.

The route staked out by ATC and surveyed
by American and Northeast Airline crews several
months earlier was designed to be flown by
Douglas C-53s—DC-3s that had been stripped,
repainted, and fitted with a celestial navigation
bubble, long-range radios, and internal fuel tanks
for added range. Reflecting the C-53's obvious
shortcomings as a long-range transoceanic transport, the route advanced in relatively short, easy
stages from LaGuardia to Presque Isle, Maine,
northward across the Gulf of St. Lawrence to
Goose Bay, Labrador, then on to the deeply in-
cised, fjord-pocked southern coast of Greenland
and that infamous box canyon leading—if one
chose the *right* box canyon—to the air field
known as Bluie West One. The final, eleven-hour
leg over the northernmost segment of the North
Atlantic, from the tip of Greenland to Prestwick
on Scotland's Firth of Clyde, was a stretch for
eastbound C-53s and well-nigh impossible for
those flying westward into the strong westerly
winds common to the northern latitudes. For this
reason, return flights routinely landed and refu-
eled at Reykjavik, Iceland, before proceeding to
Greenland.

By October most of American's converted
DC-3s and Army C-47s had been replaced by
four-engine Consolidated C-87s. With their longer
range, added speed, and greater load-carrying capacity, the 87s were far better adapted to the

11. Germany's Graf Zeppelin and Hindenburg airships
completed 144 ocean crossings (72 round-trips) between
1928 and 1937. Otherwise, Pan American was the only carrier to inaugurate transatlantic air service prior to the war.
Beginning in 1940 it advertised twice weekly flights between
New York and London—weather permitting.

The Surveyors

In April 1942 American Airlines began North Atlantic runs for the USAAF with a survey flight from LaGuardia to Greenland aboard the former AA Flagship *Cleveland*. The survey team members, pictured in front of the newly commissioned Army C-53, were (from left) Captain H. G. Robertson, Radio Operator Dick Wisenbaker, Navigator Colin McIntosh, Chief Pilot–Atlantic John F. Davidson, Meteorologist E. C. "Doc" Buell, Engineer Frank Ware, Captain J. F. "Fran" Bledsoe, and Captain M. G. "Dan" Beard. *Photo courtesy of the Mangan collection*

North Atlantic run than the smaller C-47s, or so it seemed. But the bigger ships had problems of their own—notably, a distressing habit of stalling out whenever they picked up a load of ice.

As winter approached, the weather and winds over the northern route grew steadily worse. By early December the half dozen American crews stacked up in Scotland waiting for a break in the storm cycle were beginning to wonder whether they would make it home by Christmas. Each day

the Prestwick weather forecaster's report was the same: "Grim—pretty bloody grim."[12]

Finally, ATC's North Atlantic Division Commander Larry Fritz called it quits for the winter. The American crews, with their ice-shy C-87s, were subsequently reassigned to Natal, Brazil, where they joined Eastern, TWA, and Pan Am crews in airlifting troops and supplies across the

12. James Mangan, *To the Four Winds.*

South Atlantic to North Africa throughout the winter of 1942–1943.

North Atlantic flights were resumed the following spring. In June 1943 ATC began augmenting or replacing the C-87 "Thundermugs" assigned to American crews with brand-new Douglas C-54 Skymasters—an event greeted by pilots and crew members with wild rejoicing and prayers of thanksgiving. Later that year there were more glad tidings: After lengthy negotiation, the neutral Portuguese government had agreed to let the Allies use the Portuguese-owned Azores Islands as a mid-ocean refueling base, thus opening vitally important alternative routes across the North Atlantic by way of the Azores and Newfoundland, or the Azores and Bermuda.

With more reliable planes, safer air routes, and steady improvements in weather reporting and long-range radio navigation, air traffic across the North Atlantic increased exponentially. During the climactic months of the war in Europe, from D-Day (June 6, 1944) to V-E Day (May 8, 1945), and for several months thereafter, approximately one hundred American Airlines crews were assigned to the North Atlantic run. They flew an average of 150 crossings a month—as many as 500 per month in peak periods, 7,000 in total. In the end, they proved that year-round transatlantic operations were not only feasible but also practical. In light of history, this may have been the airline industry's most significant wartime achievement.

By Whose Authority?

Like just about everyone who flew the C-87, Braznell had his own reason for remembering its eccentricities:

On one of our first C-87 flights from New York to Prestwick, somewhere between Greenland and Iceland our flight engineer went aft to transfer fuel from one tank to another. This was done by means of an exposed "U" tube, one end of which was attached to a full, pressurized tank and the other to the tank needing refueling. A spring-loaded connector device on the U-tube was supposed to prevent back-flow or spillage after the refueling was completed and the U-tube removed. This time the connector malfunctioned and a gusher of gasoline sprayed out over the cargo-compartment floor. One spark from a nearby box of electrical relays would have blown us away.

The spill was cleaned up quickly and without incident. But it didn't take an aeronautical engineer to recognize the safety hazard inherent in this crude refueling system. Later, talking to other pilots, I heard, and later confirmed, reports of C-87s mysteriously disappearing over the North Atlantic. When I got back to New York, I grounded our C-87s and arranged with American's Engineering Department to have the transfer system modified and enclosed. This was in mid-October 1942.

The following day I had a telephone call from ATC operations in Washington asking "by whose authority" the ships had been grounded, and why. When I explained, my caller, an officious bird colonel, angrily informed me the C-87s had flown "hundreds of missions without mishap," and that I could either put our ships back into service immediately or return them to the Air Transport Command.

I told the Colonel we had identified a serious operational problem, and that we were fixing it. The planes would not fly with our crews aboard until the problem was resolved—which would probably take several days. If that wasn't satisfactory, he could let us know when his crews would arrive in New York, and we would have the 87s shoved out of the hangar for them. The Colonel backed down, but wrote a stinging letter to my boss complaining about my "arbitrary" behavior.

The Thundermug

Consolidated's C-87 was a hasty and not terribly successful attempt to convert its warhorse B-24 Liberator bomber into a transport. The angular, ungainly ship looked rather like a cross between a beached whale and the packing crate for a B-17. Its thin, high-speed/low-drag wings worked very nicely in clear air, but had an unhappy tendency to stall out whenever they picked up a load of ice. Additionally, the C-87 had an oddball internal fuel transfer system that sometimes sprayed fuel onto the cargo compartment floor—a serious safety hazard believed to have caused a number of mysterious midair explosions. The last of the Thundermugs was retired in May 1944, long after they were removed from service on the North Atlantic, but not before they had gained respect for their yeoman service over the South Atlantic and the Himalayas.

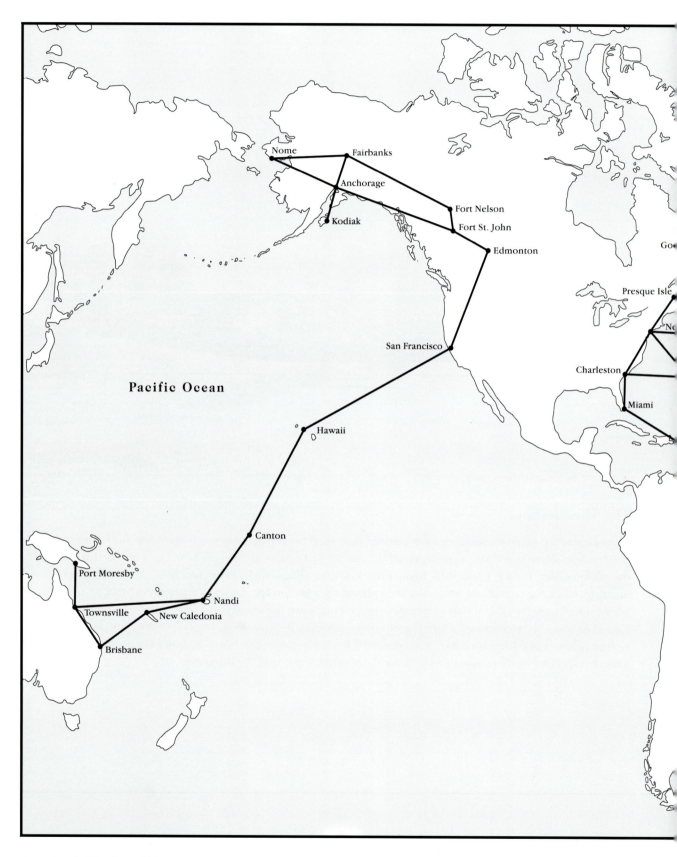

American's Wartime ATC Routes

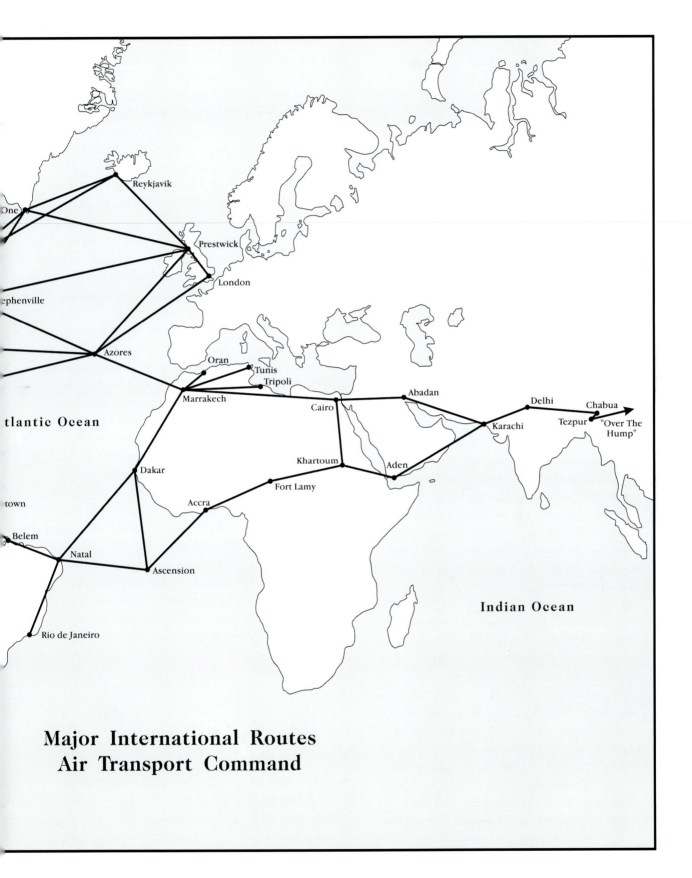

**Major International Routes
Air Transport Command**

In January 1943, a few months after American's modified C-87s went back in service, Braznell got another call from Washington.

Since the Japanese cut off the Allies' supply line from India to China via the Burma Road, the Air Force had taken on the task of provisioning Generalissimo Chiang Kai-shek's ground and air forces by air. So far, the mission wasn't going very well. Madam Chiang, China's unofficial but immensely influential ambassador to the United States, had come to Washington and threatened that her husband would pull China out of the war if the Air Force didn't get a move on. The ATC wanted us to pull some aircraft off the South Atlantic run and augment its day missions with night operations based out of Tezpur, an abandoned British bomber base in India's upper Assam valley. Feeling desk-bound and overdue for a little action, I decided to make the survey flight, and rounded up a crew including Johnny Davidson and Colin McIntosh.

Our outbound route took us from Melbourne, Florida, where we received our ATC briefing, then across the Caribbean, by way of Puerto Rico and British Guiana, to Natal, Brazil, at the easternmost hump in the South American continent. From there we flew to Ascension in the South Atlantic, on to Accra on the Gold Coast of Africa, then to Khartoum and down the Red Sea coast to Aden, on the southern tip of the Arabian peninsula. Our first stop in India was Karachi, on the north shore of the Arabian Sea. We progressed in short hops across the Indian desert to Allahabad, then to New Delhi, Gaya (a British bomber command base), and finally, eastward along the Brahmaputra River to Chabua at the base of the Himalayas.

Before running over to Tezpur for a look at our proposed Project 7A resupply base, we enjoyed a relaxing evening with our old friend (Major) Red Clark as guests of the Chabua officers club. At Red's request, Johnny, Colin and I had smuggled a couple of cases of liquor out of New York for the parched pioneers of the India-China aerial relief corps. Needless to say, we were greeted with open arms.

For a Missouri-born lad who, up to the war, had never been outside the North American continent, this trip was the experience of a lifetime, filled with adventures and images too vivid ever to be forgotten: Sighting a German U-boat in an island cove barely a stone's throw from Puerto Rico; visiting a British officer's mess in the heart of Africa, with the officers in their starched bush jackets and a quartet of native children serenading us to the tune of "You Are My Sunshine," flying low across the deserts of Sudan and India following caravan trails thousands of years old; circling over a moonlit Taj Mahal; climbing out one night into the inky blackness of a tropical rainstorm carrying a load of plastic explosives labeled *Harmless unless subjected to extreme heat or sudden shock*. But I'm getting away from my story.

After completing our mission, we took off for home with a load of tungsten, following the same route by which we had come. Arriving at Natal, we were notified by base operations that all C-87 aircraft were grounded, pending modification of their internal fuel transfer systems. Apparently the Air Force had come to the same conclusion we had about the failings of the original system. I invited the base commander's chief engineering officer aboard to inspect our ship, and showed him what an enclosed fuel transfer system looked like. The base commander immediately wanted to requisition our ship for shuttle duty over the South Atlantic, but we managed to escape his clutches and continued to New York. For some time after that, American's C-87s, with their modified fuel transfer systems, were the only ships of that type in service. I have no idea what happened to the colonel who fired off the letter about my arbitrary behavior. Never heard from him again.

Over the Hump

The Air Transport Command's mission to supply China and the air and ground forces there following the closing of the Burma Road in 1942 presented "the greatest logistical challenge of the war, probably of any war," wrote Pulitzer Prize–winning historian Barbara Tuchman.

> If natural obstacles of terrain and climate were extreme, human obstacles raised by the mutual antagonisms and soured morale of reluctant cobelligerents were no less so, and the monsoon of the summer months thickened the misery. To raise the Hump's deliveries [from 3,000 tons] to 10,000 tons a month under these conditions . . . was a struggle.
>
> "The [ATC's new] C-46 is full of bugs," [General Joseph] Stilwell noted worriedly on one of his inspection tours. "Carburetor ices up. We have lost six over the Hump and the boys' morale is lower and lower." Crews were rebellious and often bailed out as soon as an engine missed once, or refused to fly if there was a cloud in the sky . . . Defense against Japanese fighters was poor . . . The OSS rescued 125 ATC crew members in 1943 but this represented less than a third of all who went down, the rest to death or capture.
>
> Nevertheless, with reinforcements, a new ATC commander, and gradual ironing out of the C-46 faults, morale and flying conditions improved, and tonnages rose from 3,000 in May [1943] to 5,500 in July, to 8,000 in September, and after the rains ended, to an unbelievable 13,000 tons in November.[13]

Among the unnamed reinforcements Tuchman credits with having helped to achieve the "unbelievable" growth in cargo tonnage over the Hump was a small contingent of American Airlines ATC contract crews and mechanics who had been detached from duty in the South Atlantic and reassigned to the newly formed India-China wing of the Air Transport Command, headquartered at Chabua. In truth, this all-volunteer corps of "reinforcements"—seldom numbering more than

a dozen flight crews and thirty mechanics at any time during its four-month tour of duty, nursing a half dozen balky, war-weary C-87s over the most fearsome mountain ranges in the world and under some of the foulest and most treacherous weather conditions on the planet—deserves a share of the credit for the success of this historic airlift that is disproportionate to its numbers.

There is something curiously disjointed about the chronology of events leading up to American Airlines' involvement in the India-China airlift. Braznell mentions Madame Chiang's visit to the United States to drum up support for her husband's flagging cause; he recalls receiving a directive from Washington to reassign American crews from the South Atlantic to the CBI; and he describes his subsequent survey flight—the standard precursor to any major airlift operation involving American crews—in *January* 1943. But we know the first crews were not dispatched to India until late July, six months later. Braznell's memory for dates is confirmed by his log book entries and by an informal account of the journey published in American's *Flagship News* long after the conclusion of Project 7A. Further, it is a matter of historic fact that Madame Chiang began her mission to the United States in November 1942, well within the time-frame of the events Braznell discusses. But then, why the long delay in sending in reinforcements?

Almost immediately after Madame Chiang arrived in Washington to take up her three months' residence in the White House, she kicked off a political football match of titanic proportions. The stakes of the game were no less than China's participation in the Allied war effort and its ultimate place in the hierarchy of world powers. The India-China aerial resupply mission—"the greatest logistical challenge of the war," as Tuchman put it—was the football.

---

13. Tuchman, *Stilwell and the American Experience in China, 1911–1945*, 375–76.

The principal contestants, fighting for control of the airlift and the hundreds of tons of military cargo ultimately destined for the China-Burma-India (CBI) theater, were Stilwell and his boss, Army Chief of Staff George Marshall, on one side, and on the other, Generalissimo and Madame Chiang and Major General Claire Chennault, Chiang's erstwhile air commander (subsequently, commanding officer of the recommissioned 14th Air Force.)

Stilwell, in the impossible dual role as commanding.general–CBI and chief of staff to the generalissimo, urged that the bulk of munitions and supplies destined for the CBI be used to strengthen China's tattered armies, and he insisted that the increase in tonnage Chiang demanded be conditional on Chiang's promise to commit ground troops to a joint Anglo-American-Chinese campaign to reopen the Burma Road. Chiang, however, wanted no part in a jungle war. Ignoring Stilwell (they loathed one another), Chiang supported Chennault's claim that, with enough aircraft and aviation fuel, the 14th Air Force could neutralize or destroy the enemy's ground and air forces in China, recapture strategic air bases near the coast of mainland China, and use them to launch crippling air strikes against Japan's home islands. Chiang encouraged Chennault to take his proposal directly to President Roosevelt, bypassing the Army chain of command.

The infighting and political maneuvering that ensued continued for months. Finally, in May, Roosevelt settled the dispute by overruling his chief military advisers in favor of Chennault's bid for a huge build-up in the 14th Air Force's tactical strike force. The War Department was ordered to increase air shipments over the Hump to 7,000 tons a month by July and 10,000 tons by September. Chennault's demands for aviation fuel and supplies were to receive top priority.

While this fierce intramural scrimmage was going on in Washington, the ATC's India-China airlift remained plagued by all sorts of afflictions: foul weather, changes in command, continually disrupted supply channels, inadequate equipment, and the inexperience and low morale of its Air Force–trained flight crews. By mid-April supplies were dribbling over the Hump at a pace that made it virtually impossible for Stilwell and Chennault to sustain operations against the enemy, much less launch a major air-ground offensive.

The flight crews' low morale was understandable. Their unsupercharged C-47s, though dependable at lower levels, were totally out of their element in the rarefied atmosphere of Burma's high mountain passes. In a fully-loaded C-47, cruising at 20,000 feet on two *good* engines was like balancing a stack of dishes on a broom stick. An engine failure or even a temporary loss of power due to carburetor icing, a thunderstorm or sudden blast of clear air turbulence, even a moment's inattention to the air speed indicator was all it took to overcome the fragile balance of gravity and lift and send the plane spinning into the rocks below—another marker along the route pilots called the Aluminum Trail.

In late April the Air Force began replacing its C-47s with Curtiss C-46 Commandos—bigger, beefier transports equipped with twin supercharged Pratt & Whitney R-2800 engines. The Curtiss aircraft boasted a legitimate service ceiling of over 24,000 feet and a payload carrying capacity roughly twice that of the C-47. Unfortunately, the C-46 lacked the C-47's most prized quality—reliability. The first thirty Commandos to arrive from the States were so riddled with problems, or "bugs," as Stilwell put it, that they seldom made it into the air during their first few months of service and rarely completed a mission without a malfunction of one sort or another. Eventually, however, the major recur-

The Curtiss Commando (C-46)

With its smooth, elliptical profile, two-tone camouflage paint job, and broad Curtiss fluke of a tail, the C-46 looked like a fat brown trout. More than three thousand Commandos were built during the war, most of which began and ended their military careers flying the Hump or supporting the U.S. Army and Marine Corps island-hopping campaigns in the South Pacific. Remnants of this mighty fleet saw action as air cargo and troop transports in Korea and even in the early stages of the Vietnam War. War-surplus C-46s helped spark the boom in small, veteran-owned and operated nonscheduled airlines following World War II. At last report, a few ancient C-46s were still hauling freight into the interior of Central and South America. *Photo courtesy of National Archives*

ring problems were corrected, and as pressure mounted to stockpile aviation fuel and supplies for Chennault's vaunted fall air offensive, the '46s and their brave young Air Force pilots, aided and abetted by American's veteran ATC crews, would far surpass even Chiang's expectations.

The first American Airlines crews assigned to Project 7A landed at Tezpur on August 1. If anyone from ATC headquarters in Chabua had anticipated their arrival, it was not immediately evident. The site looked entirely abandoned— and was, except for the host of goats and cattle, lizards, snakes, and assorted bugs that had taken up residence in the huts which were to serve as crew quarters for the duration of their tour. More goats and cattle grazed alongside the runway.

The base's main street was a river of mud. The only latrine, a six-hole affair left over from the days of the Raj and, by the looks of it, last cleansed during Victoria's reign, was a nursery for hordes of bluebottle flies. There were no showers, no mess hall—no mess. That night, while flight-weary crews dined on C-rations, mucked out their quarters, and set up camp as best they could, mechanics working by torchlight prepared the aircraft for their initial flights over the Hump. The following morning, August 2, the first Project 7A C-87, commanded by American Airlines Captain Toby Hunt, staggered off the runway at Tezpur with a payload of 8,500 pounds of aviation fuel, bombs, and detonation fuses. Hunt and his crew circled for altitude over the Assam Valley, then headed eastward toward the glittering peaks of northern Burma's Patkai Range en route to Kunming, six hundred miles distant as the eagle flies. Thus ended the first twenty-four hours of Project 7A.

Over the next four months this round-the-clock pattern of semi-subsistence living and hard flying, of soldiering and making do, would be repeated unendingly. Veterans of Project 7A still differ over which was tougher, or riskier: facing vicious storms and attacks by enemy fighters over the high mountain passes, or enduring camp life in Tezpur. Jim Mangan writes: "Everything mildewed in the oppressive heat; food spoiled while one looked at it; and the endless rain followed by unbearable humidity bred fungus, bacteria, rot and disease." Dysentery, or "Delhi Belly," raged through the camp. As the weeks dragged by, dietary problems ranging from dizziness and fainting to impaired night vision and even temporary blindness became widespread.

A cholera epidemic among the native kitchen crew left the base so understaffed that, for weeks, everyone "from captain to junior mechanic" had to lend a hand cooking, washing dishes, serving, and cleaning up the communal mess hall during their off-duty hours. After informal complaints to the ATC wing headquarters in Chabua failed to bring relief, Project 7A's officer in charge, Captain Owen "Chuck" O'Connor, fired off a dispatch to the wing commander at Chabua, reporting, "It has now developed into a question of whether we must remove flight crews and maintenance personnel from flying cargo to China in order to assign them to camp duties, or whether other personnel (under your command) should be provided to run the camp . . ." Eventually, O'Connor's implied threat of curtailing airlift operations got results. But for the most part, the civilians of Project 7A expected and received little help through official Air Force channels.

So they took care of themselves, doing what they could to make life bearable. That pestilential latrine disappeared one night in a blinding explosion of aviation fuel. In collusion with certain unnamed contacts at Chabua and Kunming, an ad hoc operation called the "Project 7A Wholesale Supply House" was established to requisition fresh produce, eggs, and other sorely needed food supplies in China and fly them back to Tezpur. And on rare and special occasions, Major Harry Clark, the lone American Airlines veteran assigned to wing headquarters, would unexpectedly drop in with a planeload of Air Force nurses—most of them former AA stewardesses—for a grand reunion.

In all fairness, ATC India-China wing headquarters was reputed to be just as negligent in looking after its own personnel as it was in dealing with the basic human needs of civilian air crews under its command. Barbara Tuchman reports that General Stilwell arrived unannounced one day "to test reports of foul conditions" at the enlisted men's mess in Chabua. "After going through the mess line with the GIs and sitting

Joker's Wild

The vandals responsible for destroying Tezpur's infamous outhouse were never officially apprehended. But the finger of suspicion pointed like an unwavering compass needle to American Airlines Captain Si Bittner, a recent arrival at Tezpur, a man gifted with one of the world's most creative minds for practical jokes and, among American flight crews, a legend in his own time.

The Bittner legend goes back to the 1920s, when Si, flying an open-cockpit Stearman biplane for Colonial Airways, was accused of disrupting interstate traffic and causing grave discomfort to the passengers of the Pennsylvania Central Railroad's crack 20th Century Limited one night by swooping down over the highballing express and shining his landing lights squarely into the engineer's eyes. The pandemonium that followed can best be appreciated by audiences who remember the early sequences in the movie *Close Encounters of the Third Kind.*

The legend grew during the 1930s, particularly after the advent of flight attendants—lovely, innocent young maidens whom Bittner, like many other pilots of the era, delighted in teasing. On flights involving several intermediate stops, he would sometimes get off at one stop, tell the stewardess, "I'm going to stretch my legs. Don't run off without me," and then sneak back into the cockpit via the baggage chute when she wasn't looking. After takeoff, Bittner would turn the controls over to his copilot and take up a prearranged hiding place in the baggage bin. The copilot was then to buzz the stewardess and ask her to send Captain Bittner forward—a request that usually elicited an anguished cry, "Oh my god, I thought he was with you!" To cap off the joke, Bittner would sometimes exit from the baggage chute as soon as the plane came to a stop at the next airport. Running around to the passenger ramp, he would greet the stewardess with a big hug and a breathless, "Gosh, glad I caught up with you. Had to hitch a ride with United."

At Tezpur, Si was constantly surrounded by younger members of the Project 7A group, all eager acolytes fastening on the words and wisdom of the Master. When he wasn't taking his regular turn flying the Hump, Si busied himself organizing nocturnal "Hyena hunts" for his innocent admirers (the hyena always had the last laugh); instructing them in the proper techniques for stalking the Assam Valley's fearsome "Big Cats" ("Here, kitty-kitty!"); and experimenting with aviation gasoline in an attempt to find the ideal fuel-air mixture for vaporizing small wooden outbuildings and their odious contents. In an insane world, his was the inspired madness that may have kept less resilient comrades from going 'round the bend.

at filthy benches to share the 'slop,' Stilwell announced, 'All right boys, let 'em have it.' The place exploded in a flying melee of food, tin plates, and overturned tables. Stilwell then called in the base commander and said, 'There's your mess!' and told him that unless he found decent conditions at his next unscheduled visit, the commander would be relieved and sent home."

Another headquarters brass hat, informed that monsoons and heavy storms over the mountains had forced the Air Force to ground all ATC aircraft for two days, issued orders that "Effective immediately, there will be no more weather over the Hump."[14] For this godlike pronouncement, he would henceforth be known as "Sunny Tom."

The number of C-87s assigned to American's Project 7A group never exceeded ten, and de-

14. Mangan, *To the Four Winds.*

spite the Herculean efforts of its maintenance crews, seldom were more than five or six airworthy on any given day, even under the most liberal interpretation of the word "airworthy." After four months of flying the Hump, six of the group's eight remaining C-87s were rejected by the Army Air Force as unfit for further service. The Air Force did, however, permit American crews to fly their derelicts back to the States under signed orders protecting the crews from having their aircraft grounded and stripped for salvage by any overly safety-conscious engineering officer they might encounter en route.

According to official records, Project 7A crews flew a total of 499 round-trips—2,108 tons of air cargo—over the Hump from August through November 1943. Many of the 157 American Airlines pilots, navigators, flight engineers, and radio operators who participated in the airlift completed at least twenty-five round-trips—fifty "crossings"—during their tour of duty; this over terrain so awesome and under flying conditions so severe that ATC staff attrition experts rated the odds of surviving that many runs at one in three.

In fact, six American crew members lost their lives flying the Hump. On August 23 a C-87 loaded—probably overloaded—with aviation fuel and ammunition crashed and exploded a mile from the air base after at least one engine (more likely two) failed immediately after takeoff. All five crewmen, Captain Harry Charleton, First Officer Bob Dietze, Navigator John Keating, Radio Operator Bob Davis, and Flight Engineer Joe Smith, were killed instantly.

Project 7A's sixth fatality, Captain Toby Hunt, was also a victim of sudden engine failure, this time while attempting to climb out after a missed approach at his destination airfield in Kunming. Hunt went down with his stricken C-87 near Yunnanyi, China, on November 18, after ordering his crew members to bail out. The other four crewmen, First Officer Wayne Smith, Navigator

Wes Witte, Flight Engineer Gerald Toker, and Radio Operator Bob Hardeman, parachuted safely and made their way to the Yunnanyi air base, where they were picked up and returned to Chabua by an Air Force air rescue team the following day.

In the broad view, the contributions to the Allied victory made by the men of Project 7A pale in comparison to the thousands of missions, the millions of pounds of air cargo, and the thousands upon thousands of combat personnel and evacuees airlifted by American ATC crews over the Atlantic during World War II. Moreover, the efforts by American and Air Force crews to reinforce Chiang and Chennault were clearly lost causes—not only in the light of history but also in the consciousness of practically every airman who flew the Hump. These young men may not have known all we now know about the corruption and incapacity of Chiang's regime, or the inevitable failure of Chennault's quixotic air offensive, but neither were they entirely blind to the mischief going on under their very noses. That they behaved so professionally, so heroically, despite the knowledge of their mission's futility adds all the more luster to the legend of American's Project 7A.

No medals or ribbons were ever bestowed on these volunteers—not even an official commendation. A simple plaque, paid for from the project's mess fund and dedicated to the memory of the six American crew members who died flying the Hump, hangs in a place of honor at the American Airlines Flight Academy. Perhaps some day we shall get around to honoring the valiant survivors.

Tales of the South Pacific

In *High Horizons: The United Airlines Story,* Frank Taylor writes about a "remarkable" transpacific mission flown by a United crew in one of the Air Transport Command's first C-54s.[15]

General George Kenney's Fifth Air Force, stationed at Port Moresby, needed a supply of stabilizers for the bombers operating from that base. Though these stabilizers weighed only 400 pounds, they were so cumbersome that a C-87 couldn't handle a load of them. So a C-54 was called out of the ATC Atlantic service and rushed to San Francisco, where Captain Jack O'Brien [United's superintendent of Pacific Flight Operations] and Benny Howard, noted United—and, later, Douglas—test pilot, took over. Taking off at 12:05 A.M. on June 25, 1943, O'Brien and Howard averaged 226 miles per hour to Honolulu. After a fast refueling, they headed for Canton Island, from which they flew nonstop to Amberly Field near Brisbane, completing the 9,000-mile trip from San Francisco in thirty-nine hours. Actual flying time was thirty-five hours. With time out only for refueling, Captain O'Brien flew immediately to Port Moresby to deliver the stabilizers.

And now, as radio commentator Paul Harvey would say, the *rest* of the story:

In March 1943 the Air Force began taking delivery of its long-awaited Douglas C-54 transports, the first four-engine military aircraft designed specifically for long-range transport of personnel and air cargo. The C-54, which later saw service with the airlines as the DC-4, was cast in the proud tradition of its sire, the DC-3—sturdy, reliable, and so forgiving it was said to spoil pilots for other aircraft. Though not much faster than the C-47 or C-87, it could carry two to three times the C-47's maximum load and half again as much cargo and personnel as the narrow-waisted C-87. American on the East Coast and United on the West Coast were the

first ATC contract carriers to receive the new aircraft, which was to be rushed into service as the eventual replacement for all other aircraft then flying ATC's Atlantic and Pacific runs.

At LaGuardia, American's North Atlantic crews were midway through their test runs and checkout flights on the new C-54 when Walt Braznell received another one of those weekend phone calls.

Late one Saturday afternoon in June, I got a call from ATC in Washington asking if we were prepared to handle a high priority mission to the South Pacific. Our cargo was to consist of modified nose-gun turrets and horizontal stabilizers for B-24 bombers stationed in New Guinea. General Kenney's planes were getting peppered by Japanese Zero fighters and the new parts were badly needed. The only cargo ships big enough to carry the oversized load were the two C-54s Douglas recently delivered to airline contract carriers—one to United, the other to American. United said it wasn't ready to take on a long, over-water mission: Its crews were untrained in the new aircraft. Moreover, there were not enough spare parts to make the long trip over and back. Could American handle the assignment? I said we could, and would depart for San Francisco later that day to pick up the load.

As soon as I got off the phone with Washington, I called the field and asked our flight dispatcher to assign me a flight engineer and radio operator from the North Atlantic roster. Maintenance was to load the C-54 with all the spare parts it could find and get it ready to go within two hours. Then I called Colin McIntosh in Chicago and arranged for him to catch a plane and meet us in Fort Worth around midnight. Finding a copilot at this hour was no problem. I leaned out the window and called to my neighbor, American Airlines Chief Pilot–New York Harold Matheny, who was mowing his lawn. "Hey, Harold, how'd you like to go for a ride?" Harold asked where we were going, and I said I couldn't shout it out the window, but to "pack some light summer gear and tell Effie you'll be gone a couple of weeks."

15. Serling repeats Taylor's story in *When the Airlines Went to War.*

On the way to Fort Worth, Harold did most of the flying while I boned up on the C-54's performance charts and operating manual. Neither of us had more than a few hours actual flying experience in the new bird. We picked up Colin in Fort Worth and reached Hamilton Air Force Base, just north of San Francisco, early the next morning. At Hamilton we got a few hours crew rest while the Air Corps loaded our cargo.

We were 600 miles out over the Pacific that afternoon, en route to Hawaii, when the oil cooler on our No. 2 engine split and spilled all its oil. This meant shutting down the engine and returning to Hamilton. As soon as the repairs were complete, we took off again, dog-tired, and this time made it all the way to Hickam Field. Our next stop was Canton Island, a tiny atoll in the Pacific about 1,600 nautical miles south of Hickam. Captain Eddie Rickenbacker had missed it a few months back and drifted for days in a life raft before being rescued. Colin hit the island right on the nose, even though we had flown in solid clouds and heavy rain practically all the way. Taking on fuel, we cleared for Nandi in the Fiji Islands and landed there just before dark. The next morning we pushed on to New Caledonia, rested for an afternoon, and then took off for Brisbane, Australia.

In Brisbane we received a royal welcome. The Aussies must have thought Eleanor Roosevelt or some other VIP was aboard this first C-54 to cross the Pacific. A general greeted the plane, and as we were being chauffeured down the flight line, a flight of Lockheed P-38s did a low fly-by and victory roll for our benefit. It had taken us just three days to cover the 9,000 nautical miles from Hamilton to Brisbane, but we learned on arrival that United had finally gotten its C-54 airborne and was hot on our tail. Aboard were my old friend Benny Howard, now chief pilot for Douglas Aircraft, and an extra complement of United crew members. With augmented crews and auxiliary gas tanks, the United plane could easily overtake us by flying longer legs with fewer crew rests, and apparently that's what they had in mind. Soon after we departed Brisbane for Townsville, our last hop before heading into New Guinea, we learned that the United plane had arrived in Brisbane and would depart the next morning direct to our final destination, Port Moresby. Even in wartime, a friendly rivalry existed among the major carriers like American and United, and in this case we had upped the stakes by invading United's turf—the Pacific. The race was on.

During the long westbound journey Harold and I had spelled each other at the controls or stuck the plane on autopilot, while Colin had slept and cat-napped whenever his duties permitted. Clearly, Colin felt he had the tougher job, and as the flight wore on, he let that view be known in pointed little comments and snide allusions to the pilots' "cushy" job. So, from time to time, I offered to switch off with him. I would navigate while he took the controls, and we would see who had the tougher job. I always contrived to make this offer when we were in or expecting to enter clouds and heavy turbulence. This eliminated the necessity of demonstrating my proficiency in celestial navigation. While Colin wrestled to keep the aircraft upright, I would have nothing to do but read off our predetermined DR (dead reckoning) course settings, put my feet up on the navigator's desk, and tell Colin to wake me when we arrived at our next check point.

Eventually my fraud was exposed. The first time Captain McIntosh ordered me aloft to make a sunshot, I fixed our position as somewhere off the coast of Norway, and that was the end of my brief career as a navigator.

Now Colin's navigating skills were about to be put to their severest test. From Townsville we would be entering the war zone. Naturally, there would be no navigational radio aids. We were instructed to maintain complete radio silence and take maximum advantage of cloud cover to avoid being sighted, not only by the Japs, but by our own planes, which were likely to mistake our unfamiliar profile for that of the Mitsubishi bomber.

Our course would take us directly from Townsville across the Coral Sea to the mountainous coast of New Guinea. Our recognition point was to be a small native village, built on stilts out over the water. From there it would be just a short hop along the coast and then inland, through a valley in the towering Owen Stanley mountains, to an improvised landing strip near Port Moresby.

After a few hours of rest, we departed Townsville around midnight. Port Moresby weather was forecast to be low overcast with about three miles visibility on arrival. We flew in the overcast most of the way, popping up through the clouds occasionally to give Mac a chance to take a few shots with his bubble octant. I didn't have to encourage him to be especially careful in plotting our course and estimated time en route. The coastline at our check point would be virtually perpendicular, with the Owen Stanley range rising straight out of the sea.

When Colin signaled to start our descent, the cockpit grew remarkably quiet. At 1,000 feet we were still in solid clouds, though we could tell dawn was breaking. We hit 700, then 600 feet—still no bottom. At 500 feet we broke out enough to see the waves below us, though our forward visibility was still limited. At least we were over water. About three minutes afterwards, we picked up the shoreline, and Colin pointed over my shoulder, "There's your recognition point, dead ahead." It was, indeed. If a cannon had been mounted on the nose of our plane at the moment we first sighted the village, we could have fired a shell straight down its main drag.

We circled the village, turned to intercept a breakwater about four minutes down the coast, and then headed up the valley to our landing strip as a convoy of Bell P-39s circled overhead. While our cargo was being unloaded, the United plane flew over, high, obviously searching for the field. It landed at the wrong airstrip, and by the time Benny and his crew had corrected their mistake, we had barely enough time to exchange insults before taking off for home.

I didn't realize how close we had come to getting into the war until we reached Hawaii and learned that Japanese planes had bombed the airstrip a few hours after we departed, destroying a

number of aircraft. Fortunately, Benny and his crew got out in time.

Braznell and his exhausted four-man crew, Captain Harold Matheny, Navigator Colin McIntosh, Radio Operator J. I. Osborne, and Flight Engineer Frank Zion, touched down at Hamilton Field on July 1, having completed the 22,000-mile round-trip in ten days and just under ninety hours of flying time. They were the first airmen to cross the Pacific in a C-54—or not, depending upon which version of the tale you prefer. In any event, theirs was the sort of achievement that modern airline managements and pilot unions, with their strict rules governing maximum flying hours and minimum crew rest, would probably choose to forget.

Final Tally

By V-J Day, 1945, America's military and civilian air carriers were operating on a scale that would have been unimaginable four years earlier. Consider:

In 1941 the nation's combined domestic airline fleet amounted to just 359 transports. Total U.S. transport aircraft—domestic and international, civilian and military—numbered only a little more than 600 ships. By contrast, at the war's end ATC alone operated more than 3,000 planes, roughly a third of which were four-engine aircraft capable of lifting two to three times the payloads carried by prewar DC-3s.

At its peak ATC was, by almost any measure—number of personnel, number and size of aircraft, total payload capacity, passengers miles and ton miles flown—at least ten times bigger than the nation's entire prewar domestic airline industry.

During World War II, U.S. aircraft manufacturers built approximately 10,000 Douglas C-47s, 3,300

Curtiss C-46s, 400 Consolidated C-87s, and 1,000 Douglas C-54s—14,000 transports in total, or more than twenty times the number of civilian and military transports the United States possessed at the beginning of the war.

During the peak months of May, June, and July 1944, ATC and NATS averaged twenty-six scheduled C-54 flights a day across the Atlantic and thirty-eight trips daily across the Pacific. All by itself, American Airlines flew an average of ten transatlantic flights a day during that period. Indeed, for a time it looked as though American would emerge from the war as the United States' second largest international carrier, ready to give Pan Am and another budding transoceanic competitor, TWA, a run for their money. Ah, but that's another story.

When the Boys Came Flying Home Again

In June 1945 ATC's Deputy Commander, Major General Cyrus R. Smith, resigned his Air Force commission and returned to his first love, American Airlines. If *Mister* C. R. felt it a come-down to be rejoining a measly hundred-ship airline, he never let on. But certainly his wartime experience had to affect his notions of scale—had to enlarge his vision of the postwar airline industry and American's role in it. And, who knows? Maybe the downshift was just what American's boss needed to get his entrepreneurial motor revving again.

No sooner had Smith returned from Washington than the company's board of directors presented interim wartime president Alexander Kemp with a handsome plaque commemorating his services to the company and showed him to the door. Smith was invested with the new title of chairman and chief executive. And the title of

president was awarded to the man who had actually served in that capacity for the preceding year and a half, General Manager Ralph Damon.

In January 1946 Walt Braznell's long-time boss, Hugh Smith, retired as vice president of operations and was replaced by a C. R. Smith appointee, Brigadier General Larry Fritz. Fritz, a veteran TWA pilot and operations officer, served under C. R. Smith during the war as commanding officer of ATC's North Atlantic Division. Among other high-ranking Air Force veterans returning to American about this time were Colonel Tommy Boyd, Fritz's wartime chief of operations and former AA chief pilot–New York; Colonel Harry Clark (ATC, India-China wing); Colonel Bill Hooten; and Colonel—later Brigadier General— Jack Gibson, the much-decorated leader of the 8th Air Force's 44th Bomb Group. These veterans, together with a half dozen men who, like Braznell, remained at their posts with American throughout the war, formed the nucleus of the administrative team that would guide the flight operations of the nation's "leading airline" for the next twenty years.[16]

In all, more than fifteen hundred AA men and women served in the armed forces during World War II, and an additional thousand civilian crew members, mechanics, and supervisors saw extended duty with the Air Transport Command. Eighty-seven died in the service of their country or were missing in action at war's end, including eighteen who were killed while flying ATC missions.

---

16. American had to relinquish its boast of being "America's largest airline" when United acquired Capital Airlines in 1960. However, American continued to call itself "America's *Leading* Airline"—a meaningless claim, perhaps, but one no self-respecting AA flight crew member ever doubted for a minute.

Nine years after the war ended, in a speech to the Newcomen Society, C. R. Smith summarized the positive aspects of the airlines' World War II experience:

> Under the emergencies of war, the air industry acquired decades of experience in a matter of a few years. Flights of very long distances became commonplace. The operators learned how to carry heavy cargo. There were navigation aids that five years before would have seemed improbable—radar and Ground Controlled Approach. A whole generation of people was brought to a realization of what the plane meant, and what it could do.

It was a pretty good wrap-up, as far as it went. But oddly enough, Smith appears to have overlooked what was easily the most important aeronautical legacy of World War II—jet propulsion.

By the late 1930s, both Germany and Great Britain were working on prototype turbojet engines. The first operational turbojet fighter, Germany's ME 262, was test flown in 1942, but due to wartime production priorities, it did not go into full production until late 1944, and fewer than a thousand were delivered to the Luftwaffe before war's end. A British jet fighter, the Gloster Meteor, also saw limited action in the last few months before V-E Day.

We are often reminded that the pace of technological change is "ever accelerating," yet in this case, sixteen years elapsed from the initial test flight of the ME 262 to the introduction of the first American-built jet transports in 1958. That's roughly the same span of years dividing the Wright Brother's first successful experiments at Kitty Hawk from the commencement of regular transcontinental air mail service in 1921.

In our next chapter, we will explore the reasons for this remarkable postwar jet lag.

Postscript

Some splendid stories have been omitted from this brief account of the airlines' war years, mainly because those old favorites have been so often told, and so well, that there was little we could add to the existing body of literature. A case in point is the saga of American Airlines Captain Chuck O'Connor's crash landing on a frozen lake in the wilderness of northern Quebec and the eventual rescue of O'Connor, his crew, and his aircraft by his ATC comrades. Novelist Ernie Gann, who participated in the rescue mission, dined out on the tale for years, describing it in two popular nonfiction books, one novel, and one Hollywood screenplay.[17] The story has since been retold in several other books, notably James Mangan's *To the Four Winds*, Robert Serling's *When the Airlines Went to War*, and *Eagle: The Story of American Airlines*, also by Serling. We found these books both fascinating reading and indispensable material for research on the war era, and we recommend them to all true lovers of pilot yarns.

---

17. The novel and screenplay was *Island in the Sky*, the nonfiction books were *Fate is the Hunter* and the autobiographical *A Hostage to Fortune*.

Wartime Photo Album

The Uniform He Wore

Walt Braznell in his ATC dress uniform—the uniform airline pilots were supposed to wear when on official Air Transport Command business. Except for the insignia, ATC officers' uniforms were the same as the traditional olive tunic and pinkish tan pants ("pinks") worn by commissioned Army Air Force officers. Notice the ATC command wings (denoting a senior pilot) and lack of rank insignia on the shoulder. Following airline custom, flight officers were distinguished by the number of braided stripes on their sleeves—three for captains, two for first officers, one for navigators. Civilian ATC pilots seldom wore their dress uniforms. I never saw Walt in his, except in this portrait.

LaGuardia Airport

In late 1939 American moved its headquarters and headquarters staff—some eight hundred employees and their families—from Chicago Municipal Airport to the new New York Municipal Airport on Flushing Bay, Long Island. Soon after it opened, in October 1939, the airport was rechristened *LaGuardia*, after Fiorello LaGuardia, the tempestuous New York mayor who conceived the project and almost single-handedly brought it to fruition. American Airlines, an ardent supporter of the project from beginning to end, became the airport's prime tenant, leasing three of its six huge hangars—"each as large as Madison Square Garden!" according to one of the company's promotional brochures. For years these buildings served not only as aircraft hangars but also as the company's corporate headquarters and East Coast operations and maintenance center. After the war, American's top management moved to swank offices in midtown Manhattan. By the dawn of the Jet Age, LaGuardia Airport had been eclipsed by the new Idlewild (later Kennedy) International Airport. But American's Flight, Engineering, and Maintenance Departments continued to occupy those cavernous red-brick hangars until the late 1960s. To Walt Braznell, the last occupant of C. R. Smith's old office in Hangar 3, LaGuardia was a home away from home for twenty-six years. *Photo courtesy of American Airlines C. R. Smith Museum*

North Atlantic Run

October 1942—On a stopover at Presque Isle, Maine, en route to Prestwick, Scotland, Braznell (in Air Force–issue flight jacket, center) chins with Chicago Chief Pilot Fred Bailey (right) and an unidentified crew member. It was Walt's first transatlantic ATC mission and his first flight in one of the Air Force's new C-87 transports.

Pathfinder

Colin McIntosh at his plotting board somewhere over the North Atlantic. McIntosh, American's chief navigator, set up schools that turned hundreds of raw recruits into Air Transport Command navigators, both military and civilian. None of his boys ever lost a plane due to navigational error.

War Hero

Braznell and associate Walt Hughen welcome a returning war hero, 8th Air Force Group Commander Jack Gibson (October 1944). Gibson would soon return to American as Walt's right-hand man in the Flight Department. The two would work side by side for the next twenty-three years. Gibson is recognized as the father of American Airlines' Flight Academy, a project conceived in 1964 and initiated in 1969, the year after Walt retired.

Into the Jet Age

Today the guns are silent. A great tragedy has ended. A great victory
has been won . . . A new era is upon us.

—General Douglas MacArthur, Tokyo, September 2, 1945

lick forward to 1947. America is briefly and uneasily at peace. Twenty-four months have passed since Japan's surrender aboard the battleship *Missouri* officially ended World War II. The first major confrontations of the Cold War—the Soviet blockade of Berlin, the Berlin Airlift, the Korean War—are still to come, but the dimensions and portent of the conflict that will engage the world's superpowers for the next forty years are visible even now, in the ashes of Hiroshima and the lengthening shadow of the Iron Curtain.

At home, five million former servicemen and women are flocking to college campuses, buying their first houses, or starting new businesses with GI loans and grants provided by a grateful nation. Production of consumer goods and office, factory, and farm equipment is in full swing once more. Customers flush with wartime savings are emptying salesrooms of new automobiles, television sets, and all manner of home appliances.

A surge in business and personal travel, now that wartime restrictions have been lifted, is feeding an aviation boom reminiscent of the Lindbergh era, though on a vastly larger scale. Domestic scheduled airlines have carried close to twelve million passengers in the past year—still a drop in the bucket compared with the railroad's intercity passenger traffic, but more than three times the prewar record of 3.6 million airline passengers set in 1941.

The nation's obsolete airways and airports are swamped with traffic. Terminals, most of them built in the 1930s to Depression-era standards, are a disgrace—littered, chaotic, bulging with waiting passengers who have nowhere to wait. Traffic control system bottlenecks at busy destinations such as Chicago Midway, Newark, and La-Guardia keep arriving planes stacked in holding patterns for hours. Late departures, overbooked flights, no shows, and standby lines are becoming endemic—part of the routine of air travel in the postwar era.

Since 1944, when the War Department lifted its embargo on the manufacture and sale of commercial aircraft, the major airlines have been in a race to augment their aging fleets of twin-engine

DC-3s with converted war-surplus C-54s and, to a much larger extent, with orders for the new generation of fast, high-altitude airliners being built by Lockheed, Douglas, Consolidated-Vultee, Martin, and Boeing. In the early months of 1946 TWA's Howard Hughes had stolen a march on the rest of the industry by inaugurating transcontinental service aboard his secret weapon, Lockheed's sleek 280-miles-per-hour, sixty-passenger Constellation. Now United and American are about to introduce their entry in the postwar transcontinental sweepstakes, a stretched, pressurized, souped-up version of Douglas's DC-4 called the DC-6.

Aside from figuring out how to pay for all these new aircraft, the biggest problems facing the major airlines revolve around a simple but unfamiliar concept, one scarcely ever mentioned in the snugly insulated, federally subsidized airline industry of the 1930s: Competition!

Competition!

With the rapid growth in domestic air travel during and immediately after World War II, U.S. government policy respecting the airlines underwent a sea change. Beginning around 1943, the original 1930s model of an industry dominated by three or four strong domestic trunk lines, of protected markets and exclusive route franchises, was progressively replaced by one aimed at promoting the maximum level of passenger service a market could support. Between 1943 and 1947 the Civil Aeronautics Board (CAB) leveled the playing field for the major transcontinental carriers—United, TWA, and American—by allowing all three lines direct access to the five leading coast-to-coast destinations: Los Angeles, San Francisco, New York, Washington, and Boston. Northwest Airlines became the fourth transcontinental operator in 1945, when the CAB extended its Great Lakes–Pacific Northwest system eastward from Milwaukee to New York. By the mid-1950s further CAB route awards would promote several other second-tier carriers—Delta, Western, Capital, Continental, Braniff, and National—into the big leagues, creating a new subset of major transcontinental, north/south, and interregional carriers.

As if the increase in competition from other scheduled carriers were not enough of a challenge, established airlines faced unrelenting and decidedly ungentlemanly competition from the hundreds of small, hungry nonscheduled passenger and air freight carriers that sprang up immediately after the war. The "nonscheds," predominantly owned and operated by veterans, took advantage of the government's postwar fire sale of surplus C-47s, C-46s, and C-54s—and the plethora of service-trained pilots—to set themselves up in business hauling passengers and cargo wherever and whenever there was a demand for low-cost air transportation. Economy was the nonscheduled airlines' unique appeal: Their aircraft may have been war-weary and poorly maintained, their pilots somewhat lacking in professional polish, their departures and arrivals unpredictable, their passenger cabins unbearably cramped, and their pre-flight and in-flight service nonexistent, but their fares were often less than half those charged by the regulated scheduled carriers, and that was enough to pack in the customers.

To the airlines' marketing moguls, these upstarts represented the worst of all possible competitive challenges: They were not only taking large bites out of the major carriers' passenger and air freight business but also undercutting the government-regulated fare and tariff structure upon which the scheduled airlines depended for survival. In fact, though the airlines would be the last to admit it, the nonscheds were doing more than that—more than the marketing moguls had ever dreamed possible: They were actually making air travel popular.

In retrospect, those cheeky charter airlines deserve much of the credit for the boom in air tourism that occurred in the late 1940s and early 1950s and, ultimately, for liberating the airline industry from its near-total dependence on the upscale business travel market. At the time, however, the growing appeal of the nonscheds was looked upon with unalloyed horror by airline officials and civil aeronautics authorities alike. Something had to be done to restore order and sanity—and profitability—to the airline industry. Attempts by the airlines' Air Transport Association to lobby the nonscheds out of existence through the passage of restrictive or burdensome legislation proved ineffective, as did the CAB's efforts to curb their activities by limiting the number of charter flights a nonsched could operate over a given route within a given period. The obvious alternative—to fight the nonscheduled airlines on their own terms—was resisted by industry leaders such as American's C. R. Smith and United's Pat Patterson until all else failed.

In November 1948 Capital Airlines broke ranks, announcing a new, supplemental coach-class service between New York and Chicago with essentially the same no-frills service and rock-bottom fares offered by its charter-line competitors. American and TWA responded almost immediately, instituting coach flights between New York and Los Angeles for $110 one way. United reluctantly joined the fray some months later.

At first the scheduled carriers went to extremes to justify the very substantial difference in coach and regular fares. Coach service was restricted to off-hours "red eye" flights aboard unpressurized DC-4s whose cabins had been configured to carry the maximum number of customers in the least possible comfort. Gradu-

ally, however, competitive pressure forced scheduled and nonscheduled lines alike to improve the quality of coach service. By 1950 American was offering daily coach flights between New York and Los Angeles aboard a stripped-down, eighty-one-passenger model of its new DC-6.

With the upgrading of equipment and service, coach travel gained a measure of respectability. Ticket sales rose sharply. A year after the upgrade, one out of eight American Airlines passengers was flying coach. Within three years the ratio was one in four. Then, in 1955, the major airlines began offering passengers a *choice* of coach or first-class seating on most intermediate and long-range domestic flights. Almost immediately coach class became the default standard for air travel.

Few of the nonscheduled airlines that developed and popularized the concept of coach service survived the established lines' massed counterattacks on their principal markets. Some subsisted on military contracts in support of the Berlin Airlift and Korean War; others found a profitable niche promoting domestic and international "affinity group" charter flights. A few eventually made it into the ranks of scheduled carriers. But by the late 1950s the domestic air travel market as a whole was once again under the firm control of the major scheduled airlines.

Two's Company, Three's a Crowd

From the late 1920s to the onset of World War II, while American, United, TWA, and Eastern battled among themselves for top ranking among the nation's domestic airlines, one U.S. carrier, Pan American Airways,[1] reigned solitary and serene over an air mail and passenger route

1. The name of the airline became Pan American World Airways in 1950.

system covering most of the rest of the world's surface. Its franchise extended from Florida to the Caribbean and Central and South America; from San Francisco to Hawaii and Manila; from New York to London; and virtually anywhere else it chose to fly outside of the continental United States. With its close ties to the State Department and its uncommonly lucrative air mail contracts,[2] Pan Am was widely considered and, indeed, considered itself, the United States' "chosen instrument" for worldwide air service—the American equivalent of British Overseas Airways, Air France, SAS, Swissair, and other state-supported monopolies.

Then came World War II, and as we have noted, Pan Am became simply one among several contract carriers supporting the armed services' global logistical mission. Immediately following the war, Pan Am attempted to restore the old order—to put Humpty Dumpty together again—by proposing a pooling concept, or cartel, in which all U.S. airlines desiring to participate in the anticipated boom in international air travel would be welcome. In addition to putting up most of the capital for this operation, members of the cartel would be expected to feed their overseas-bound business to Pan American, which would retain exclusive control over all international operations. Naturally, prospective participants were assured a fair share of the pool's profits, if any.

It was the sort of scheme that only someone with the monumental ego of a Juan Trippe could have concocted. The industry's reaction was predictable: Sixteen carriers joined in a formal protest to the CAB, calling the Pan Am plan monopolistic and demanding open competition for new overseas routes.

Competition focused on the North Atlantic routes nominally pioneered by Pan Am in 1938, but largely developed by American Airlines under contract to the ATC during the war. Projections of postwar transatlantic traffic ranged from epic to insignificant. United's top strategists predicted that as few as forty-three four-engine transports could handle all of the scheduled passenger traffic across the Atlantic for the foreseeable future. Since eight nations were planning to enter the market, fewer than six planes per nation would be needed to "do the job," by their calculations. Accordingly, United's management decided it was not interested in Europe just yet.

On the other hand, Pan Am and Transcontinental & Western Air saw glorious opportunities for transatlantic business travel and tourism and visualized themselves fighting one another for dominion over the North Atlantic air corridor.[3] At first, however, they had to settle for somewhat smaller pieces of the European pie than either had expected. In 1945 the Civil Aeronautics Board granted TWA permission to begin service between New York and Paris. Pan Am got London and Frankfort.[4] And a virtual unknown, American Export Airlines, was awarded access to "the whole of Northern Europe north of 50th parallel," including London.

By the fall of 1945, when the three lines initiated passenger service over the North Atlantic,

2. A report issued by the postmaster general's office in 1940 noted that Pan Am had received more than $47 million in mail payments over the previous ten years. This compared with $60 million in payments for all domestic air mail carriers *combined*. See R. E. G. Davies, *Airlines of the United States since 1914*.

3. Transcontinental & Western Air was renamed Trans World Airlines in 1950.

4. Naturally, access to overseas destinations was also subject to negotiation with the host nation's civil aviation authorities. These gatekeepers were, in turn, strongly influenced by the International Air Transport Association, a voluntary, self-regulating organization established in 1945 to promote fair pricing and competitive practices among its forty-one member airlines and twenty-six host countries. The organization's primary mission during the immediate postwar era was to prevent powerful U.S. carriers such as Pan Am and TWA from running rough-shod over the smaller, weaker flag carriers.

American Export Airlines was no longer inconspicuous little AEA, but rather American *Overseas* Airlines (AOA), the proud new international arm of American Airlines.

Established in 1937 as a subsidiary of American Export Lines, AEA/AOA was hardly a newcomer to the North Atlantic. In 1940 it won CAB permission to operate scheduled air mail, passenger, and freight service between New York and Lisbon. Because the Civil Aeronautics Act barred control of an airline by any other common carrier, the award was made subject to AEA's spinoff from its parent steamship company. Even after the divestiture, Pan Am challenged the CAB's $1.2 million air mail contract award in court, and when that failed, successfully lobbied its friends in the Senate Appropriations Committee to cancel the contract. AEA went ahead with its plans anyway and had already set up a base at LaGuardia and purchased a few flying boats by the time the United States entered the war. All through World War II it flew the North Atlantic for the Naval Air Transport Service. Later, in 1945, it flew C-54 runs for the Air Transport Command between New York and Casablanca.

Following the war it was only natural for the orphaned AEA to team up with a friendly rival, the North Atlantic operating division of American Airlines and its deep-pocketed parent. In an agreement approved by the Civil Aeronautics Board in June 1945 and completed between the two parties six months later, American acquired a 51 percent interest in AEA for $3 million, and various assets and personnel of American's North Atlantic division were merged into AEA to form American Overseas Airlines. By May 1946 AOA was operating regularly scheduled flights from New York, Boston, Chicago, Washington, and Philadelphia to Shannon, London, Copenhagen, Oslo, Stockholm, Amsterdam, Frankfurt, and Berlin. Its transatlantic fleet,

originally consisting of six converted Air Force C-54s (DC-4s), gradually expanded to include a melange of DC-4s, Lockheed L-049s, and Boeing 377 Stratocruisers.

Then, on December 13, 1948, in a move that surprised even their own boards of directors, American's C. R. Smith and Pan Am's Juan Trippe announced that American had agreed to sell AOA to Pan American for $17.5 million. Pan Am's application to acquire AOA was rejected by the CAB in May 1950, but four months later President Truman overrode the board and approved the combination.

Of the eight-hundred-odd AOA employees declared surplus following the merger, only a handful actually lost their jobs. But for veteran American administrators, pilots, mechanics, and staff personnel who had transferred to AOA following the war, the Pan Am deal was a bitter and bewildering disappointment. Despite Pan Am's promise to recognize their prior service and seniority, many old American Airlines hands felt they had been sold down the river.

Why did Smith sell AOA? Certainly no one disputes the fact that competition for transatlantic traffic was fierce; that AOA, like most other carriers, was having trouble filling seats; and that it was leaking copious quantities of red ink. But anyone who knew the airline business as well as C. R. Smith would have expected nothing less—or more—in the first few years of such a pioneering venture. In all likelihood, it wasn't *just* the red ink that led Smith to his decision, but also the cash drain associated with equipping this upstart subsidiary to compete head-on with heavyweights such as TWA and Pan Am. There was even speculation that Smith sold AOA partly to get rid of the eight Boeing Stratocruisers it owned and operated. "Those Pratt & Whitney 'corncob' engines Boeing hung on the Stratocruiser were enough to drive any

Boeing 377 Stratocruiser

The double-bubble-shaped Stratocruiser was an adaptation of the C-97 and the KC-97 aerial tanker that Boeing began building for the Air Force late in World War II. It was fully pressurized, carried anywhere from 55 to 117 passengers, depending upon the cabin configuration, and featured a cocktail lounge on its lower deck— very popular with the pre–jet set. With its four huge Pratt & Whitney R-4360 Wasp Major engines, the biggest and most powerful piston-driven aircraft engines ever built, the Stratocruiser was competitive with the Lockheed Constellation and DC-6 in range (over 4,000 miles), load-carrying capacity (62,300 pounds), and cruising speed (280–300 miles per hour, purportedly). Persistent problems with those gas-guzzling Wasp Major engines made it hideously expensive to operate, however. Only fifty-five were built, more than half of them for Pan Am. Many 377s ended their brief airline careers as cargo ships. *Photo courtesy of American Airlines*

airline into bankruptcy and any sane mechanic to drink," said one observer.[5]

Others, however, claim that economics had little to do with the decision. They view the AOA sale as the culminating act in a clash of wills between C. R. Smith—who was on military leave when AEA was acquired and never felt particularly keen about the deal—and American's president, Ralph Damon, who championed the acquisition and served as a director of AOA from 1945 onward. The fact that Damon left American for TWA five weeks after Smith's surprise announcement gives credence to that argument.

Whatever Smith's motives for selling, Trippe's reason for buying AOA was perfectly clear: In his view, one U.S.–based World Airway was ideal; two were company; three were a crowd.

American's Postwar Pilot Factory

The airline industry suffered no shortage of pilots during the early postwar period. There were thousands of returning war veterans eager to resume their prewar jobs on the line or in flight administration. There were seasoned airline captains and first officers who had spent most of the war on extended duty with the Air Transport Command. There were, in addition, large numbers of pilots who had been hired during the war to fill in for employees on military leave of absence. And lastly, there were great, seething masses of young service-trained pilots waiting in line for a crack at flying for the airlines.

At American Airlines, Walt Braznell and his staff had the unenviable job of unraveling the knotty problems of postwar integration and making the reassignment of war veterans and displaced nonveterans as painless as possible. The task was complicated by the industry's tradition

of permitting captains and first officers to bid for route assignments strictly on the basis of their seniority, or years of service, without regard for relative experience or ability.[6] Thus, an American pilot who had been flying as a DC-3 captain out of Dallas throughout the war might be "bumped" by any returning veteran possessing a higher seniority number. The bumpee would then have the choice of accepting a demotion to first officer or bidding for a captain's slot at another, less desirable station. In either case, one bump led to another, and another, and another, all the way down the ladder to the most junior copilot—who, having no one to bump, would be laid off or furloughed until the next job opening occurred. The combination of a rigid seniority system and the unprecedented turnover and realignment of flight personnel following demobilization created an atmosphere of friction and resentment within American's traditionally "big happy family" that only time and patience would erase.

A related and equally urgent problem—transition training—occupied the attention of American's thirty-seven-year-old director of flight in the months immediately preceding and following the end of the war. Before the war, most of American's pilot training had been performed by the airline's regional chief pilots and their staffs at the airline's four main operating centers—New York, Chicago, Los Angeles, and Dallas. Walt

5. The "corncob" engine got its name from its bristling array of cylinders—twenty-eight of them, stacked four-deep around the engine's "cob" or drive shaft.

6. Seniority alone was not enough to qualify for a route assignment. A pilot had to be "checked out" or certified by both an American check pilot and a CAA examiner in the type or types of aircraft flown on that particular route. After qualifying in the aircraft and successfully bidding for the route, he also had to pass a route check demonstrating his knowledge of terrain, weather conditions, landing facilities, emergency fields, and navigation aids along his assigned route.

Braznell's experience in operating military contract schools during the war convinced him that this decentralized and somewhat haphazard approach would be totally inadequate to the company's anticipated postwar training needs. By 1946, he estimated, more than a thousand pilots would be in American Airlines uniform. Between 1946 and 1948, each of them would require training and certification in one or more of the new generation of twin-engine Convair 240s and four-engine DC-4s and DC-6s that were scheduled to replace American's DC-3s. In addition, hundreds of first officers would be ready for upgrading to captain, and hundreds of new hires would have to be trained to fill the seats those new captains vacated.

In 1945 Braznell approached General Manager Ralph Damon with a plan and an urgent request for funds to establish a centralized flight crew training center in Fort Worth, Texas.[7] Damon agreed in principle, but chose a different site for the center, an abandoned Air Force base and Army hospital in Ardmore, Oklahoma. Ardmore, with its in-place housing for more than two hundred trainees and staff, its large hangars, its four 7,000-foot runways, and its excellent year-round flying weather, was an inspired choice for a flight school. Furthermore, the rent was dirt cheap.

American reopened the base in June 1946 and began operations almost immediately under the administration of Captain William Arthur and his flight training director, Captain Donald K. Smith. Eventually the Ardmore complex grew to

include training facilities for stewardesses, flight engineers, mechanics, even passenger and cargo agents. At its peak it employed a staff of 187 and graduated about 135 students per month. During its three years of operation, nearly 1,000 mechanics and flight engineers, 500 flight attendants, 2,000 American DC-4, DC-6, and Convair 240 captains and first officers, and scores of other pilots trained under contracts with foreign carriers such as SAS and Royal Dutch Airlines passed through Ardmore. It was, in its time, "the largest flight and ground school ever established by a commercial airline," according to American's *Flagship News*.

Ardmore was also the first airline flight crew training center to employ exact mock-ups of aircraft cockpits "with instruments and controls rigged to respond just as they do in the real aircraft." These mock-ups—crude prototypes of our modern, fully computerized flight simulators—made it possible to practice normal and emergency flight procedures in absolute safety and without tying up costly airplane time.

So urgent was the need for qualified captains and first officers, and so shorthanded and overworked were the CAA's flight examiners, that Donald Smith and a few of his senior staff members were deputized as CAA airline transport examiners, with authority to certify pilots on their own, without the usual CAA check ride. Any pilot who thought this arrangement would make it easier to pass his qualification exam was in for a surprise, however. Recognizing that part of their job was to weed out the few marginal or substandard pilots who had managed to slip through during the war years, Ardmore's instructors and deputy examiners could be tough as nails—particularly on pilots who had doped off in ground school and failed to memorize the operating systems and emergency procedures every qualified captain and first officer was expected to know

7. "Knowing that the lack of better facilities for flight training was costing money and making it difficult to do a thorough job, and that training volume would increase in the postwar transition period, Director of Flight Walt Braznell early in 1945 obtained approval from top management to investigate the establishment of a training center for pilots." American Airlines *Flagship News*, March 1949.

They Wrote the Book

This photo, taken in Fort Worth around 1948, includes a number of supervisors and regional chief pilots who played prominent roles in directing American's flight operations through the 1940s, '50s, and '60s. Standing, left to right: Dave Little, Al DeWitt, Si Bittner, Sam Nuckles, "Pop" McFail, Tom Copeland, Fran Bledsoe, Roy Pickering. Around the table: Joe Anderson, Harry Clark, Fred Bailey, Al Schlanser, Bill Dunne, Walt Braznell, Don Ogden, Dick Fagin, Ted Melden, and Jack Gibson.

Old-timers speak sentimentally about the close-knit American Airlines family of that era. The legend is not exaggerated. Fifty years after this photo was taken, the writer (who was a teenager at the time) could not only identify most of the men in the group but also remember the names of their wives and children.

by heart. Even a few of the company's top line pilots and supervisors suffered the ignominy of flunking a check ride with one of Ardmore's no-nonsense examiners.

By 1949 Ardmore had served its purpose: The postwar surge in pilot employment, training, and upgrading had subsided, and the number of new pilots being added to the company's roster no longer justified the cost of maintaining the huge training facility with its full-time staff of instructors and support personnel. Accordingly, the base was closed in March 1949, and primary responsibility for pilot training was handed back to the regional chief pilots, under the general direction and guidance of the company's New York–based Flight Department. While the idea of a centralized crew training facility was set aside for the time being, it wasn't forgotten. It would reemerge in 1970 with the establishment of one of the airline industry's premier pilot schools, the American Airlines Flight Academy at Dallas–Fort Worth International Airport.

An Earthward-Bound Projectile

Seven months after V-J Day, in March 1946, TWA led the airline industry into the postwar era with the introduction of eleven-hour, one-stop transcontinental service aboard its new pressurized Lockheed Constellation. With the introduction of the 280-miles-per-hour, sixty-passenger Connies, American's low and slow-flying DC-3s and -4s were doomed, and the company was forced to mark time until its first DC-6s went on the line a year later.

Although similar in appearance to the DC-4, the Douglas DC-6 represented a considerable advance in power, air speed, cruising altitude, and payload, and was competitive with the new

Connies in all respects. Both were fully pressurized and powered by supercharged engines that permitted them to operate comfortably at altitudes of 19,000 to 21,000 feet, twice the normal cruising altitudes of the older aircraft.

Captain Braznell remembers his first impressions of American's new flagship:

The DC-6 may have looked like a stretched DC-4, but the two aircraft were worlds apart in performance. From a pilot's perspective, the transition from the older aircraft to the DC-6s and the comparably equipped twin-engined Convair 240s was even more difficult than our later transition from piston-driven aircraft to jets.

The big difference was in the new aircraft's rate and speed of descent. Pilots at that time were used to climbing and letting down at a leisurely 500 feet per minute—not because the DC-3s and -4s couldn't change altitude any faster, but because quicker changes in an unpressurized environment were hard on the ears. Now, suddenly, we were making high-speed descents at 1,000 to 1,500 vertical feet per minute without perceptible change in cabin pressure.

On my first flight in command of a DC-6—we had flown to Douglas's plant in Santa Monica to pick up our first plane, and were en route to Mexico City to test the aircraft's high-altitude takeoff performance—the sensation of making a night letdown into El Paso from 20,000 feet was like flying an earthward-bound projectile. Later, when the jets came along, we would have Q-bells to warn us when we were approaching maximum air speed and altimeter "bugs" set to go off as we reached assigned altitudes. But the DC-6 had neither bells, whistles, nor warning lights—not even the familiar pressure on the inner ear to help a pilot gauge his rate of descent. I found myself concentrating harder on instrument descents in the DC-6 than ever before or since, and I know that other veterans of the DC-3 era had similar problems adjusting.

Lockheed Constellation

The Constellation, an aircraft of rare beauty and technical sophistication, even by modern standards, was conceived in the late 1930s by TWA's Howard Hughes and Lockheed's genius designer, Kelly Johnson. Hughes envisioned the Connie as the secret weapon with which TWA would surpass American and United as the leading transcontinental air carrier of the 1940s. Had World War II not intervened his plan might well have succeeded. As it happened, the first production model of the Connie wasn't delivered until April 1944, and the recipient was not TWA, but rather the U.S. Army Air Force. At war's end, Lockheed began production of a commercial version of the plane, the L-049, which was built with parts from war surplus C-69s (as the military Connies were designated) and outfitted with only forty-eight seats. This was quickly followed by the all-new L-649 model, with seating for sixty-four passengers, and subsequently by a succession of bigger, faster models, culminating in the mid-1950s with the introduction of the long-range, 350-miles-per-hour L-1049 Super Constellation series and the ultra-long-range transatlantic L-1649 Starliner.

TWA inaugurated one-stop transatlantic Constellation service between New York and Paris in February 1946. Transcontinental service between Los Angeles and New York via Kansas City or Chicago began the following month. Even then, four years after its intended introduction, TWA's new flagship totally outclassed the best that American and United were able to put up against it. Unhappily for TWA, its Constellations were grounded in July 1946 following a series of nonfatal accidents involving the failure of their cabin pressurization systems. By September, when they returned to service, American and United had received the first of their new DC-6s, and the decade-long race for transcontinental air supremacy was underway between TWA, with its Connies, and American and United, with their Douglas aircraft.

Douglas DC-6

Though obviously patterned after the DC-4, the Douglas DC-6 boasted improvements that made it far superior to the '4s and fully competitive with Lockheed's Constellations. Like the Connies, its fully pressurized body and increased service ceiling afforded passengers a new level of above-the-clouds comfort and safety. Its Pratt & Whitney R-2800 engines gave it an advertised cruising speed of 280 miles per hour, nearly 80 miles per hour faster than the DC-4. And its somewhat longer fuselage provided seating for fifty-two passengers—up to eighty-six in coach configuration—as opposed to the DC-4's forty-four-passenger seating capacity. After an extended break-in period, American and United introduced DC-6 service simultaneously in April 1947—American on its New York–Chicago run; United between San Francisco and New York. By the following month both were offering coast-to-coast one-stop service. American ordered fifty DC-6s initially, and subsequently purchased twenty-five stretch models, the DC-6B.

Three incidents, discussed in the accompanying texts, led to the grounding of American's DC-6s soon after the aircraft entered service. But from that point on, until the last of the fleet was retired from service in 1966, the "Sixes" built a record for durability, reliability, and efficiency unmatched by any other piston-driven aircraft in the company's history, including their fabulous forebear, the DC-3. *Photo courtesy of American Airlines*

Convair 240

Consolidated Vultee Aircraft Corporation (later, the Convair Division of General Motors) was one of several aircraft manufacturers American Airlines looked to as a possible source for the planes that would replace its DC-3s on secondary, short-haul routes. Martin, Douglas, Boeing, Lockheed, Republic, and Curtiss-Wright submitted proposals, but Convair won the bidding with its design for the CV 110, a thirty-passenger, fully pressurized aircraft powered by two Pratt & Whitney R-2800 engines—the same power plants used in the DC-6. However, American was not satisfied with the specifications for the prototype CV 110. It wanted a wider body that would accommodate four-abreast seating, forty seats rather than thirty, and—a new wrinkle—a self-contained passenger ramp or staircase that would fold up into the cabin after the passengers were aboard. American got all that and more in December 1946, when it signed an $18 million contract for one hundred CV 240s (the revised model's new designation). With its agile short-field takeoff and landing capability, cruising speed of 240 miles per hour, and comfortable air-conditioned passenger cabin, the CV 240 was a hit with passengers and crew members from the day it was introduced in June 1948 until the last 240 was retired in June 1964. American was the the original sponsor of the CV 240. Other major carriers followed—Continental and Western in 1948, then Pan Am, and finally United in 1951. *Photo courtesy of American Airlines*

Another challenge was learning to cope with the previously unknown hazards of high-altitude flight—or what we then considered high altitude. One such phenomenon was summer thunderstorms, which could be particularly murderous at altitudes of 10,000 to 20,000 feet. Another was the narrow band of 100-plus miles per hour westerly winds called the jet stream. Older, lower-flying planes seldom encountered the jet stream except in the dead of winter, when the current would sometimes drift south across the Canadian border and descend to as low as 10,000 to 12,000 feet. Later, meteorologists would learn how to track these high-altitude airstreams, and pilots of eastbound planes would often intercept and ride them across the country. Similarly, later aircraft could be vectored around electrical storms by ground and airborne radar. But during these transition years, a DC-6 pilot would occasionally run head-on into a jet stream or stagger blindly into a granddaddy of a thunderhead and get turned every way but loose.

Anatomy of a Thunderhead

The typical summer thunderstorm has been likened to a slow-motion explosion—an explosion of hot, moist air pushed aloft by powerful thermal updrafts. As this saturated, super-heated column of air rises through the colder surrounding atmosphere, it condenses into visible moisture. In doing so, it undergoes a thermal exchange similar to the cooling effect of evaporation, but in reverse. (Just as evaporation absorbs heat energy, condensation releases it.) The faster the column rises, and the more moisture it carries aloft, the warmer it grows relative to the surrounding atmosphere. And the warmer it gets, the higher it climbs. In a granddaddy thunderstorm, this chain reaction may continue right up to the tropopause, the absolute ceiling for cloud formations, which ranges up to 40,000 feet in the temperate zone and over 65,000 feet in the tropics. The heat energy generated by a rising column of water vapor as it condenses into rain, snow, and hail may exceed 100 kilowatt hours, or the equivalent of ten 20-kiloton atomic bombs.

A large thunderhead is usually made up of several individual storm cells, each in a different stage of development. As a cell matures, precipitation forms at its upper level and begins to fall through it, creating downdrafts of cool, moisture-laden air running parallel to the cell's warm updrafts. The velocity of downdrafts and updrafts in a fully developed cell tends to increase with altitude and may range from a few hundred feet per minute to more than 100 miles per hour.

The extreme turbulence or shearing action caused by the interaction of these vertical winds can put more stress on an aircraft's wings than they were designed to withstand—particularly if the plane enters an active cell at excessive speed or the wrong altitude. (In thunderstorm penetration, lower is better, and complete avoidance best). Once caught in a thunderhead an experienced pilot knows he must immediately slow his plane to a safe penetration speed and concentrate on keeping his craft flying as straight and level as possible, ignoring the wildly fluctuating readings of his altimeter and rate of climb indicator, and avoiding violent or abrupt maneuvers that would put added stress on the plane's wings.

Lightning (and/or the discharge of static electricity from aircraft to cloud) has been known to cause damage to planes caught in thunderheads—half dollar–sized holes, popped rivets, and burnt-out radios and electrical wiring, for example. But for the most part, lightning's bang is worse than its bite. Far more serious, from an airman's standpoint, are the hailstones that can pulverize a plane's nose, windshield, wings, and tail section in a matter of seconds. One needn't be flying within a thunderstorm to witness the effect of golf-ball-sized hailstones impacting an aircraft at several hundred miles per hour: Mature thunderheads have been known to spew hail several miles to the leeward of their anvil-shaped tops.

Arguably the most dangerous aspects of thunderstorms are the buffeting surface winds, downdrafts, and sudden, violent shifts in wind direction (wind shear) that typically precede an advancing storm. Accidents caused by these treacherous low-level winds during final approaches and landings have probably claimed more lives than all other thunderstorm-related aircraft accidents combined.

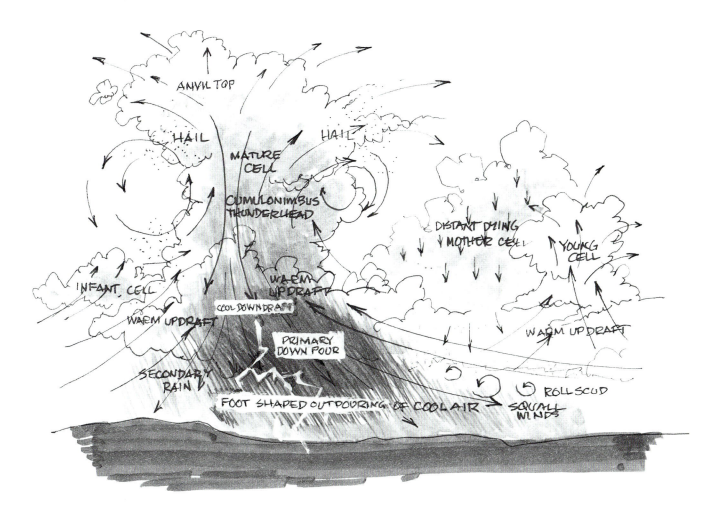

Disaster and Near Disaster

In October 1947, barely six months after the DC-6 went into service, a United Airlines plane en route from Los Angeles to Denver caught fire and shed a wing while making an approach to an emergency landing field near Bryce Canyon. All fifty-two passengers and crew members died in the crash. The Civil Aeronautics Board, Douglas, and United were in the midst of investigating this tragedy when an American Airlines DC-6 caught fire west of Gallup, New Mexico. Fortunately, the American pilots, Captain Evan Chatfield and First Officer V. B. Brown, were able to make an emergency landing before the plane disintegrated. No one was injured. All DC-6s were immediately grounded pending determination of the cause or causes of the two incidents.

Braznell:

> I flew to Gallup to participate in the investigation of the American accident. As soon as the Douglas crew was able to make emergency repairs and add some angle-iron supports, (Captain) Don

V1, VLOF, and V2

V1 is the speed at which an aircraft is committed to takeoff, even if an engine fails at or beyond that point. VR stands for "rotation velocity"—the speed at which the nose wheel is supposed to come unstuck. VLOF is lift-off speed. V2 is the optimum speed to be maintained during climb out after failure of one or more engines. Each of these critical velocities is computed before each flight. Variables include aircraft gross weight, temperature, altitude, wind speed, and runway length and gradient.

Ogden and I were given a waiver to fly the ship to the Douglas plant in Santa Monica for further inspection, investigation, and repair. We anticipated that getting the plane out of Gallup's snowbound airstrip might pose a few problems, and it did. In the first place, the engines had been cold soaking for some time, and we had trouble getting them started and running properly. Then there was the altitude of the airfield, and the snow, and the fact that the Douglas engineers had deactivated the flaps and wired them in the fully retracted position. I calculated our takeoff roll under these conditions and paced off the estimated distance to our estimated V1 "go–no-go" and VLOF (lift-off) points, sticking a flag in the snow at each spot. Someone from the CAB set up his camera to film the take-off—just in case we figured wrong or the angle irons didn't hold—and off we went. Our damaged plane lifted off right at the VLOF marker. We flew on to Santa Monica and made a no-flap approach and landing without incident.

At this point, I should introduce Glenn Brink, one of American's top test pilots and aeronautical engineers of that period and, for my money, one of Benny Howard's few peers as an aircraft handler. While Don Ogden and I had been trying to decide how to get our plane out of Gallup, Glenn had been busy investigating and analyzing every possible cause for the fires that had gutted the two DC-6s. When he thought he knew the answer, he ordered a test plane's tanks filled with red-dyed fuel and painted the entire belly of the ship with a chalky substance resembling Milk of Magnesia. As a precaution, he shut off the suspect gas combustion heaters used to de-ice the DC-6's wings and heat its cabin and flight deck. During the test flight, Glenn transferred fuel from one wing-tank to another, deliberately overfilling the receiving tank. When he landed, the solution to the mystery was clear for all to see. Overlaying the milky undercoating was a bright red streak of fuel streaming back from the tank overflow vent into the air scoop for the gas combustion heaters. It was the perfect set-up for an uncontrollable midair fire.

No sooner had the necessary modifications in the aircraft's overflow venting system been made and the DC-6s put back in service than one of American's ships became involved in a spectacular midair incident. The plane, piloted by Captain Bob Baker, was flying at 20,000 feet when the tip of a propeller blade on one of the inboard engines flew off and sliced through the plane's fuselage, severing several flight control cables and hydraulic lines and causing sudden, explosive decompression of the pressurized cabin and flight deck. Captain Baker safely executed a high-speed emergency descent and landed the crippled plane without further incident. His outstanding feat of airmanship earned him an American Airlines Distinguished Service Citation. Subsequently, the company replaced all the original steel-bladed props on its DC-6s and Convair 240s with Hamilton Standard aluminum propellers. Once these early problems were resolved, the DC-6s and the companion Convair 240s (same engines and propellers) proved to be remarkably reliable aircraft. Both continued to give good service until well after the advent of the Jet Age.

"V2—for God's Sake!"

Around 1950 the airlines began operating under new federal aviation regulations that required a preflight computation of the maximum gross weight at which the aircraft could lose an engine at V1, "the point of no return," accelerate to safe climb-out speed (V2) and clear all obstacles by at least 50 feet. The calculations were routinely performed by the captain or first officer, using Engineering Department tables that incorporated variables such as runway length,

effective headwind, runway temperature, and altitude. Pilots tended to distrust these tables—occasionally with good reason.

Braznell:

Around midnight one summer evening, soon after we had installed the new Hamilton Standard props on our DC-6s, I got a call from La Guardia Dispatch reporting that the captain of our transcontinental flight was refusing a maximum gross weight takeoff on the airport's short Runway 22. I told our dispatcher to reduce the takeoff load to whatever the captain considered reasonable and to send out a message cancelling, until further notice, an order increasing gross weight limits that had been issued by the Engineering Department a few days earlier.

The next morning I asked Engineering to set up a test flight for a maximum gross weight takeoff from La Guardia, using its new calculations. Glenn Brink would act as captain, with me in the right seat—and I specifically requested that the engineer responsible for approving the new takeoff criteria occupy the cockpit jump seat as an observer.

Shortly after noon we taxied out to Runway 22. As usual, our takeoff performance had been precalculated, based on air temperature, wind direction, and the new gross weight formula. For this test we had also posted signs at estimated V1 and VLOF points on the runway, as Don Ogden and I had done in Gallup. At our computed V1 air speed I was to cut an outboard engine, and we would see what happened after that.

Glenn started his takeoff roll. The outside air temperature was warm—over 80 degrees—and the plane's initial acceleration was sluggish. We were well past the V1 stake when, eyes glued to the air speed indicator, I called out V1 speed and retarded the throttle on our number one engine to idle. From that point, our grossed-out ship refused to accelerate any further. I kept calling "V1 . . . V1 . . . V1" as the end of the runway rushed up to meet us. Beyond lay a short stretch of grass, a fence, and the Grand Central Parkway. At the last possible moment, Glenn rammed the outboard throttle forward. The ship came unstuck from the runway in a big ugly yaw and drifted over the Grand Central like a wind-blown balloon. Somewhere between unstick point and our passage over the freeway, still with my head down and eyes fixed on the air speed, I called "V2, for God's Sake!" If you think I was white-faced, you should have seen the look on the engineer riding in the jump seat when I finally had a chance to glance his way. Suffice to say, a critical error had been made in calculating the new gross weight limits for our retrofitted DC-6s. Although Douglas, which conducted the CAA certification tests, was mainly to blame, our engineers should have caught the mistake. Henceforth, I was sure, this particular engineer would be more careful in computing and checking takeoff performance data.

The captain who put his own judgment on the line the night before was commended.[8]

Stretching

Competition among the Big Three transcontinental air carriers stiffened during the late 1940s and early 1950s, as TWA introduced progressively improved and extended models of the Lockheed Constellation, and American and United countered with a longer, faster, and more luxurious version of the DC-6—the DC-6B. TWA and Lockheed once again upped the stakes in October 1953 by introducing the L-1049C or "Super Connie." This aircraft carried bigger fuel tanks and was equipped with the hot new Wright turbo-compound engines—literally the last word in reciprocating engines. With the Connie's added

speed and range, and an augmented flight crew, TWA became the first airline to inaugurate nonstop service from Los Angeles to New York—a flight of about ten hours. Due to the prevailing westerly winds in the Northern Hemisphere, westbound flights took roughly an hour longer and required a refueling stop en route.

American's response was to order an even longer and sleeker version of the DC-6—the DC-7, featuring four-bladed Hamilton Standard props and a more powerful version of the revolutionary Wright turbo-compound engine, the R-3350. With its sleek new "Sevens" American was able to offer, beginning in November 1953, the first *two-way* nonstop transcontinental service, with an advertised cross-country flight time of less than eight hours either way. Sounded great. This time, however, someone had stretched the rubber band too far.

Braznell:

By the time the Flight Department was consulted on the purchase of the DC-7, the decision had already been made, and we were brought in to be briefed on "the shape of things to come" by our engineering and financial people. At this meeting we learned that the company was committed to developing and operating a nonstop transcontinental airliner. Because civil air regulations limited domestic pilots to no more than eight hours flying time in any twenty-four-hour period, the new plane would have to be capable of flying westbound nonstop in less than eight hours. Douglas had insisted that the new DC-7 would be capable of doing so, and the American engineers assigned to bird-dog the project had assured management it could.

But there were a couple of flaws in the data Engineering presented to us. First, the average wind factor used to project westbound performance was less than half the force our Flight Department records told us to expect during winter months. The second consideration had to do with the en-

---

8. In a *Smithsonian Air & Space* article, "Stretch Six" (February/March 1993), William Walter recounted the same incident from his perspective as a young aeronautical engineer who had been invited to accompany Brink and Braznell on the test flight. Mr. Walter's version was originally titled "Aw, Come On Airplane—FLY!"

Two-Way Stretch

The DC-6B (not pictured), which American began operating on transcontinental flights in February 1951, was a stretch version of the DC-6 (six feet longer, nose to tail), with slightly more powerful R-2800 Double Wasp engines and a seating capacity of anywhere from 60 to 107 passengers. American purchased twenty-five aircraft of these planes at an average cost of about $1.2 million—quite a bargain as it turned out. With its low operating cost per seat mile, reliability, and long service life (for an aircraft of its day) the 6B proved to be more profitable to operate than any other passenger aircraft of the pre–Jet Age.

(Above) The DC-7, American's counter to TWA's Lockheed L-1049C Constellation, was about two feet longer than the 6B and initially carried a payload of 65 passengers. Powered by the same engines as the "C Connie," the brilliant but cantankerous Wright R-3350 Turbo-Compound engine, the DC-7 claimed— or rather, American claimed for it—the ability to fly nonstop from New York to Los Angeles in eight hours, cruising at 365 miles per hour. Actually, the 7s seldom made it from East to West Coast in less than nine hours.

American introduced DC-7 nonstop transcontinental service in November 1953. Within five years the 7s would be made obsolete by the arrival of the jet and turboprop transports. By 1963, when the last of them was retired from passenger service, their resale value was so low that C. R. Smith, only half in jest, offered one to a *U.S. News and World Report* editor in exchange for a subscription to the magazine.
Photo courtesy of American Airlines

Walt and Harry's Grand Adventure

Ironically, two of the DC-7's most outspoken critics, Walt Braznell and Chief Pilot–New York Harry "Red" Clark, got the honor of flying the plane's maiden transcontinental nonstop flight. This was not its first scheduled passenger flight, but rather a special media event for reporters and show business celebrities that American's PR department had dreamed up to ballyhoo the new nonstop service. A few hours after the plane took off from New York's Idlewild Airport its cabin pressurization system developed an ear-splitting howl that soon had the flight's distinguished guests climbing the walls. Braznell and Clark elected to set down in Denver to fix the problem—thus sparing their passengers' eardrums, but throwing a monkey-wrench into the PR department's big promotion. The celebratory shindig went on, as planned, and was a great hit. On the return flight, Clark and Braznell set a new coast-to-coast record of 6 hours and 31 minutes.

gine cowl-flap settings used in projecting the DC-7's long-range cruising speed. Wright had based its estimates on a closed-flap configuration. Our sources indicated the new R-3350 required a flap setting of 4 to 6 degrees open at normal cruise power to prevent the cylinder head temperatures from exceeding safe operating limits. We estimated the added aerodynamic drag produced by those open cowl flaps would knock several miles per hour off the cruising speeds the manufacturer had forecast. The combination of these two miscalculations, we concluded, would compromise an already tight schedule and, consequently, make it virtually impossible for American to comply with CAA crew rest regulations on the transcontinental flights.

At a strategy meeting held in C. R. Smith's downtown apartment one night, I stated our position and recommended we immediately petition the CAB for a waiver of the eight-hour rule on domestic flights. There was precedent for this: The CAA permitted ten-hour crew-days for international flights by U.S. carriers. Such a rule change would probably require expensive concessions to the pilot's union, the Air Line Pilots Association, which had already announced it would challenge the proposed schedule and refuse to

allow pilots to fly trips of more than eight hours. Most of the senior executives at the meeting didn't want to hear anything about rule changes or concessions to the union. Top engineers from both American and Douglas had convinced them the less-than-eight-hours schedule was achievable. That was the end of the argument as far as they were concerned.

In practice, the DC-7 transcontinental flights had a miserable on-time record, averaging closer to nine hours than eight westbound. Ultimately, the matter of crew-rest was settled by changing the rules.

That didn't end our problems with the DC-7s, however. Their Wright R-3350 turbo-compound engines proved to be an operational and economic disaster. They broke down constantly and seldom gave us more than 500 to 600 hours of service—two or three months of normal operation—before requiring costly overhauls. The main problem lay with the engine's three small gas turbines, which were designed to generate additional horsepower by recapturing energy from escaping engine exhaust gases. This was a case of stretching the capabilities of internal combustion engines to their absolute limit—and beyond. Fortunately, jet-powered airliners were just a few years away.

Air Speed, True Air Speed, and *Real* Air Speed

Speed is a tricky business. There is, of course, ground speed—which tells us how fast we are traversing our track from one point on the map to another, taking winds en route and off-course wanderings into account. Then there is indicated air speed (IAS)—the reading we get from our shipboard air speed instrument. The air speed indicator is supposed to measure the aircraft's velocity relative to the stream or envelope of air in which it is traveling. Unfortunately, old-style indicators—which are essentially pressure gauges designed to measure the difference between ram air pressure and static air pressure—are only accurate at sea level, or rather, at normal sea-level barometric pressure of 29.92 inches of mercury. The higher we fly, the lower our indicated air speed relative to our true air speed (TAS). Modern airliners carry true air speed indicators that automatically adjust for changes in the density of the atmosphere. In the old days, pilots had to compute TAS by adjusting IAS for altitude and ambient air temperature.

To further complicate matters, air speed may be expressed in either statute miles or nautical miles per hour. Most aviation texts prefer miles per hour (MPH), whereas the airlines and armed services express air speed in nautical miles per hour (knots). One nautical mile is equal to approximately 1.15 statute miles.

When we speak of an aircraft's cruising speed, we're talking about its average true air speed under normal flight conditions, using standard cruise power settings for that type of aircraft. Sounds simple and straightforward, but it isn't. Aircraft engines are designed to be flown at a wide range of cruise power settings, depending upon considerations such as gross weight, desired cruising speed, cruising altitude, fuel economy, endurance, and service life. In general, the more power an engine pulls, the more fuel it will burn per flight and the shorter its service life is likely to be. Aircraft manufacturers naturally want to claim the highest possible cruise speed for each new model and are inclined to base their claims on operating the aircraft's engines at the highest sustainable cruise power setting. Usually it is the manufacturer's figures that are quoted in aviation magazines, texts, and history books. Bear in mind, however, that actual operating experience often varies considerably from published figures, and may differ from airline to airline—even from pilot to pilot. Retired American Airlines Captain Kelly Owen provides the following comparisons of published and actual cruise speeds for the Douglas aircraft he flew during the 1940s and 1950s:

Aircraft	Published MPH*	Actual MPH
DC-3	207	165–180
DC-4	227	180–200
DC-6	315	240–260
DC-7	355*/ 365**	280–300

* Source: *The Complete Encyclopedia of World Aircraft*
** American Airlines' engineering and advertising claims

Strike One

On July 31, 1954, American Airlines was hit with the first pilot strike in its history. The proximate cause of the walkout was American's insistence on operating nonstop DC-7 service from coast to coast in violation of a union work rule prohibiting flights of more than eight hours duration by a single, unaugmented flight crew. (Federal regulations containing the same eight-hour stricture had been conveniently waived on transcontinental flights a few months after American inaugurated the nonstop service.) No one really wanted a strike, least of all the DC-7 pilots, who, according to American's official historian, Robert Serling, "loved the nonstops . . . (and were) perfectly willing to fly in excess of eight hours."[9] Union officials, however, claimed that "the issue was not so much the eight-hour rule, but American's refusal to renegotiate a contract that had been technically violated." American's choice of chief negotiator, Senior Vice President–Operations Orval "Red" Mosier, contributed mightily to the impasse. Even his assistant, Bob Tuttle, says Serling, admitted that Mosier was "out of his league . . . the worst choice C. R. could have made."

Mosier thought it terrible that anyone would dare argue with management. He simply wasn't used to dealing with a union, and when he went to bat against the pilots, he never knew what hit him, according to Tuttle.[10] The strike dragged on for twenty-five days. In the end, the pilots agreed to waive the eight-hour rule on transcontinental flights—never a serious issue—in exchange for the "expensive concessions" Braznell had predicted two years earlier.

9. Serling, *Eagle: The Story of American Airlines*, 272.
10. Ibid., 273.

Relationships between Mosier and his director of flight, never cordial, hit a new low during the strike. Apparently Mosier had never forgiven Braznell for his outspoken opposition to the DC-7 project; certainly Braznell never forgave Mosier for relegating him to an insignificant advisory role in negotiations with *his* pilots. Braznell's career with American would mark time from this point until Mosier's retirement in 1963.

Britannia Bids to Rule the Air

All through the immediate postwar years, while U.S. airlines and their equipment manufacturers wrestled among themselves to wring ever more speed, capacity, and efficiency out of the last of the "recips" (that is, aircraft powered by reciprocating piston-driven engines), Great Britain's aviation industry was marching boldly into the dawn of a new air age—one in which its leaders envisioned British-built airliners ruling the skies as Britannia had once ruled the waves. Urged on by Winston Churchill, and with the full support of Britain's new Labour government, de Havilland, Rolls Royce, Vickers, and other industry leaders agreed to pool their resources in a bid to challenge the near monopoly of the United States in commercial aircraft design and manufacture. Conceding the immediate postwar market for conventional, piston-engine aircraft to the Americans, the British concentrated instead on building the next generation of medium- and long-range passenger transports using jet turbine technologies they had developed and advanced during the war. And give them credit: Having accepted the manifold risks of being first-to-market with a revolutionary new product and technology, they pursued their aims with remarkable resolution.

So, for the first time in modern memory (but not the last), the traditionally conservative

British, with their "muddling" Labour government and quasi-socialized aviation industry, gave their proud American cousins a lesson in technological and economic enterprise. The early results of these strikingly divergent Anglo/American policies are shown in the accompanying table.

Note especially:

In 1947, the year American and United put their first postwar transports into service, Britain's de Havilland was already taking orders for its 400-miles-per-hour Comet I jetliner.

Three years later, Vickers introduced its 350-miles-per-hour, turboprop-powered Viscount 630. Eight more years would pass before the first American-built "prop jet" took to the air.

And in May 1952, sixteen months before the inaugural flights of the last of the Douglas and Lockheed piston-engine aircraft, BOAC began regular jet service aboard its long-awaited de Havilland Comets.

Who could say, given their respective circumstances, which industry pursued the wiser course? The British appeared to have little to lose and much to gain by aggressively exploiting their one clear advantage over their strongly entrenched American competitors. The major U.S. airlines, on the other hand, had every reason to avoid leaping precipitously into the Jet Age. The first generation of transcontinental and transoceanic jets promised to be hideously expensive—$4 million to $5 million apiece, or roughly three times the cost of a new DC-7. And jet engines were notorious gas guzzlers. Granted, jet fuel was cheaper than the 100 octane gasoline burned by the recips; even so, the engines used in the B-47 and other high-performance military aircraft of that era burned two to three times more fuel per air mile than the most powerful piston-driven engines—so much fuel, in fact, that the Air Force's

biggest jet-powered bombers could not fly across country nonstop without aerial refueling.

Then there was the practical issue of where and how to launch those monster jetliners when they did at last materialize. How many metropolitan airports had runways long enough to handle the estimated 10,000-foot takeoff roll of a fully loaded passenger jet? No more than a handful: New York's Idlewild, Los Angeles's new International Airport, Chicago's O'Hare—possibly a half dozen more.

Then there was the noise factor . . . and the air pollution . . . and the fact that the nation's air traffic control facilities, barely adequate to their current task, would be overwhelmed by the advent of high-speed jet traffic. And beneath all that, possibly, an unspoken resistance to change— to the huge burden of pilot and ground crew training, the accidents and casualties that such an incredible leap in aviation technology would surely entail.

Yet, when all was said and done, one indisputable fact remained: The British had a jet airliner—a wildly successful jetliner—and the Americans didn't. From the very first, BOAC's Comet flights were booked solid, often weeks in advance. Passengers extolled the aircraft's quiet, vibration-free ride, its incredible speed: London to Johannesburg, five stops en route, in less than twenty-four hours. America's Pan Am Constellations needed forty hours to cover the same route. Orders for the new British triumph piled up: Air France, UAT, Japan Air Lines, Canadian Pacific and, not to be left out, Pan Am. "Whether we like it or not," Wayne Parrish wrote in *American Aviation,* "the British are giving us a drubbing in jet transportation."[11]

11. Parrish is quoted in T. A. Heppenheimer's *Turbulent Skies.*

Into the Jet Age: Britain and the United States March to Different Drummers

Britain

1939   By the beginning of WWI British and German engineers had developed and test flown air craft powered by experimental jet engines, and by the end of the war, both had operational jet fighters

1944   de Havilland with backing of British govern ment begins development of first commercial jet transport, the Comet

1947   BOAC commits to purchase of eight Comets

1950   Vickers Viscount 630, first turboprop-driven commercial airline, enters service

1952   Comet enters service and is an immediate popular success. "Every seat filled." Pan Am places order for three Comet IIIs—first order of a British aircraft by an American carrier

1954   Comets grounded, then permanently removed from service after two mid-air explosions found to have been caused by metal fatigue, structural failure

United States

1942   Test flight of first U.S. jet fighter, Bell XP-59, powered by twin GE J-31 engines of British (Whittle) design.

1944   U.S. airlines place orders for postwar replacement of DC-3 fleets—four-engine, pressurized Lockheed Constellations, Douglas DC-6s, and Boeing 377s, plus smaller twin-engine Convairs and Martins

1946   TWA introduces first commercial version of the Connie

1947   American and United introduce transcon DC service.

1951   Test flights of jet engine (P&W J-57) that will ultimately power the F-100, B-52 and first U.S. commercial jets

1953   Major airlines introduce "the last of the recips"—the Super Connie L-1049 and Douglas DC-7

1954   First flight of Boeing 367-80, prototype for the KC-135 airborne tanker and Boeing 707 Jet Stratoliner

1955   Pan American orders 20 Boeing 707s, plus 25 "paper" Douglas DC-8 jet transports. Orders from other airlines follow immediately

Capital Airlines first U.S. line to introduce turboprop service—Vickers Viscount 810

American first airline to order Lockheed L188 Electra turboprop midrange trans port

Britain		United States	
1958	Comet IV enters service with BOAC—not competitive with new Boeing and Douglas jets in range (3,000 miles) or cruise speed (500 mph)	1958	Pan Am introduces the 707 on transalantic routes
		1959	American begins domestic 707 service in January, United and Delta introduce DC-8 ninc months later
			American and Eastern inaugurate Lockheed Electra service
1962	Agreement among British and French governments, BAC, and Sud-Aviation (SNIA) to develop a Mach 2 supersonic transport, the Concorde	1960	American begins converting entire jet fleet to new fan jet engines (Pratt & Whitney JT-3D)
1969	Flight testing of Concorde begins	1966	Boeing awarded SST Mach 3 transport development contract by FAA
		1970	Pan Am inaugurates Boeing 747 "jumbo jet" service
		1971	Congress pulls the plug on SST project
1976	British Airways and Air France inaugurate transoceanic Concorde service		
			Note: Only nine Concords built and sold to date

Then, in 1954, just as America's domestic airlines were awaking to the downside risks of their "easy does it" postwar strategies, fate struck Britain's dream of aerial supremacy a crushing blow. In January a routine voice transmission from a BOAC Comet climbing out of Rome en route to London was suddenly cut off. Minutes later, fishermen off the island of Elba radioed reports of seeing the flaming wreckage of an aircraft hurtle through the overcast and disappear into the sea. There were no survivors, no clues to the cause of the acci-

dent, though sabotage was strongly suspected. After a two-month stand-down and investigation, the Comets returned to service.

Weeks later a second Comet crashed at sea near Stromboli under almost identical circumstances. All Comets were grounded once again. This time authorities were able to recover and reconstruct enough of the ship's remains to commence a full-scale investigation. Preliminary findings suggested that the second accident, and very likely the first as well, had been caused by a midair explosion—an explosion caused not by saboteurs, but by stress-induced cracks in the aircraft's metal skin. Investigators posited the simultaneous structural failure and explosive decompression of the Comet's fuselage as the ship climbed to altitude. These findings were later confirmed by exhaustive stress tests on a sister-ship of the two doomed aircraft.

The tests showed that the Comets were fatally flawed. Nothing could be done to correct their structural deficiencies, short of a complete redesign and recertification. That would take years, and by then the American star would again be ascendant.

Fire for Their Chariots

In 1953 C. R. Smith summed up his arguments against the jets—and American's rationale for investing, instead, in the ultimate stretch model of the Douglas postwar flagship series: To justify its outrageous price tag, said Smith, a jetliner would, at the very least, have to be able to fly nonstop from coast to coast, as the DC-7s and Super Connies did, and do so at a lower cost per seat mile than the airlines' existing equipment. At the time Smith issued that challenge, no such aircraft existed. And the reason no such aircraft existed was that British and American engine manufacturers had yet to produce a commercial jet power plant efficient enough to get a plane from here to there on one tank of gas.

The most energy-efficient turbojet in production at the time was the Pratt & Whitney J-57 engine used to power the Air Force's new B-52 strategic bombers and F-100 fighters. The J-57 employed a radical "twin-spool" design—basically a turbojet within a turbojet—to produce

nearly twice the thrust per gallon of jet fuel generated by single-spool engines. It wasn't exactly a meter miser, but it was close enough to merit serious consideration by major airframe manufacturers as the prospective power plant for future transcontinental jetliners. The J-57's one serious drawback was that it was still classified, its use restricted by the Pentagon to high-performance military aircraft—and likely to remain so for several years.

Even if declassified sooner, the J-57 would have to be considered an interim solution—something to hang on the first generation of jetliners until a better engine became available. That "something better" was the J-57's beefy kid brother, the J-75, an advanced version of the twin-spool design promising more than enough thrust and range to fly heavy loads nonstop across the Atlantic. But, alas, the J-75s were still under development and would almost certainly not be available to the airlines before the end of the decade.

In the meantime, a few American aircraft manufacturers and airlines were placing side bets on that largely ignored stepchild of the Jet Age, the turboprop (or propjet). Britain's Vickers Viscount, a small, mid-range transport powered by four Rolls Royce Dart propjet engines, had been operating successfully in Europe since 1950, and wherever they went into service the faster (350 miles per hour), smoother-riding Viscounts were stealing customers away from conventionally powered airlines. By 1953, BEA was operating a sixty-five-passenger stretch model of the Viscount between London and Cyprus, and several U.S. lines, including Capital, Eastern, and American, were considering ordering them as replacements for their obsolete recips on high-density short-haul runs.

Capital Goes for Broke—and Succeeds

In 1955 TransCanada Airlines introduced Viscount turboprop service to the United States. Capital Airlines, which competed against TransCanada on several routes through New England and the Middle Atlantic states, retaliated by acquiring its first Viscounts a few months later. Then, in a daring preemptive strike against Eastern, American, and United, Capital went on to blanket the East and Midwest with turboprop service, acquiring sixty new 810 Series Viscounts. By mid-1957 Capital's Viscounts were mopping up on its competitors. By 1959, bankers and suppliers were mopping up on Capital. Financially overextended, facing deadly cash-flow problems and defaults on its lease payments, and now confronted by competition from the bigger, faster turboprops and pure jets being introduced along its key Chicago–New York and Chicago-Washington runs, Capital desperately sought a savior.

The following year, with Vickers threatening to repossess practically its entire fleet, Capital entered into an agreement to merge with United Airlines. The marriage of convenience, effective June 1, 1961, brought together the second and fifth largest U.S. carriers, with a combined fleet of 267 aircraft and a route structure covering 116 cities. Henceforth, United, not American, would claim bragging rights as "the largest airline in the western world".

Lockheed, developer of the brilliant C-130 Hercules military turboprop transport,[12] was one of the few American manufacturers to express an interest in building projets for the commercial market. However, it did not find a serious prospect until 1955, when American and Eastern Airlines agreed to help underwrite the development and production of its proposed L-188 Electra propjet with firm orders for thirty-five and forty planes, respectively. Conceived as an interim solution—a forerunner of the pure jets—the Electra did not enter commercial service until 1959, a few months *after* the introduction of the Boeing 707. It was subsequently used by American and Eastern primarily on high-density short and mid-range flights, including their bread-and-butter New York–Chicago runs.

Boeing Lifts Off

On the morning of July 15, 1954, a glistening yellow and brown leviathan of an aircraft turned onto the 5,400-foot runway at the Renton Municipal Airport, Renton, Washington, and paused, dead still, like a diver gathering herself at the end of a springboard. The ear-piercing whistle of

12. Conceived in 1951 and commissioned by the Air Force in 1955, the aptly named Hercules was a brute that flew like a Greek god. With its four immensely powerful Allison T56 engines and huge four-bladed props, a fully loaded C-130 could easily take off from a 3,000-foot unprepared strip and climb to 2,000 feet before its wheels were fully retracted. It cruised at nearly 350 miles per hour on all four engines and close to 300 miles per hour with two engines "caged" (a fairly common long-range cruise regimen in the author's Air Force days). But why use the past tense? The last time we checked, the C-130s were still in service; they were, in fact, still being manufactured in small quantities.

Notes on Propulsion

TURBOPROP ENGINES are relatively simple machines with substantially lower weight-to-horsepower ratios than the most efficient reciprocating engines and no moving valves or pistons to break down or shake loose. Ram air entering the engine intake is compressed by a series of rotary compressor fans, then mixed with fuel and ignited. The explosive force of the combusted gases drives a set of turbine wheels, which are mechanically linked to a front-mounted

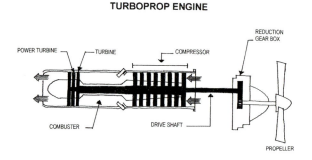

TURBOPROP ENGINE

propeller via a drive shaft and reduction gear assembly. Although they were never as popular with airline passengers, propjets of the 1950s and early 1960s were considerably more efficient than "pure" jets on short flights, where the propjet's inherently slower speed was not a critical factor. (The top speed a prop-driven aircraft is capable of attaining in level flight is about 500 miles per hour. As a plane approaches that speed, shock waves develop along the leading edges of its propeller blades, disrupting the airflow over their surface and spoiling their aerodynamic efficiency.) At 300 to 450 miles per hour, however, propjets actually outperformed the pure jets, which tended to be quite sluggish in the low subsonic speed range. Furthermore, the propjet's short-field takeoff and landing capabilities were vastly superior.

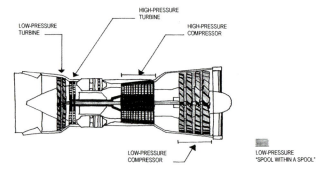

TURBOJET ENGINES operate on the same principle as the turboprop, but without the prop. This is a simplified diagram of the earliest twin-spool turbojet—virtually a turbojet within a turbojet. The additional spool consists of a series of high-pressure compressor fans mounted behind the low-pressure compressors and linked by a hollow shaft to a set of high-pressure turbines immediately aft of the combustion chamber. The slower-rotating low-pressure spool

TWIN-SPOOL TURBOJET

(compressors and turbines) are connected by a separate core shaft running down the hollow channel of the high-speed drive shaft. Turbojets have no inherent speed limitations. On the contrary, the faster a jet flies, the greater the volume and velocity of ram air drawn into its intakes and, consequently, the greater the thrust its engines can generate.

FAN JETS: The first turbofan "bypass" engine to enter commercial service in the United States, Pratt & Whitney's JT3-D, was basically a twin-spool turbojet with the first three rows or stages of compressors replaced by a two-stage compressor (fan) of much wider circumference. Some of the accelerated airflow from the fan blades was directed into the combustion chamber, then to the turbines, just as in conventional jet engines; the rest flowed

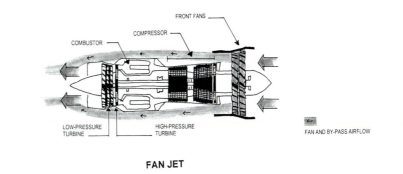

FAN JET

around (bypassed) the engine, blending with the hot engine emissions at the instant they were exhausted. The bypass feature was a relatively simple modification of the standard twin-spool turbojet, but one that produced phenomenal increases in thrust with virtually no increase in fuel consumption. Almost as important as the added power, range, and fuel economy afforded by the fan jets was the noise-dampening effect of their bypass airflow. *Illustrations by Tron Bykle*

the plane's four underslung JT3P engines slowly swelled and deepened to the roar of a blast furnace.[13] She began to roll, gathering momentum with deceptive ease, nose slowly lifting from the horizontal, wheels barely skimming the tarmac. With a little toss of her head, she rose. Boeing's new jet transport, the 367-80, was airborne. And with her maiden flight, civil aviation in the United States was launched into the modern era.

At the time it was conceived, in 1952, Boeing's "Dash-Eighty" figured to be a life-or-death gamble on breaking into the commercial airliner market long dominated by Douglas and Lockheed. Except for Pan Am, no U.S. airline had as yet expressed much interest in bankrolling the development of a U.S.-built jet transport—and

Pan Am was noncommittal. Even the Air Force, by far the company's biggest customer, had declined Boeing's previous proposals to build a new military jet transport and high-altitude aerial tanker. As if that were not enough to dissuade the company's directors, the new twin-spool jet engines Boeing engineers intended to hang on their when-as-and-if-built transport were still under wraps—classified and restricted by the Defense Department.

But Boeing President William Allen knew that sooner or later the Air Force's Strategic Air Command would require a high-speed, high-altitude jet tanker to replace its piston-driven KC-97s. And judging from the rousing commercial success of the new British Comets, he felt certain it would only be a matter of a year or two before U.S. airlines were also in the market for jetliners. Allen proposed to cover both bets by committing his company to a $16 million investment in the

13. The engines were the civilian version of the military J-57.

development of a plane that would serve as the prototype, first for its proposed military tanker, the KC-135, and later for a commercial transport version of the same plane, to be designated the Boeing 707.

Allen's daring plan worked out exactly as he had envisioned it—up to a point. In October 1952 Boeing's board agreed to fund the prototype's initial development costs. In October 1954, a few weeks following the Dash-Eighty's maiden flight, the Air Force placed an initial order for twenty-nine KC-135s. The following year, Boeing gained permission to use the Air Force–owned Renton plant to build 707s side by side with the KC-135s. And then, in October 1955, the company won its first 707 order from Pan American World Airways.

So far, so good. But Pan Am's initial order was split between Boeing and Douglas—twenty 707s and *twenty-five* DC-8s. This was hardly a vote of confidence in Boeing and its new commercial transport, considering Boeing's vastly greater experience in designing and building jet aircraft and the fact that Douglas's plane was, at the time, still on the drawing board. Furthermore, Pan Am and United were demanding that the fuselage of both the 707 and DC-8 be expanded to accommodate six-abreast coach seating. Douglas, with its paper airplane, agreed to these demands without a second thought. But for Boeing, which had visualized punching hundreds, even thousands, of virtually identical C-135s, KC-135s, and 707s from the same preexisting "cookie cutters," the new specifications called for an agonizing reappraisal. Without commonality of tools and dies, the 707's added production costs would eat up most of Boeing's projected profits. It would be years before the company recovered its research and development outlays. On the other hand, refusal to accommodate demand for a mere four-inch

increase in the width of the fuselage would cost Boeing not only the Pan Am and United contracts but also its last realistic chance of breaking back into the commercial aviation industry.[14] Not yet prepared to concede that market to its powerful and deeply entrenched rival, Boeing abandoned its Hobson's Choice strategy once and for all. From then on, its policy with respect to airline customers and prospects was, *"What can we get you?"*

Even with Boeing's new spirit of accommodation, the fate of the 707 twisted in the wind. Twelve days after Pan Am announced its split-decision, United unequivocally opted to go with Douglas, placing an initial order for thirty DC-8s. American's C. R. Smith, whose motto in those days seemed to be, "We may not be first, but we damned sure don't intend to be last," pondered United's move and his own company's long and cordial relationship with Douglas for a fortnight. Then, recalling the old adage about a bird in hand, he committed American to an initial purchase of thirty new Boeing 707s.

Airborne

Having filed our flight plan, completed a walk-around inspection, and run through the standard preflight and engine-start procedure, it's time for the writer to slide into the right seat and turn the controls over to Captain Braznell for our takeoff into the Jet Age:

American Airlines was the first major domestic carrier to operate jets, beginning in January 1959,

14. The airlines wanted, and eventually got, a body 148 inches wide, versus 144 inches for the production model of the KC-135 and 132 inches for the original 367-80.

with the introduction of Boeing 707 service between Los Angeles and New York.[15] Since American would be leading the way for the rest of the industry, it fell to our Flight Department to work with the FAA on all the preliminary aspects of testing, proving, and certifying the 707 for domestic flights entering and departing each of the major airports American served. In addition, we would be responsible for training not only our own pilots but the FAA's flight examiners as well.

As project leader, I began preparations by taking a group of fifteen supervisory pilots and flight engineers, plus several FAA people, to a special 707 school Boeing had set up at Harbor Island, Washington, near Seattle. This was in October 1958. At Harbor Island we were joined by members of American's engineering team, including acceptance test pilot Kelly Owen, who had been working with the Boeing people for weeks before our arrival.

On our first night, we were visited by Tex Johnston, the head of Boeing's flight test group, and a few of the flight section chiefs. Without beating around the bush, Johnston informed us that the planes we were about to put into service had a small problem, which he described as "not enough feathers on the arrow." He explained that the 707's rudder control was marginal at low speeds, and the plane had a tendency to wallow, or roll on several axes at once, during takeoffs and landings. This phenomenon was called "Dutch Roll," and a considerable amount of our training would be devoted to learning how to avoid or recover from it.

Subsequently, American and most of the other airlines that flew the first series of 707s had serious problems with this Dutch Roll. After we experienced two fatal 707 crashes during training flights, the aircraft were sent back to the factory and outfitted with new power-controlled rudders. The retro-

fit didn't eliminate the Dutch Roll, but it did make it easier for pilots to recover from it. About a year later, Boeing came out with further modifications to the tail section and rudder controls that effectively eliminated the problem of the missing feathers. We had little trouble with the 707s from then on.

In November our 707 task force returned to New York and began crew training in earnest. As soon as we had a few qualified crews checked out in the plane, we formed them into teams and took off across the country, "proving" the jet takeoff, approach control, and landing capabilities for each airport, revising flight and ground operating procedures to take into account the size and speed of the new aircraft, training airline ground personnel in their handling, and so on. For example, we had to explain to tower operators and traffic controllers that there was no point in issuing pilots the customary instruction to report climbing through 1,500 feet, because a 707 would pass through that altitude before its wheels retracted.

In a typical instance of proving, the pilot's union (ALPA) challenged the company's intended use of the old Dallas Airport's 7,500 foot runway for jet traffic. To demonstrate that jets could operate safely into and out of the airfield, we took a 707 down to Dallas and shot several heavily loaded landings and takeoffs while union photographers recorded our performance with motion pictures and still shots. Union reps even weighed the sandbags we had loaded on the plane, just to make sure we weren't cheating.

Another critical aspect of our proving operations involved working with air traffic controllers on the problem of vectoring high-speed, high-altitude aircraft around thunderstorms. In those days, airborne radar and ground-based radar traffic control hadn't progressed to their present stage of sophistication. Controllers were inclined to underestimate the amount of clearance a plane going 600 miles an hour needed in order to avoid running into the extreme turbulence generated by the storm cells that appeared on their radar. I had a couple of incidents, early on, of having to talk a controller out

---

15. National Airlines claimed the honor of being the first domestic carrier to introduce jet service, which it did in December 1958, leasing a couple of 707s from Pan Am to augment its New York–Miami service during the peak winter travel period.

Into the Jet Age

JET SCHOOL: A Boeing instructor briefs American Airlines' project team on the aerodynamics of the new 707. Braznell sits directly behind the model's left wingtip. Chief Pilot–Los Angeles (and future VP-Flight) Ted Melden is on the extreme left. Chief Pilot–New York Harry Clark sits with folded arms just forward of the model's bow. Assistant Director of Flight Bill Reedholm (white hair) is in the next-to-last row, on the right. And Captain Charlie McAtee, who will command the first transcontinental jet flight, sits front row center (in suitcoat and dark tie). Others not identified.

BON VOYAGE: Film star Anne Baxter does the honors at the dedication ceremony preceding AA's (and the airline industry's) first transcontinental jet flight, January 23, 1959. Captain Charlie McAtee leans out the copilot's window to accept a posy. Braznell, beaming in the background, accompanied the inaugural flight as project supervisor.

In the DC-8 mock-up, Braznell (center), American Airlines' flight director, discusses controls with associates Frank Kolk (left) and M. G. Beard.

Photos and captions from a Life *article featuring America's jet transition project team, October 1958*

With Boeing Pilot Tex Johnston, who is head of flight testing for Boeing, [Walt] Braznell asks questions about 707's handling. The 707 has 300 hours in air.

of vectoring me onto a course that would have cut straight through the leading edge of a towering thunderhead.

This proving operation went on for months and played an important part in the introduction of domestic jet travel. Being a working member of the proving team took me away from my office much of the time during the early months of 1959, but as head of the group responsible for developing the flight procedures and training programs for these radically new additions to the American fleet, I felt I should have as much hands-on experience and operating perspective as possible. Besides, I couldn't keep my hands off those marvelous flying machines. For all of us, the coming of the jets was a tremendously exciting experience.

The Fan Jets

Next to the introduction of commercial jet aircraft, the most dramatic development in this new age of air travel was the Pratt & Whitney JT3-D fan jet engines American introduced in March 1961.

In the fan jets, the forward compressor turbines used in standard turbojet engines were replaced with much larger fan blades and the engine housing was substantially enlarged to allow some of the airstream to flow around rather than through the combustion chamber. These refinements added considerably to the engine's overall thrust. The new JT3-Ds were not only 30 percent more powerful than the original engines but also burned about 25 percent less fuel. They were cleaner burning and quieter as well.

American worked closely with Pratt & Whitney on the development of the fan jet and was the first domestic airline to reap its benefits. The cost advantages alone were staggering. On a typical "AstroJet" flight from Idlewild (JFK International) to Los Angeles International, for example, we would burn roughly 65,000 pounds of fuel, compared with the 90,000 pounds consumed by our competitors' most advanced turbojets.[16] As late as January

1962, when the last of American's 707s and 720s were converted to fan jets, all of the other major airline fleets were still predominantly or exclusively equipped with the older, less efficient turbojets.

Technology progresses; human nature never changes. Just as air mail pilots of the 1920s delighted in pouncing on slower-moving planes, pilots of the Jet Age enjoyed flaunting any competitive advantage. One morning, soon after we began flying fan jets, I was in line for takeoff at Idlewild, just behind a TWA 707 equipped with the latest, hottest, non-fan jet engines, the J-75. Both flights were bound for Los Angeles. The TWA plane took off, streaming black smoke.[17] We were cleared onto the runway a minute or two later. Climbing like a rocket, we easily overtook the other ship before crossing the Hudson River. As soon as he saw us, the TWA pilot poured on the fuel. Once again his engines streamed smoke as his water injection system kicked in. We kept flying along beside him at normal cruise power, keeping a safe but sociable distance, in full view of his passengers. And he kept shoveling the coal to his laboring engines in an effort to keep pace. I was thoroughly ashamed of myself for having so much fun at the TWA pilot's expense, and would have broken off sooner, had I not been curious to know how long it would take him to realize he wasn't going to make Los Angeles nonstop at the rate he was burning kerosene.

The two planes breezed by Chicago neck and neck, and continued that way until just south of Omaha, when the TWA flight broke off and headed south toward Albuquerque. We continued on to Los Angeles, never having altered our normal cruise regimen, and landed a half hour before the other flight with enough fuel to fly halfway home again.

---

16. American's fan jets were dubbed "Astrojets" by the company's advertising agency.

17. The smoke was caused by the injection of water into the engine's combustion chamber. This was done to increase the volume and thrust of escaping gases during takeoff and climb. The early 707s were called "water wagons."

Gallery of Jet Transports: 1952 to 1966

DE HAVILLAND COMET: De Havilland's 480-miles-per-hour, thirty-six-passenger jetliner, the D.H.106 Comet (pictured here), was quite literally in a class by itself from the time it entered service with BOAC in January 1952 until the discovery of fatal weaknesses in the structure of its fuselage led to the permanent grounding of the entire series in mid-1954. A substantially redesigned seventy-eight-passenger series, the Comet IV, returned to service with BOAC in 1958, just four weeks before Pan Am inaugurated Boeing 707 service over the Atlantic. The reincarnated Comet may have been first—again—but it was no match for the American ships in speed, range, or size. *Photo courtesy of Jesse Davidson Aviation Archives*

BOEING 367–80: Boeing began developing this prototype for the KC-135 jet tanker and 707 Stratoliner in 1952, test flew it in 1954, and delivered the first of some 820 C-135s and KC-135s to the Air Force in 1957. The raked wings, suspended engine pods, and distinctive tail configuration of the "dash eighty" were borrowed from Boeing's famous B-47 medium bomber. Other structural elements were cobbled from its KC-97 aerial tanker.
Photo courtesy of Boeing Company

Boeing hoped to sell the commercial model of the 367–80 more or less as is. But Pan Am and other prospective buyers insisted on expensive alterations, notably a slightly wider body. Worried about losing the market to Douglas's paper airplane, the DC-8, Boeing capitulated, and a long series of customized 707 variants followed. The most important of the 707 series were:

BOEING 707–120, an 111-seat medium-range aircraft powered by P&W JT3C-6 engines. This was the aircraft introduced by Pan Am on North Atlantic routes on October 26, 1958. American Airlines, the first of the Big Four domestic lines to enter the Jet Age, inaugurated 707–120 service between Los Angeles and New York in January 1959. *Photo courtesy of American Airlines*

BOEING 707–320 (not pictured), a larger intercontinental version of the 707, entered service with Pan Am in August 1959. With larger wings, a lengthened body, greater fuel capacity, and more powerful P&W JT4 engines in place of the 120's JT3s, the 707–320 was the first jetliner capable of nonstop flight between New York and the major capitals of Europe.

BOEING 707–20 (see page 204)

DOUGLAS DC-8 (not pictured): Aside from the smaller size of its windows and the less pronounced sweep-back of its wings (30 degrees versus 35) the DC-8 was practically identical to the Boeing 707 in appearance and performance. Like the 707, it was produced in a variety of configurations, including the long-range DC-8 Series 30 model and a Series 50 fan jet economy version with an interior redesigned to accommodate 189 passengers. United breathed life into the DC-8 program by being the first major domestic airline to choose it over the 707. The DC-8 flew its first flight in May 1958 and entered service with United and Delta in September 1959—eight months after American began 707 transcontinental service. A worthy successor in a long line of distinguished Douglas airliners in every other respect, the DC-8 proved to be a financial failure. Only about 290 aircraft were built and sold over a nine-year period—hardly enough to recover the DC-8's horrendous development costs.

CONVAIR 880 AND 990: Under TWA's sponsorship, the CV 880 was originally conceived as a faster, sleeker replacement for the 707–120. A major drawback was its narrow fuselage, which would only accommodate five-abreast seating, compared with the six-abreast seating standard in 707 and DC-8 coach sections. TWA and Delta placed their bets on the 880 in June 1956. American ordered a lengthened version of the aircraft, later designated the CV 990, in 1958, committing to twenty-five ships with options for twenty-five more. Delta and TWA put their first CV 880s into service in May 1960.

Production problems delayed American's introduction of the 990 until March 1962, and the first ships delivered had to be returned to correct design problems that severely inhibited their performance. Even with the modifications, the aircraft was a great disappointment, both to the manufacturer and to the airlines stuck with them. American dumped its 990s in 1968. After taking a $425 million write-off on the 880/990 project, Convair permanently abandoned the commercial jet market. *Photo courtesy of American Airlines*

Short Haul Jet Liners

The immediate and intense popularity of jet travel following the domestic introduction of the 707 took the airlines by surprise. Most of the major U.S. lines planned to reserve the jets for their high-density intermediate and long-range flights and expected to eke out many more years of service from their aging recip fleets on shorter, less traveled runs. But air travelers had other ideas, and within a year or two after the transcontinental jets went into service Boeing, Douglas, and Lockheed rushed to market with small and midsized transports proporting to offer a combination of the jet's smooth, whisper-quiet ride with the economies of operation and short-field performance of the recips and propjets. Once again, the Europeans got a jump on their American competitors, having begun development of short-haul jet transports, the French Caravelle and British BAC 1–11, in the early 1950s.

CARAVELLE SE.210 was the first in a long line of successful Caravelle jet transports built by France's Sud-Aviation. Its innovative tail-mounted engine pods and clean wings eventually became the design standard for short-range jets. The sixty-four-passenger SE.210 first entered service with Air France and Air Inter (France's domestic line). United purchased twenty Caravelles in 1960 and put them in service on its New York–Chicago run the following year. Larger and more powerful models followed, culminating with the 140-passenger Mk 12 Super Caravelle in 1964. *Photo courtesy of Jesse Davidson Aviation Archives*

BOEING 720, originally called the 707–20, was a shorter, intermediate-range adaptation of the 707 with substantially improved short-field takeoff performance and faster cruising speed. United and American put the first 720s into commercial service in mid-1960. The fan jet–powered 720B began service with American in March 1961. *Photo courtesy of American Airlines*

BOEING 727, the first of the tri-jets, was designed for short- and intermediate-range, high-density routes. Eastern introduced the 727 in February 1964, and within a year or two all the major U.S. lines were flying them.
With its three powerful tail-mounted Pratt & Whitney JT3-D fan jet engines and an advanced wing design featuring leading edge flaps, spoilers, and triple-slotted rear flaps, the 727 was unique, for its day, in its ability to
transport large numbers of passengers into and out of airports that were inaccessible to the 707s and DC-8s.
Photo courtesy of American Airlines

British Aircraft Corporation's BAC 1-11 went through several major design modifications and engine changes before emerging in the mid-1960s as Britain's answer to the Caravelle—an eighty-passenger liner powered by twin tail-mounted Rolls Royce Spey engines. Braniff and Mohawk were the first U.S. lines to put the BAC 1-11 in service (1965). American Airlines followed in March 1966—and wished it hadn't. By 1972 they were gone. *Photo courtesy of American Airlines*

BOEING 737, a twin-engine version of the 727, was initially meant to compete head-to-head with Douglas's midsized DC-9 and was scaled accordingly. Since the introduction of the 100 series in 1968, each succeeding model has grown in size, power, range, and popularity, making the 737 the best-selling and certainly one of the most versatile and long-lived airliners ever produced. *Photo courtesy of American Airlines*

Pressure Pattern Flying

The principles of pressure pattern flying were developed during World War II and used by Air Transport Command crews on long hops over the North and South Atlantic. Rather than plot straight-line or great circle routes from point to point, navigators would vector their planes north or south of course to take advantage of the counter-clockwise airflow around low-pressure areas and clockwise airflow emanating from high-pressure areas forecast en route. With the advent of high-altitude jetliners in the 1950s and the introduction of ever more sophisticated techniques for tracking and measuring upper air movement, including the jet stream, pressure pattern flying has become standard procedure on long-range transcontinental and transoceanic flights.

Proliferation

Following the introduction of the first 707 series in 1959, American rapidly expanded its jet fleet, and for a long while it seemed as though we were taking delivery of a new series or model of aircraft every few months. Aside from the long-range 707-320s and mid-range Boeing 720s, major additions included the short-lived Convair 990, the work-horse Boeing 727—introduced in 1964 and still in active airline service at last report—and the twin-engined BAC-1-11s. By 1966 we were operating eleven different models of aircraft including, in addition to our 134-plane jet fleet, an assortment of DC-6s and -7s left over from the piston era, plus twenty-four Lockheed Electra turboprops. Still in the development stage when I retired in 1968 were the Boeing 747 and what was billed as the United States' answer to the Concorde, the SST, or Supersonic Transport. Developing training programs and procedure manuals for all our new aircraft and consulting with the manufacturers on the cockpit layout and flight instrumentation for the two developmental aircraft occupied a good part of the Flight Department's time during my last few years with American.

Following the Wind

One thing I loved about flying cross-country in the late 1950s and 1960s was the freedom to vector off-airways, following the wind, tracking whatever route offered the smoothest and fastest ride. You might fly from New York to Los Angeles by way of Green Bay or Cheyenne one day and via Dallas, El Paso, and Phoenix the next: Today the Oregon Trail; tomorrow the Santa Fe.

This freedom of movement was made possible, in part, by the steady advances in aerial navigation since the low-frequency radio range stations of the 1920s and 1930s. By the mid-1950s, most of the old range stations had been replaced by very high frequency omnidirectional ranges (VOR) or "Omni" stations,[18] whose line-of-sight radio signals could be picked up hundreds of miles away at cruising altitudes of 30,000 to 40,000 feet. Unlike low-frequency radio signals, the Omni stations' transmissions were static-free—unaffected by electrical storms, rain, or snow.

Along with Omni came sophisticated radio navigational instruments that made it easy to identify the compass bearing to any station within range and maintain a precise track inbound or outbound. Later, these directional VOR receivers were supplemented with distance measuring equipment (DME) that clicked off the mileage to or from a station. Knowing both your compass bearing to a station and your distance from it, you could almost in-

18. In 1948 Congress authorized the establishment of a VOR (Victor) airway system to replace the nation's outmoded low-frequency ranges. The first VOR airway was commissioned in October 1950. By 1952 there were nearly forty-five thousand VOR stations in operation throughout the country. The last of the low-frequency range stations were decommissioned in 1974.

stantly fix your exact location anywhere in the country.

Still later, toward the end of my flying career, airlines began equipping their transoceanic planes with gyro-based inertial guidance systems that made our VORs and DMEs seem like toys. Departing Los Angeles, a pilot could crank the longitude and latitude for Honolulu into his inertial guidance system, and it would do practically all the rest of the navigation, continuously reading off true course, estimated ground speed, wind velocity, and miles to destination.[19]

With the freedom afforded by off-airways navigation came the obligation to assure the safe separation of military, commercial, and private air traffic, not just on designated airways and around congested terminals, as before, but everywhere planes flew—border to border, coast to coast, sea level to stratosphere. Making our crowded skies safe for all manner of air traffic has been a slow, painful, and unending quest, but at the time I retired we were making progress. By the mid-1960s the CAA and its successor, the Federal Aviation Administration, had completed construction of a superb system of Air Route Traffic Control Centers with long-range radar blanketing virtually the entire continent and direct radio contact with all aircraft flying within designated control areas. Most airlines had airborne radar to help guide their planes around thunderstorms and to warn of approaching traffic. We also had precoded airborne radio transmitters, called *transponders*, that signaled or "painted" a plane's identity and precise altitude on the air traffic controllers' radar scopes. And, just as important as these technological advances, we had, at last, a single set of rules and procedures controlling all flights, military and civilian, within prescribed areas and altitudes. Ironically, in my

forty-year career as a pilot, we had come full circle, from a time when no one flew by Instrument Flight Rules to a time when everyone flew by them, even in clear, cloudless skies.

I wish it could be said that all these progressive steps, and the many more that followed, eventually put an end to the midair collisions that have cost so many fatalities in my lifetime. But I fear that such catastrophes—so unnecessary, so avoidable in most instances—will occur as long as human beings fly airplanes.

Golden Age

The first decade of the Jet Age, from the beginning of coast-to-coast jet service in 1959 through the 1960s, was, to my mind, the golden age of air travel. In the 1960s flying was no longer a luxury, but it was still luxurious. There was always plenty of leg room, commodious seats, and excellent food service, even in economy class. In first class, service was incredibly grand. Passengers were wined and dined from the minute they came aboard until they deplaned at their final destination. Airlines vied to see which could pamper its customers the most.

At long last, the airline industry was making money—piles of it. Jet travel proved enormously popular, rapidly displacing all other modes of long-distance mass transportation. Between the advent of efficient fan jet engines and the beginning of the oil crises of the 1970s, fuel costs plummeted. So did maintenance costs. Where, in the old days, we were constantly changing and overhauling those cranky piston-driven engines, the new fan jets required little upkeep and could operate for thousands of hours between engine changes.

And flying those early jets—what a difference! What a joy, compared with the droning, wallowing piston-driven planes we flew for so many years. The first 707s may have been "short a few feathers," but they were arrows nonetheless—swift, silent, high-arching projectiles—and the fan jet–powered ships that followed were simply awesome. No air-

19. Today, of course, all manner of vehicles, from long-range missiles to commercial jets to automobiles, are equipped with simple and inexpensive satellite-based navigation systems capable of pinpointing their exact location, anywhere in the world.

man who has been through the experience ever forgets the sensation of strapping one of those missiles to his backside and pushing the throttles to the wall.

Try to imagine how a pilot who, thirty years earlier, had spent his afternoons hedge-hopping from St. Louis to Chicago, doing 85 miles per hour, wiping snow off his goggles, dodging trees and water towers—imagine how such a person might feel sitting in the cockpit of a 707, cruising along at 40,000 feet with a panoramic view of thousands of miles of towering summer cumulus, mountains, desert, and prairie, while a tiny electronic measuring device clicks off ten nautical miles per minute. A dozen years after my last flight as an American captain, I still imagine myself at the controls, still feel the surge of those powerful engines. It is an incredible experience: beautiful, endlessly fascinating—heart-swelling.

—Walt Braznell, December 1979

Postflight

A few old-timers who flew "The Threes" are still around, and when they make an appearance at a gathering of American's Grey Eagles, younger retirees attend them with the same reverence and listen to their hoary stories with the same rapt attention that pilots of their generation once bestowed on the grizzled air mail veterans of the 1920s. And deservedly so. The airmen of the '20s were the airline industry's pathfinders, blazing trails through a vaulted wilderness. The young men who came up through the copilot ranks in the late 1930s were its colonizers—its yeoman pioneers. With their sturdy workhorses, the DC-3s, they tamed the wilderness and made it bloom.

These lines, repeated from chapter 4, are not quite Walt Braznell's words, but they're close. No shrinking violet himself, he stood in awe of the older crowd of air mail pilots—"pathfinders" such as Slim Lindbergh, E. L. Sloniger, and Dean Smith. He felt privileged to have flown with many of them during the last few years of the open-cockpit era—privileged, and thankful to have survived the experience. But the younger generation of American Eagles, the thousands of "pioneers" whom he trained during the 1930s and 1940s and ultimately led into the Jet Age, were his pride and joy, his heirs and successors.

Braznell's proudest boast was that, in forty years of flying and more than 15,000 hours of flying time, he never dented an airplane. If it ever crossed his mind that he may have had something to do with another, far more impressive safety record—that of American Airlines and the rest of the airline industry during the quarter century he served as first or second in command of American's "Flagship Fleet"—he

made no mention of it in all the years we corresponded on the subject of his memoirs.

Not that he wasn't proud of American's record. He was immensely proud of it. But there were certain protocols. First of all, safety was a taboo subject among airline people. Bragging about your company's good fortune was tempting fate, and a sure way to gain the enmity of less fortunate competitors. More to the point, flight safety was his job—a job he shared with every flight administrator and every pilot who ever wore an airline uniform, not to mention the aircraft builders and engine manufacturers, the mechanics and ground crews, the meteorologists, the FAA air traffic controllers and supervisors, and all the thousands of other people responsible for getting the passengers of a modern jetliner safely to their destination. You didn't take bows for doing your job, or credit for what others helped to accomplish.

Well, then, perhaps the entire industry should stand and take a bow.

Fatal Accidents Per Million Air Miles
Scheduled Airlines 1938–1968

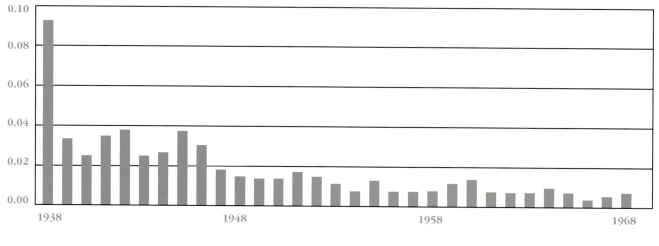

Source: Air Transport Association

The accompanying chart illustrates the decline in the incidence of fatal accidents among scheduled domestic airlines over a thirty-year period, from roughly one incident in every ten million aircraft miles (.09 per million miles) during the dark days of the late 1930s to one incident per 167 million aircraft miles (.006 per million) by the end of the 1960s. In 1998, for the first time in airline history, the ratio shrank to zero—*zero* fatal accidents involving scheduled airline passengers. In the early 1930s flying across country was an adventure comparable to setting out across the Pacific in a rubber raft—so risky most insurance policies excluded aviation-related death or injury from coverage. Today air travel is by far the safest mode of mass transportation—vastly safer, certainly, than taking to the highways in the family station wagon.

In the course of our narrative we have chronicled the evolutions in aircraft and engine design, cockpit instrumentation, navigation aids, air traffic controls, and instrument landing systems that contributed so significantly to this record of progress.

Without question, technology has played a central role in making yesterday's "vaulted wilderness" safe for human habitation.

But let us not overlook the human side of the equation, as aviation writers and historians are apt to do. If, as most experts agree, "pilot error" is, was, and probably always will be at least a contributing factor in the majority of fatal airline accidents (we have seen estimates as high as 87 percent), then clearly there must have been at least an equivalent reduction in accidents attributable to the human factor over the period covered by our chart. Assume for the sake of argument that the ratio remained relatively constant over the years—say 50 percent, to be on the conservative side: This would mean that the number of fatal airline accidents attributable to pilot error declined from 0.045 per million air miles in 1938 to 0.003 per million in 1968—a *fifteen-fold* decrease. That's quite a trick, considering human nature hasn't changed appreciably since man first sprouted wings.

How do we account for this remarkable

achievement? I submit that much of it was due to better *flight management:* Higher pilot selection standards and qualifications, vastly improved training (from the self-taught air mail pilots of the 1920s and early 1930s to the American Airlines Flight Academy graduates of the 1970s and beyond), better pilot supervision and regulation, steady improvements in flying technique ("attitude" instrument flying and safer thunderstorm penetration procedures, for example), and last but not least, a constant focus on standardization.

One could write a book on standardization and what it means—or what it meant in Walt's era. I know he took pride in the claim that cockpit procedures in an American Airlines Astrojet were so standardized he could assemble a flight crew at random, choosing a captain from one station, a first officer from another, and a flight engineer from another, and this motley team would perform so smoothly, so seamlessly, that "even a trained observer would scarcely believe they hadn't flown together for years." What a change from the old days, when copilots had to adapt to a completely new set of operating procedures every time they were assigned to a new captain. ("Don't touch nothin' till I tell you!")

But standardization meant more than training flight crews to do the same things the same way every time; more than making pilots and flight engineers commit volumes of routine and emergency procedures to memory. I think what Walt Braznell, Jack Gibson, Harry Clark, and their contemporaries had in mind was establishing a work environment in which every crew member strove to conduct his or her part of the flight mission according to the *highest* standards and *best* practices recognized by the airline industry. Standardization, in other words, was a synonym for professionalism, discipline—excellence.

Whether they knew it or not, what Braznell and his associates were doing between 1937 and 1968 was nothing less than redefining—or reinventing—the airline pilot. The pilots of Walt's youth were basically airplane handlers, a term he used with great respect, and applied to the best of the breed, virtuosos like Benny Howard and Bud Gurney. The airplane handler was, first and foremost, an individualist. His basic approach to flying for the airlines was neatly expressed by another great airplane handler, Ham Lee: "If I get there, so will my passengers."

But by the time Braznell was promoted to chief pilot, the airlines were flying close to a half-billion passenger miles a year, and airline managements could no longer simply delegate responsibility for their passengers' safety and comfort to a small, elite corps of airborne egoists. Thus, out of necessity was born the concept of flight management and the new model of the airline pilot as the ultimate *flight manager*—a concept that was continuously expanded and refined during the years Braznell ran American's Flight Department.

Actually, no one really "invented" the model of the pilot as manager: It evolved. And certainly no one person deserves credit for that evolution. On the other hand, as Woody Allen once remarked about the nature of success: "Eighty percent of it is just showing up," and Walt Braznell showed up earlier and stayed longer at his post as chief pilot of America's "leading airline" than any of his predecessors, successors, or industry peers. On that basis, if for no other reason, he might legitimately be considered the father of modern flight management.

But then, I may be prejudiced.

William Braznell
August 2000

Father and Son

My earliest recollection of Walt Braznell is that he often slept till noon. While he slept, my sister and I had to be quiet, or my mother would shoo us out the screen door and make us play in the back yard. I also recall that he was sometimes gone for a day or two at a time, and when he left or returned, he would always be carrying an impossibly heavy black leather satchel and wearing a dark blue uniform with a set of miniature wings clipped to the blouse. From this I gradually deduced that my father was not like my grandfather or uncles, who came to breakfast every morning and read the newspapers, and drove to work each weekday in business suits and hats. When I asked my mother about Walt's odd dress and behavior, she explained that he flew airplanes for a living and sometimes had to work all night, so that he would be tired and need rest when he got home.

Later, she showed me an old clipping from the *St. Louis Post-Dispatch* with a photo of a young man in fleece-lined leather coveralls, helmet, and goggles standing next to a small, fragile-looking airplane with two wings on each side. This was a picture of my father, taken when he first began "flying the mail," she told me. I was very impressed to have a father whose picture was in the newspaper, but thought it odd that a grown man would dress up in a snowsuit.

When I was three, we moved from St. Louis to Memphis and then, a year or so later, to a suburb of Chicago. During that time my mother, my sister, and I became frequent fliers, shuttling off to St. Louis to visit Mother's family as often as company rules and Dad's patience would permit. On some of these flights, Walt would be at the controls, and I can remember strutting up and down the aisle of a Vultee or Ford TriMotor telling the plane's few paying passengers that my father was the pilot, and I was going to be a pilot, too, when I grew up.

My parents were a gregarious couple, and throughout most of their lives, their closest friends were airline people. We lived in airline enclaves—La Grange, Illinois, and later Manhasset, Long Island—surrounded by American Airlines pilots and their families. Our neighbors and occasional house guests included some of the legends of commercial aviation—Doc Ator, Duke Ledbetter, Si Bittner, Fred Bailey, Joe Hammer, Kit Carson, Bobby Jewell, Red Clark, Charlie Allen, Ken Case, Fran Bledsoe, Roy Pickering, Johnny Davidson. These were my heroes. On nights when we had company, I would stay up past my usual bedtime, listening to them swap yarns ("lies") about their flying experiences. They were an extraordinary lot: individualistic, self-assured, good-humored and, on the whole, remarkably gentle men, with none of the macho swagger one would expect of a profession in which careers and life expectancies were once measured in hours. When a group of them gathered at our house for dinner or a game of poker, it was not hard to imagine them as knights of the Round Table and my father as a young Arthur. I made up my mind to remember their stories and to write them down for my children and for future generations when I grew up. That was a long time ago, and I have promises to keep.

Walt obviously enjoyed parenthood. In an era that long predated Little Leagues and other organized recreation programs for tiny tots, he somehow found time to coach me, all by himself, in the rudiments of baseball, football, basketball, track, boxing, wrestling, tennis, golf, sledding, skating, fishing and fly casting, hunting and marksmanship, carpentry and mechanics. He also taught my sisters and me how to pedal a trike, ride a bike, and drive a car. Although he could be a stern and demanding instructor, he had a remarkable reservoir of patience—a quality I don't think I fully appreciated until I began teaching my own children to drive.

Paradoxically, the one thing Walt refused to teach me was what he knew best: *flying*. I suspect he recognized long before I did that my interests and aptitudes were more attuned to words and pictures than mechanical things, like airplanes. Besides, he would remark whenever the subject came up, if I wanted to fly, the only proper place to learn was in the service.

He was right, of course. After earning a degree in journalism from the University of Missouri, I accepted an ROTC commission in the Air Force, signed up for pilot training, and spent the next four years learning all I could about the art of flying. I'm still not entirely sure why I did it, since I hadn't the slightest notion of making aviation or the military my career. All I know is, the day Walt and Diddy pinned my Air Force wings on me was the proudest of my young life.

Walt and Bill Braznell at Bill's graduation from pilot school, Webb Air Force Base, May 1955. Walt was commencement speaker.

Appendix

Major Events and Developments in the Airline Industry, 1925–1968

1925   Post Office awards air mail routes
            to private carriers

1927–1929   Industry consolidation, formation
            of aviation holding companies:
            Universal Aviation, AVCO, North
            American, United Aircraft and
            Transport (Boeing)

1930   Origins of major transcontinental air
            routes and carriers

1930–1934   Cuts in air mail rates force airlines to
            scramble for passenger business

1934   Franklin D. Roosevelt abruptly can-
            cels commercial air mail contracts,
            orders Air Corps to take over mail
            routes. Restructured airline industry
            resumes air mail service following
            hasty passage of Air Mail Act of
            1934.

1942–1945   Army Air Corps and Navy team up
            with airlines to create huge global
            carriers, Air Transport Command
            (ATC) and Naval Air Transport Ser-
            vice (NATS)

1946–1950   Raging competition among "scheds"
            and "non-scheds," rapid growth in
            business travel and air tourism,
            worldwide

1952–1958   De Havilland Comet jet liner intro-
            duced in Europe and United King-
            dom. United States lags far behind
            in jet race, but, fortunately, gets it
            right the first time

1958–1968   Period of phenomenal growth and
            prosperity for domestic airline in-
            dustry—a brief pre-oil cartel, pre-
            deregulation "golden age of air
            travel"

Bibliography

Speeches

C. R. Smith, "A.A.: American Airlines since 1926." Address to the Newcomen Society, 1954.

Periodicals

"The Air is How Safe?" *Fortune* (April 1937).

"American Airlines Flies World Routes for ATC." *American Airlines Flagship News* (December 1943).

"Burma Roadsters: American Airlines' Indian Summer." *American Airlines Flagship News* (February 1944).

"Teamwork in Alaska." *American Airlines Flagship News* (March 1944).

"They Call It Routine." *American Airlines Flagship News* (April 1944).

"Star-Wise Globe Girdler." *American Airlines Flagship News* (July–August 1945).

Books

Allen, Oliver E. *The Airline Builders.* Time-Life Books, 1981.

Cearley, George W., Jr. *American Airlines, An Illustrated History.* Published by the author, 1981.

Davies, R. E. G. *Airlines of the United States Since 1914.* Putnam, 1972.

Davis, Kenneth S. *The Hero: Charles A. Lindbergh and the American Dream.* Garden City, N.Y.: Doubleday, 1959.

Day, Karl S. *Instrument and Radio Flying.* Air Associates, Inc., 1938.

Donald, David, ed. *The Complete Encyclopedia of World Aircraft.* Orbis Publishing Ltd., 1997.

Fishbein, Samuel B. *Flight Management Systems.* Praeger Press.

Gann, Ernest K. *A Hostage to Fortune.* Alfred A. Knopf, 1978.

———. *Ernest K. Gann's Flying Circus.* Macmillan Publishing Co., 1974.

———. *Fate is the Hunter.* Simon and Schuster, 1961.

Glines, Caroll V., *Jimmy Doolittle, Master of the Calculated Risk.* Van Nostrand Reinhold Company, 1972.

Handleman, Philip, *Aviation, A History Through Art.* Howell Press/The American Society of Aviation Artists, 1992.

Heppenheimer, T. A. *Turbulent Skies: The History of Commercial Aviation.* John Wiley and Sons, Inc., 1995.

Horgan, James J. *City of Flight: The History of Aviation in St. Louis.* Patrice Press, 1984.

Jaynes, Jack, *Eagles Must Fly.* Taylor Publishing Co., 1982.

Lindbergh, Charles A. *The Spirit of St. Louis.* Charles Scribner's Sons, 1953.

———. *We.* New York: G. P. Putnam's Sons, 1928.

Kelly, Charles J., Jr. *The Sky's the Limit: The History of the Airlines.* Arno Press, 1972.

Jordanoff, Assen, *Through the Overcast.* Funk and Wagnalls Co., 1938.

Mangan, James M. *To the Four Winds.* Turner Publishing Co., 1990.

Morison, Samuel Eliot. *The Oxford History of the American People.* Oxford University Press, 1965.

Murchie, Guy. *Song of the Sky.* Houghton Mifflin Co., 1954.

Rashke, Richard. *Stormy Genius: The Life of Aviation's Maverick, Bill Lear.* Houghton Mifflin Co., 1985.

Serling, Robert. *Eagle, The Story of American Airlines.* St. Martin's Press, 1985.

———. *Loud and Clear.* Doubleday and Co., 1969.

———. *When the Airlines Went to War.* Kensington Books, 1997.

Smith, Dean. *By the Seat of My Pants.* Little Brown and Co., 1961.

Taylor, Frank. *High Horizons: The United Airlines Story.* McGraw Hill, 1962.

Tuchman, Barbara W. *Stilwell and the American Experience in China, 1911–1945.* Macmillan Co., 1970.

Young, Charles H. *Into the Valley: The Untold Story of USAAF Troop Carrier in World War II.* PrintComm, Inc., 1995.

Wilson, C. Lloyd, and Leslie Bryan. *Air Transportation.* Prentice-Hall, Inc., 1949.

Index

relationship, 76, 80, 95–97; war service (ATC), 137, 154–57; opts out of transatlantic competition, postwar years, 168; postwar competition, transcontinental flights, 174–76, 180, 182–84; Bryce Canyon disaster (1947), 180; becomes largest U.S. carrier with acquisition of Capital Airlines, 191; choice of DC-8 over Boeing 707, 194, 201

U.S. Air Corps, 11, 14, 17, 131, 132; takes over mail routes, 1934, 83. *See also* Air Transport Command

—Bases: Kelly Field, Texas, 2, 11; Brooks Field, Texas, 17, 114; Chanute Field, Ill., 17; Hickam Field, Hawaii, 156; Hamilton Field, Calif., 156, 157; Webb AFB, Texas, 215

U.S. Air Force, 193, 215

U.S. Army Air Force (USAAF), 131, 132, 134, 137, 140. *See also* Air Transport Command

U.S. Army Air Service, 2, 11, 94

U.S. Army Corps of Engineers, 138

U.S. Department of Agriculture, weather reports, 67

U.S. Department of Commerce, 1, 4, 26, 39, 67, 70, 93

U.S. Department of the Navy, 131, 134

U.S. Department of State, 131, 168

U.S. Department of War, 131, 132, 134, 136, 165

U.S. Marine Corps, 131, 136, 151

U.S. Navy, 131. *See also* Naval Air Transport Service

U.S. Postal Service: Air Mail Service, 15; Postmaster General Walter F. Brown, 23, 57, 58, 60, 67, 83, 91, 92; air mail "subsidies" and rate changes, 58, 89, 91; policy toward contract air mail carriers, 58, 67, 91; regulation of airlines, 58, 117

U.S. Signal Corps, 2, 12

Universal Air Lines, 3, 43, 54; facilities and fleet, 26, 44, 60; passenger and airmail services, 60, 68

Universal Aviation Corporation, 14, 26

University of Missouri, 54, 215

Velocity (V1, VLOF, V2), 180, 181–82

Vertical speed (rate of climb) indicator, 71, 116

Vertigo, 38

Vickers aircraft company, 186, 187–88, 190

Visual flight rules (VFR), 39, 69

Vultee, Jerry, 75

Vultee V-1A, 75, 80, 96, 214

Walter, William, 182

Ware, Frank, 143

Wassall family: Charlie, Kate, Cliff, Jack, Warren, 4, 5; Ray, 2, 4, 5, 9–11, 17, 26

"Water wagons" (pre–fan jet jetliners), 198

Weather. *See* Meteorology

Webb Air Force Base, Texas. *See* U. S. Air Corps, Bases

Western Air Express, 1, 58, 60, 94

Western Airlines, 137

Wind shear, 63, 178–79

Wing-walking, 9–10

Wisenbaker, Richard, 143

World War I, xv; biplanes, 1, 8, 13, 15; veterans, 1, 2, 35, 70, 94

World War II, 131–63; fighters, 13, 155, 157, 159; D-Day, 144; V-E Day, 144; China-Burma-India theater, 148–54; veterans return to American Airlines, 158, 163; veterans, postwar assimilation and benefits, 158, 163, 165, 172–74; wartime aircraft production, U.S., 158; jet fighters, British and German, 159, 188; jet propulsion, research and development, 159; V-J Day, 165; pressure pattern flying, introduction of, 207

Wright brothers, ix, 1, 4, 159

Wright engines: J-5 Whirlwind, 13, 18, 33, 64; Cyclone, 76, 80, 96; G-102, 98; R-3350 (turbo compound), 182–84

Young, Charles, x, 131

Zion, Frank, 157